JEWS IN CONTEMPORARY
VISUAL ENTERTAINMENT

JEWS IN CONTEMPORARY VISUAL ENTERTAINMENT

Raced, Sexed, and Erased

Carol Siegel

INDIANA UNIVERSITY PRESS

This book is a publication of

Indiana University Press
Office of Scholarly Publishing
Herman B Wells Library 350
1320 East 10th Street
Bloomington, Indiana 47405 USA

iupress.org

Manufactured in the United States of America

First printing 2022

Cataloging information is available from the Library of Congress.

ISBN 978-0-253-06022-8 (hardback)
ISBN 978-0-253-06023-5 (paperback)
ISBN 978-0-253-06024-2 (ebook)

To my beloved self-appointed entertainment director, Gerhard.

And in memoriam, David Siegel and Eva Fuchs,
my love for you both will never die.

CONTENTS

ACKNOWLEDGMENTS

THIS BOOK COULD NEVER HAVE BEEN POSSIBLE WITHOUT the love and support I received from my father, David Siegel, who taught me everything I needed to know about living my life as a Jew. I am proud to be his daughter and miss his presence every day of my life. The other person without whom this book would not have been possible is my wonderful film enthusiast husband, Gerhard Magnus, who is always an enormous help and an inspiration. He also has my eternal gratitude for acting as my personal IT assistant after the COVID-19 pandemic closed on-site instruction at my university so that I could continue teaching classes and working with graduate students without having to put this book aside to learn all the online teaching technologies the move off campus required. I am happy for this opportunity to thank Spike Lee and Charles Burnett for their help and support of the film series I organized on minoritized directors' work for the Washington State University Vancouver Diversity Council. The generosity of these great filmmakers was inspiring to me and my students. I am also very grateful to my friend and colleague Steffen Silvis for reading and invaluably commenting on the manuscript. Other people whose interest in this book was crucial to its development include all the members of my chosen family but especially Christopher Toomey, Eva Fuchs, Lillian Taiz, and my magnificent godson, Ezekiel Abel (Tefari) Casas, because they listened to my ideas and encouraged me. I so much wish Eva could have lived to read the finished version of the book as she wanted to do and will never forget her saying to me in the last week of her life, "Please tell me about your revisions to the book. Hearing about it brings me joy in this dark time." My heartfelt thanks also go out to my former graduate students and dear current friends Robert Richardson, Amber Strother, and Jenna Leeds for their useful input. I additionally thank my Fulbright postdoctoral student Abhik Mukherjee for educating me about how differently Jews are seen in India. I am also very grateful to Linda Mizjewski, Sophia Forslund, Jonathan Branfman, Pamela Raintree, and Laura Frost for their ideas and suggestions. A special thank-you goes to my colleagues at Washington State University Nicole Campbell, Chris Rhoads, Aaron Oforlea, William Hamlin, Kandy Robertson, Sue Peabody, Thabiti Lewis, Desiree Hellegers, Pavithra Narayanan, Donna Potts, and Todd Butler for all their help and support. Thanks also to my undergraduate and graduate students whose political engagement and response to my work gives me hope. And without the Hadassah-Brandeis Institute and the great people there— Deborah Olins, Debra Kaufman, Sharon Pucker Rivo, Lisa Rivo, and Sylvia Barack Fishman—I would have been lost in a never-ending forest of films. In every sense they helped me focus, as did those who attended my talks at the Society for Cinema and Media Studies, the Association for Jewish Studies, the American Literature Association Film Group, and the Popular Culture/ American Culture conferences. I also profited greatly from my conversations with my editor at Indiana University Press, Dee Mortensen, and am very grateful to Ashante Thomas and Gary Dunham for taking over and making the transition easy for me when she retired. Special thanks are due to project manager Carol McGillivray, who was always there with the answers when I needed her, and to Julia Turner, who did a lovely, intuitive job of copyediting.

Washington State University Vancouver provided me with a semester's sabbatical in the fall of 2015 to allow me time to finish my initial research for this book and draft two chapters, for which I am thankful. I am also grateful for the internal grant that allowed me to go to Brandeis to do research for the book during this sabbatical and for the six weeks of summer freedom to write provided by a Washington State University Humanities Research Center grant in 2018.

Chapter 1 is a revised version of an essay I previously published, "Talking Cures? Jews and Sex Therapy in *Nymphomaniac* and *A Dangerous Method*," in *Jewish Film & New Media* 5.1 (Spring 2017). It is reproduced here by permission of Taylor and Francis Group LLC, www.tandfonline.com. I thank them, and I also thank Nathan Abrams and Nir Cohen for their editorial help and suggestions that very much strengthened the argument.

An early version of chapter 5, "Two Funerals and a Wedding: Not So Nice Jewish Girls in *Transparent* and *Broad City*," appeared in *Intercourse in Television and Film: The Presentation of Explicit Sex Acts* (2018), edited by Lindsay Coleman and myself. I thank Lexington Books Press for permission to reprint material in it here. And I warmly thank Lindsay Coleman, whose work with me on the essay was absolutely essential.

Finally, I thank the members of the Portland Antifa for keeping the various fascists and white supremacists who constantly threaten us from attacking me and everyone else these alt-right bullies hate—and especially the young masked man who ran two blocks through the downtown park blocks to warn me that "the Nazis are coming!" and advise me to retreat from the battle area as I am too old to successfully fistfight young men.

JEWS IN CONTEMPORARY
VISUAL ENTERTAINMENT

INTRODUCTION

Jewish Racialization Matters

I. Notes of a "Nominal" Jew

In this book I seek to illuminate, through examples taken from visual entertainment media of the late twentieth and the early twenty-first centuries, how Jews have been raced and sexed in the time period leading up to today. As the book's subtitle indicates, representations in visual entertainments contribute to the racialization of Jewishness, its sexualization, and even its erasure. This erasure derives from lack of attention to a group history that might do much to explain the truly unique position of Jews as contributors to the development of the sex-positive strand of American culture. Jews, in America and elsewhere, have frequently contested the racist belief that white people are naturally drawn to the sexual practices that the mainstream deems valuable, decent, and proper, while people of color are by nature perverse and drawn to sexual practices that undermine society. Furthermore, many Jewish public intellectuals have argued that far from being a force against social good, sexual diversity is beneficial to society, while the repression of consensual forms of sexual expression is detrimental not only to individuals but to the societies in which they live. For this reason, Jews were leaders in the sexual revolution that took place from the mid-1960s up until the AIDS pandemic began in the early 1980s. And for that reason, I have chosen to focus on the representation of Jews as raced and sexed subjects in films and television series that were made during and after the sexual revolution.

The end of enforcement of the Motion Picture Production Code in the 1960s resulted in a rise of attention to sexuality as a major plot element in many films. The sexual revolution had a similar impact on television. When we think about the loosening of censorship in American entertainment media, many of us tend to think of the ubiquitous sex scenes in films made during this time. However, as Elana Levine argues, by the 1970s,

"Sexualized popular culture became a taken-for-grant element of everyday life. Nowhere were [the] new forms of sexual expression more prominently or more surprisingly, felt than in commercial network television" (2). One effect of the turn in visual media to dramatizing sexualities was an increase in the sexualization of minoritized people, very much including Jews.

Because of my intersectional focus on sexualization as a part of racialization, as well as the appearance of Jewish characters in thousands of films and television programs, I do not aim to cover the representation of Jews in every film or television series released in this time period, let alone in the whole history of moving pictures. Patricia Erens's classic *The Jew in American Cinema*, Omer Bartov's *The "Jew" in Cinema: From "The Golem" to "Don't Touch My Holocaust,"* and Eric A. Goldman's *The American Jewish Story through Cinema* provide reasonably wide coverage. This book, instead, gives an overview of the Jewish presence in a selection of films and television series that reflect the construction—or deconstruction—of American sexual norms. While I concentrate on American films and television series, I also include some films made by international directors who had reason to expect a substantial American audience and who depend on American film critics' reviews to attract the widest possible audience of art cinema enthusiasts. My contention is that such films reflect a view of Jewishness that is widespread in the Western world and so informs American films and television. However, I have selected for discussion films and television series that stand out to me as exemplifying specific meaningful and often contrasting ways of intertwining race and sexuality in representation of Jews.

This is a book about matters involved in the racialization of Jews, but it is also about why this racialization should matter to everyone. My intended audience includes anyone interested in Jewish studies, film and television studies, or sexuality studies. If we read my introduction's title as a statement, it has a force resembling that of the movement that gave a name to African American resistance to state-sanctioned violence committed against Black people in the United States: Black Lives Matter. Some may be angered that I would suggest, with this introduction's title, that there can be any significant comparison between the racialization of African Americans and that of Jewish Americans. Whatever persecution Jews have undergone in this country, if we are understood to be Ashkenazi (European), we now belong to a group that is officially designated on the US census as "white," while Americans of African heritage bear the full weight of race; they can never be merely "ethnic" so long as color-based racism exists.[1] However, to those familiar with African American history, the Holocaust stands as a sort of condensed version of the sufferings of Black people in the United States with many stark parallels: the cattle train transport to concentration camps and the Middle Passage, slave labor under inhuman conditions and subjection to unrestrained sexual abuse for both groups, the medical experiments on the concentration camp prisoners and those done on impoverished Black people, and the forced sterilizations and the post–Civil War lynching of freed Black Americans and the attempted extermination of the Jews.

In defiance of the general American concept of the Holocaust as the worst crime against humanity ever committed, I must point out that the grotesque crimes against African Americans have gone on for centuries and that Black people in America continue to be victims of what can be understood as an ongoing attempted genocide, while the majority of American Jews now enjoy most of the privileges of whiteness because most of us look white. And while in Europe and throughout the United States many memorials exist to the victims of the Holocaust, until recently there were none in America honoring the Black or Native American victims of white racial violence. Yet I will contend that Jews are racialized and this does matter to everyone because of the unique way that this particular racialization affects the formation and continuation of America's dominant sex and gender politics.

II. A Matter of Focus

One of the most difficult decisions I made when I started this book project was to not discuss films made in Israel. I made this decision because Jews are not a racialized minority in Israel. While Israeli filmmakers, like filmmakers anywhere, may decide to draw on stereotypes of Jews to develop characters, they do not do so in a country where the majority of citizens consider Jews Others who are, by definition, only provisionally of the same status as those who are always considered racially unmarked white people. Moreover, while Jews are a minority of the population in every other country on earth, Jews are the majority in Israel. As a consequence, Jewish stereotypes cannot have the same impact on Israeli audiences, Jewish or Gentile. Nor can Israeli films, which generally make Jewish characters and experiences central, be understood as what Gilles Deleuze calls minoritarian cinema. In the rest of the world, Jewish characters are always representations of people who are seen as Jews first and universalized humans second, whether or not the filmmaker attempts to challenge stereotypes and provide new visions. Sadly, as I will show throughout this book, many films and television series made in America do not attempt this sort of resignification of Jewish identities but instead carry on the European tradition of depicting Jews as a threat to Gentiles by attributing to Jews dangerous levels of perversity, greed, and general subversive tendencies.

III. Placing Myself in the Jewish Story

Terry Eagleton's book *Literary Theory: An Introduction* (1983) was one of the greatest influences on critics of my generation. I remember waiting in the San Francisco airport for my flight to New York in 1986 and being able to tell who else was heading to the Modern Language Association conference by seeing, all around me, job candidates poring over the paperback. Throughout this time period, when many senior professors and journal editors were wont to chastise us for what they saw as an inappropriate focus on the political in our analyses of texts, many of us turned for support to Eagleton's central claim that all criticism is based on ideologically determined theories. Eagleton argues that all criticism makes use of literature "to further certain moral values . . . which are in fact indissociable from certain ideological ones, and in the end imply a particular form of politics. It is not that it reads the texts 'disinterestedly' and then places what it has read in the service of its values: the values govern the actual reading process itself, inform what sense criticism makes of the works it studies" (208–9). Those of us who veered off from the study of literature into the study of film and took positions informed by our opposition to the dominant narratives of our culture, immediately saw the relevance of this argument to our interpretations of how specific films, and images within them, made meanings as part of a larger system of signification.

Embroiled in the 1980s culture wars, we thrilled to think that no longer would feminist approaches be treated as a lesser type of criticism practiced by those who were too caught up in their personal issues to pay proper attention to aesthetics. For scholars in feminist studies, like me, Eagleton's insight strengthened our belief that the personal is political, and since we rejected T. S. Eliot's view that literature should be impersonal, we saw all writings, creative and critical, as inevitably personal. And in that visual media is composed of images that constitute a vision, we saw the personal infusing the political, and vice versa, in cinema. Throughout that decade, as feminist professors fought lawsuits against the universities that denied them tenure because their research was not seen as serious and important, but instead, as dealing only with minor—that is women's—issues, the battle was far from won. However, we struggled on and finally reached our current respectable, if not always respected, position as "tenured radicals" in academe. It is in that spirit that I begin this, the most obviously personal and political book I have ever written.

As a true child of my academic generation, I have always written as a situated speaker, and so I will, throughout this book, discuss Jews as a Jew rather than from a distance that renders Jews "them" instead of "us." But this is far from being a book only for Jews. Instead, I intend it to add to studies of intersectionality in the representation and consequent identity formation of various groups traditionally considered Other, minoritarian, and outside the dominant group that define what it is to be an American. And in relation to current events, you might even think of it as a warning of the "and then they came for me" genre.

In a detailed historical overview of the history of Jews in America, Cheryl Greenberg explains that while many of us have considered Jews generally to be "white by color," the majority of American Jews "did not consider themselves White racially," and "most American Jews today still do not consider themselves Whites" (40–41, 46). Debra Renee Kaufman found, through an extensive study of young Americans who identified as Jews, that this identification can be based on religion, family history, social practices, concepts of race, or a combination of any of these (78). In addition, for her young respondents, social justice activism, especially as it concerned racial issues, was often an important component of that identification whether they were religious or secular (78–79). As Eric L. Goldstein discusses, Jewish identification with and as people of color has grown from the 1990s on as "an increasing number of Jews are becoming frustrated with the constraints of acceptance in white America and are expressing a sense of alienation and disengagement from whiteness" (235). They are hardly alone in such thinking. In *Rooted Cosmopolitans: Jews and Human Rights in the Twentieth Century*, James Loeffler traces the development of current concepts of human rights through examining the role of Jewish activists and thinkers who advocated for the minority rights of their own group and others.[2] This history suggests why Jewish identity issues should matter to Gentiles as well as to Jews. The racialization of Jews should matter to everyone concerned with social justice, first because it sheds a unique light on how racialization works, due to the way it encompasses all the factors (physical appearance, historical descent, culture, and religion) that comprise a racial or ethnic identification. Second Jewish racialization should matter to all Americans with progressive views of sexuality because of the leadership role Jews have played in sexuality studies since their inception. Anti-Semitic and sexually repressive philosophies are so closely intertwined that the majority of social media condemnations of instances of support for sexual freedom also blame Jews for fostering a climate of tolerance—or celebration—of sexual liberation, women's reproductive rights, and LGBTQ rights.

Yet to bring the focus back to Jews as subjects and creators of visual entertainments, we must also acknowledge the complexities of the history of relations between Jews and other racialized subjects within the American film industry. And there seems no better place to start than with consideration of Michael Rogin's influential study, *Blackface, White Noise*. Although Rogin's book ends its deep investigation of the representations by Jews of Black people in American cinema with a look at the developments brought about by the civil rights movement, and so discusses few films made after 1960, his work is still relevant to this book, whose coverage begins with films made in the early 1960s. His study is relevant because it fills in the historical background of the depiction of race in American film. He goes beyond close reading of plots to unpack specifically cinematic aspects of the ways films represent race through his discussions of casting, framing, montage, and music, as this book also does. I will show how the films in the period on which I concentrate, the time from the beginnings of the sexual revolution to today, reflect the realities Rogin points out, that "Jews were the most black-identified immigrant group" and that, beginning with the use of blackface in the first sound film, *The Jazz Singer* (1927), our cinematic representations have been consistently marked by racialization (165).

Confronting this history of exploitation and appropriation includes examining the situation of Jews as consumers of visual entertainments, which is why this book draws on theories of spectatorship as one of its primary modes of analyzing the impact of representation of Jews. The book began for me in 2010, after I saw on video two films that had been released the previous year, *A Serious Man* and *Inglourious Basterds*. Situating my own viewing experience in relation to those of others whose responses to the films diverged greatly from my own made me more aware than I had ever been before of the phenomenon that is the secondary topic of Henry Bial's excellent study, *Acting Jewish: Negotiating Ethnicity on the American Stage and Screen*. While Bial's primary concern is how Jewishness is performed in popular entertainments, he finds this inextricable from the way such performances are interpreted and mainly how they are interpreted by Jews in ways that inform our identity constructions.

As Vivian Sobchack argues, "There are always two embodied acts of vision at work in the theater, two embodied views constituting the intelligibility and significance of the film experience," as the vision of the film and that of the spectator "meet in the sharing of a world and constitute an experience that is not only intrasubjectively dialectical, but also intersubjectively dialogical. . . . Cinematic vision, then, is never monological" (53–54). This world sharing becomes especially fraught with conflicts when race is introduced into the mix. A good example of how this happens is provided by bell hooks's analysis of how the "oppositional gaze" of Black women viewers of television and film has historically been informed by their exclusion from the production of these entertainments and their place as actors with little leeway to interpret their assigned parts in a mass media "system of knowledge and power reproducing and maintaining white supremacy" (230). She is right that the inclusion of race complicates theories of film spectatorship (235), and one must add that the odd position of a significant number of Jews as racialized subjects who have the power to construct cinematic images complicates theories of spectatorship even more. Consequently, matters of double address and double consciousness in filmmaking and the reception of films are especially pertinent to Jews because of our prominence in developing American film and television cultures.

Of course, anti-Semites often accuse us of controlling visual media for nefarious reasons. But a more favorable view of our role was voiced by Jean Renoir in an interview when he claimed that Ernst Lubitsch "invented the modern Hollywood" (Bogdanovich). In an appreciation of Lubitsch that begins with this quote, Phillip Lopate attributes the director's refusal of didacticism in depicting people struggling with racism and sexism to his consciousness of the importance of Jewish culture's insistence on comedy as a form of resistance (53–54). Elana Levine and Michael Z. Newman point out that "the Jewishness of [visual] media creatives historically has been tamped down in their work, often ignored and occasionally coded in terms invisible to the non-Jewish world" (43). Bial shows that it is through "reading Jewish," a process of "decoding of Jewishness or non-Jewishness," that Jews form what Benedict Anderson called "imagined community" as a basis for identity construction (Bial 146).

When we watch films, this process is complex because it entails comparing our responses to those of others both inside and outside the group with which we identify. Because Jewish identity essentially means not being Gentile, a term that simply means "not Jewish," we know what it means to be a Jew in large part through recognizing ways we differ from Gentiles. My experience of home viewing *A Serious Man* brought to my attention as never before just how much my Gentile husband and I belong to different interpretive communities. At the conclusion of the film, which I discuss in chapter 6, I began laughing so uncontrollably that I fell off the sofa onto the floor and began to roll around gasping for air. My alarmed husband, who did not see the film's conclusion as humorous and had recently read in the newspaper that women present different symptoms of heart attacks than men, became convinced that I was, as he later put it, "either having some sort of fit or else a heart attack." A few days later I described this scene to a Jewish friend who told me that he had had almost exactly the same experience with his Gentile partner. This inspired me to talk with numerous other Jewish friends, family members, and acquaintances about similar incidents of audience response differences between Jews and Gentiles in their lives. So far so good. We all agreed that we found some things hilarious that Gentiles couldn't see any humor in at all. As Bial puts it, "for the in-group audience, the laughter . . . is the creation . . . of a kind of *communitas*, a sense of belonging that binds a group together through shared experience" (136).

Things became even more complicated with *Inglourious Basterds*. As I discuss in chapter 3, my experience of this film was blissful. It is the World War II revenge fantasy I have waited my whole life to see. Although my husband liked it very much, too, I felt confident that any Jew would find it enjoyable for exactly the same reasons I did. But when I began to research both critical reviews and nonprofessional online responses to the film, I quickly discovered that many considered it a film that Jews would and should find objectionable because it substitutes a fantasy for history and, worse, presents Jews in Nazi Germany not as innocent victims but as violent aggressors who fight back effectively. Thomas Doherty argues that the film is not only objectionable but devoid of sense because "the basterd squad" comes across as a "tribe of psycho killers" (60). He did, as I shall discuss, find some agreement among Jewish reviewers but not many. Again

I began an informal survey of Jews I knew and discovered that, just like the majority of Jewish reviewers of the film, they loved it as much as I did.

That is when things became especially interesting. I realized that Jewish identity formation in America includes not only anti-Semitism and the reactions of Jews to it but also a sort of shadow Jewishness constructed by friendly Gentiles to reflect what they think we should think and feel—and, inevitably, our reaction to that. So thinking of ourselves as American Jews entails reacting to at least three different imagined communities: one in which we are sinister figures who control the media in order to undermine the American way, one in which we are a separate (but good) culture with our own shared codes and interpretations, and one in which we are noble victims to be defended by virtuous Gentiles. That latter sense of a Jewish community is probably what makes so many Gentiles think Jews universally love *Schindler's List* when, in fact, many of us hate it—and more about that later, as well.

Drawing on my understanding of double address in critical race studies, I began writing about the various ways that identifying as a Jew impact interpretation of film and how, in turn, visual media representations of Jewishness influence Jews' personal identity constructions. What especially interested me, because I am a scholar in sexuality studies, was how racialization and sexualization intersect in this process. I was surprised when my first essay on this topic was rejected by a film journal because, as the editor wrote to me, "This essay would be of interest only to a Jewish audience." The explanation was that because, in the view of this editor, Jews are not racialized in the United States; our sexualization in media representations is the same as that of any other racially unmarked white people, and so it is of limited interest to anyone interested in sexual politics. Subsequently I learned that this view was not unusual. In fact, the ways media racialize Jews and our responses to this racialization are often met, by Gentiles and Jews alike, with the claim that Jews in America are not racialized but rather, all of us who are not practitioners of Judaism, are free to choose or reject our American Jewishness as an ethnicity. This view is supported by many academic and other serious studies.

The most provocative to me of these studies is Steven M. Cohen's "The Shrinking Jewish Middle—And What to Do About It" because of Cohen's insistence that those of us who do not practice Judaism should be considered (as we often have been) only "Nominally Jewish" (9), a designation he relates to the 2013 Pew Research Center's study, "A Portrait of Jewish

Americans." Cohen does note that "the major shift over the decades is not so much a change in Jew's religiosity, but a change in their ethnicity—the full texture of social relationships, culture, and collectivity that distinguishes Jews from others. Jews aren't so much losing their faith (which they never had much); rather they're losing their family-like ties and sense of collectivity" (18). Yet his proposed solution entails getting the merely nominally Jewish back to the synagogue as the only place such a sense of collectivity can be regained.

I resent this because I have always considered myself a Jew, was persecuted as a Jew when my family moved to Texas in the late 1950s, and retained my father's surname because I want people to know I am a Jew. Yet Jews like me who are not practitioners of Judaism and do not intend to become religiously observant are apparently doomed to a life in which we lack all meaningful connection to other Jews, since we are Jews in name only. This has not been my experience, and solidarity among nonreligious American Jews may be increasing, because things have changed dramatically for Jews since the 2016 presidential election.

IV. Things I Didn't Want to Be Right About, Volume 2[3]

Many Jews who considered themselves fully integrated into the American mainstream watched in horror on August 11, 2017, as neo-Nazis and other white supremacists marched in the Unite the Right Rally in Charlottesville, Virginia, chanting slogans that included "Jews will not replace us," "blood and soil" (a Nazi motto), and "gas the Jews." Emma Green reported in the *Atlantic* that "as Jews prayed at a local synagogue, Congregation Beth Israel, men dressed in fatigues carrying semi-automatic rifles stood across the street, according to the temple's president. Nazi websites posted a call to burn their building." Numerous other reporters and commentators on public events have observed the steep rise in anti-Semitic speech and hate crimes since the beginning of Donald Trump's campaign for the presidency. As Michelle Goldberg reported in the *New York Times*, "The Republican candidate in California's 11th District, John Fitzgerald, is running on a platform of Holocaust denial. Russell Walker, a Republican statehouse candidate in North Carolina, has said that Jews descend from Satan and that God is a 'white supremacist.'" Trump's responsibility for encouraging this sort of behavior seemed to many people to have been established beyond debate by his now infamous remark that some of the Unite the Right marchers were "very fine people."

However, others defend Trump against charges of anti-Semitism pointing out that his daughter Ivanka is married to a Jew and is a convert to Judaism and to his support for Israel, which included moving the US embassy from Tel Aviv to Jerusalem. Yet for the majority of US Jews, who do not equate Jewish identity with support for all of Israel's policies, what seemed a more significant indication of his position on anti-Semitism was his choice of the pastor of the First Baptist megachurch in Dallas, Robert Jeffress, to deliver the prayer of dedication in the new embassy's opening ceremony. Jeffress, as reported by Matthew Haag, in the *New York Times*, has made clear his view that Jews are condemned to hell. The ceremony also included remarks from John Hagee, founder of Christians United for Israel who has been criticized for his praise of Hitler for pushing Jews to return to Israel.

For many Jews the crucial issue is how we identify as Jews. Are we a special group of white people who have no common cause with people of color? A vast majority of Americans of color opposed the Trump presidency because he fostered, rather than attempting to diminish, systemic racism. Should we advocate for those disenfranchised people only in a spirit of altruistic liberalism, not because we ourselves are subjected to systemic racism? Or are we ourselves racialized people who are being discriminated against? The first step in answering these questions is to notice that while both news and entertainment media in the United States and Europe tend to ignore the existence of Jews of African heritage, who are obviously not white, we Jews need to remember that Ashkenazim are not the only Jews. So the question then becomes, are the fair-skinned Jews racialized?

In discussing the Charlottesville march in the *Washington Post*, Yair Rosenberg writes:

> Jews and non-Jews are drawn to debates about whether Jews are white. It's the sort of question that captivates academics and activists, roping in everyone from Israeli "Wonder Woman" actress Gal Gadot to African American literary luminary James Baldwin. On the one hand, Jews have been discriminated against for centuries, including by white cultures from Nazi Germany to the United States. On the other, many Jews have attained a significant measure of acceptance, and many can often "pass" as white when not wearing traditional Jewish symbols. . . . Personally, I've found this debate beside the point, and this weekend's disturbing events in Charlottesville perfectly illustrate why: The white supremacists have already made their decision.

This seems simple, but the debate rages on. We may look back on 2016 as the beginning of the most confusing era so far for American Jews, the one in which Jewish identity became the most vexed issue it has ever been in this country. The arguments among Jews that I have come to consider a variation on the old joke "one Jew, two opinions" now seem to be more like one Jew, three opinions when it comes to the topic of racial identity.

As Jews receive increasingly organized and publicly displayed resistance to our very existence in America, the question of Jewish identity becomes more troubled than it has been in decades. The problem may be familiar to those of us who recall the early days of feminism's second wave, when the developing field of gender studies raised the question of whether identification as women was a valuable political position or whether such identification was harmful to the cause of gender equality because it reified the myth of gender binarity. Inspired by Gayatri Chakravorti Spivak's work on strategic essentialism in postcolonial studies, feminist critics hotly debated the issue throughout the 1990s, with Diana Fuss, Judith Butler, and Elizabeth Grosz taking major roles. My favorite compromise is represented by the name of a famous feminist bookstore in Toledo, Ohio: People Called Women. But for some, even acknowledging that we are classified as people according to gender is anathema, as is now recognized in the many official forms that give us the choice not to identify as any specific gender. Similarly, some Jews passionately dislike the idea of agreeing with Nazis that Jewishness is a race.

Which leaves us with the question of whether Jewish identity is a religious affiliation determined by one's practice of Judaism, a racialization determined by being designated a Jew based on one's ancestry, or an ethnicity determined by cultural practices generally recognized as belonging to Jews. Most Jews, when pressed, as we often are in academic discussions, will express opinions that in some circumstances any of these three sources of identification do make one a Jew; however, many of us are also of the opinion that some people who fit only one definition of the three are not Jews.

Identities derived from religious affiliation are problematic because while they are not actually races or ethnicities, they have been historically and still are currently a source of personal and group identification that transcends actual spiritual beliefs and often inspires participation in violent conflict. For example, Catholics and Protestants in Ireland and Shia and Sunni Muslims throughout the Middle East function as (opposed) identity groups into which the individual is born. So, even religion, the seemingly least controversial identification, is problematized. People who practice some version of Judaism may not be recognized as Jews outside their specific religious sect. For example, a convert who adopts some Jewish religious practices but not others, as is the case with some celebrity followers of the Kabbalah, is likely to be seen by many Jews as not truly Jewish. And in more extreme cases, some ultra-Orthodox Jews refuse to recognize any converts as Jews.

When it comes to ancestry, few Jews are willing to recognize as Jews people who are Jewish through the maternal line—the traditional way of tracing Jewish ancestry—but have never identified themselves as Jews and refuse to do so. While Gentile anti-Semites may and often do racialize such people as Jews, Jews ourselves usually do not. But now with research on DNA coming into play, this distinction seems less valid. Harry Ostrer, a geneticist, argues in *Legacy: A Genetic History of the Jewish People* (2012) that Jewish identity can be established through DNA. And while this remains a controversial claim, it is gaining support as research on the human genome progresses.

A human interest article, "DNA Test Results in Century-Old Mystery," in the *Washington Post* suggests the many questions about identity raised by DNA evidence of Jewishness. It tells the story of Alice Collins Plebuch, who believed herself to be Irish American until a test revealed that she had some Jewish DNA. She asked her cousin Bill, related to her on her maternal side, to undergo the test, and on finding that he had no Jewish DNA, she then began a search for her roots that culminated in her discovery that her biological father was accidentally switched with a Jewish family's baby boy shortly after they were both born at Fordham Hospital in the Bronx in 1913. So her father, Jim Collins, was actually the child of a Jewish family. In discussing her cousin's test results, she remarked to the interviewing reporter, Libby Copeland, "Darned if Bill's X chromosome wasn't lily white." This phrasing indicates Plebuch's understanding that Jews are people of color, although Copeland refers to Jewishness, in the article, as being a matter not of race but of ethnicity. Toward the end of the story, Copeland paraphrases a question asked by Plebuch: "Was Jim Collins a Jewish man because he was born that way, or an Irishman because he was raised as one?"

If, as many argue today and as Copeland's own terminology supports, Jewishness is merely an ethnicity, then why would it matter that Collins's birth parents were Jews? Is Irishness a race? If not, then it, too, must be an ethnicity and that means it is culturally transmitted not genetically determined. So obviously Collins was an Irishman since his (unwittingly) adoptive parents raised him as an Irish Catholic very engaged with that heritage. Yet the article confidently labels him a Jew. What then, one must ask, is a

Jew? If Jewishness is conferred by DNA then it would seem to be a race, yet many people are considered Jews by virtue of their religious beliefs and practices irrespective of their DNA. The weirdness of this story shows the difficulty of identifying someone as Jewish.

My own DNA says that no matter what my religious practices are, I am a Jew. Is my adopted-at-birth sister who has no Jewish DNA and does not practice Judaism a Jew? Is the fact that we ate Jewish food at home and in delis, used many Yiddish expressions, and were told repeatedly that we were Jews enough to make her one in the absence of DNA or religious practice? These are the sorts of questions that vex Jewish identity construction and make a mockery of the many surveys that ask participants to list their religion and then count as Jews only those who identify themselves as religiously observant.

These cases are not just curiosities; they are representative of a problem many of us face in trying to form our identities. They matter because race matters. In Karen Brodkin's influential 1998 book, *How the Jews Became White Folks and What That Says about Race in America*, she affirms the view of many that Jewishness is no longer racialized. But we certainly are not "lily white" to many of our fellow Americans. And Brodkin's view utterly denies the motivation behind the continuation of hostile and often violent actions against Jews by white supremacists, not to mention the experience of many of us who encountered—and those who still are subjected to—intense anti-Semitism in America. It also raises legal questions about hate crimes. If someone attacks me because he believes that I am a Jew, yet Jewishness is not a race and I do not practice Judaism, can he be said to be committing a hate crime?

And finally we come to ethnicity. This is, in my view and the view of many theorists in critical race studies, a highly problematic term. For instance in *Ethnic and Racial Studies*, a discussion between Howard Winant and Andreas Wimmer raises questions about the common usage of the term *ethnicity* to signify a group identification not based on race but on cultural heritage. Winant argues that not only is ethnicity always already racialized, he calls ethnicization a type of racism. Wimmer responds that racism is a specific form of ethnic boundary construction. In other words, for these and many other scholars in the social sciences the claim that Jews are an ethnicity rather than a race fails because race and ethnicity are not separable in scientific discourse.

My own mother is a good example here. She used my father's surname, which is easily recognized as Jewish as it is one of the most common Jewish surnames in America. She learned to cook from his mother, a Russian Jewish immigrant, and loved traditional Ashkenazi foods like blintzes and kugel. Many of our family practices were typical of American Jews, and she fit in well in his old Cleveland neighborhood, where many of her close friends, all Jews, lived. When people assumed she was Jewish she never corrected them. But she was of Irish and Cherokee ancestry and, like my father and his friends, practiced neither Judaism nor Christianity. So was she an ethnic Jew? No Jew I have ever known thought so. Yet the majority of American religious Jews and, so far as the right to immigrate, the State of Israel would recognize her children, who also do not practice Judaism, as Jews, so long as we do not practice any other religion. But what if we do? Opinion, official in Israel and unofficial in the United States, differs widely on this. I like the quote attributed to David Ben-Gurion, founder and first prime minister of the State of Israel: "A Jew is anyone crazy enough to stand up in this world and declare that they are a Jew." Nonetheless, this has not been the policy of the Jewish state.

V. How the Jews Did Not Become White Folks

Although the title of this section obviously responds to Brodkin's book title, she is far from the only scholar to make the claim that after World War II, Jews in America began to be considered white. Her book title and theme came from Noel Ignatiev's 1995 book, *How the Irish Became White*. The shared contention of all the scholars who argue that American Jews are to be considered white is that when the Holocaust was generally known in the United States, due to the discovery by our troops of the concentration camps, ordinary, mainstream Americans stopped talking of and treating Jews as a racial group and started to see Jewish identity as an ethnicity. This claim makes some sense in that during the postwar period Jews began to enter the American mainstream in terms of housing, employment, and recreation. No longer banned from country clubs or subjected to admissions quotas for the professions, they rose to social and economic prominence as a group, and were no longer generally represented in popular culture as impoverished tenement dwellers. Yet as Emma Green notes in "Are Jews White?," whiteness is "a category marking power. American Jews do have power, but they are also often viewed with suspicion; and having power is no assurance of protection. According to the FBI's hate-crime statistics, a majority of religiously motivated hate-crime offenses are committed against Jews each year." And as Atiyah Husain observes in an article about a court ruling that Jews belong to a legally protected race: "Religion has never been an afterthought in systemic racism, but a racial classifier, weaponized to maintain whiteness." Since the popularization of the term *white Jew*, numerous articles by Jews have protested this concept.[4]

Furthermore Jewish identity is understood differently than other generally recognized American ethnicities, especially when it comes to sexuality. A current example can be seen in the responses to the #MeToo movement's exposure of Harvey Weinstein as a sexual criminal. In a controversial response to the #MeToo movement, J. E. Smyth discusses the ways that sexual misconduct and predation have been closely linked to Jewishness in critiques of the American film industry, concluding that "anti-Semitism fueled the anti-Hollywood establishment" (7). Smyth considers some of the rhetoric in discussions of Weinstein to be a continuation of this sort of attack on Jews. And this view is not entirely unreasonable because unlike the response to the accusations of sexual harassment or rape brought against men of Irish heritage, for example, Weinstein's disgrace is frequently discussed on social media as relevant to the view that Jews control popular media and that this control damages the country. One might argue that the people making such claims are members of small, extreme right-wing groups, and I do not dispute this. It is also quite possible that the large number of anti-Semitic discussions of Weinstein's behavior include Russian internet trolls paid to cause racial unrest in the United States. But these possibilities do nothing to establish that Jews are universally seen as belonging to a white ethnic group rather than being racialized. And in fact many of the discussions make clear the difference between academic and common, nonacademic understandings of ethnicity and of race.

Ethnicities are commonly understood as social and cultural whereas races are seen as biological. When individual Jews are discussed as being sexually immoral because they are Jews, the accusers do not talk about social or cultural reasons Jews may act in prohibited ways. Instead the accusers take as given that there is something inborn in Jews that makes us inclined toward behavior that violates sexual decency. This is the essence of racism, as is evident in a mountain of written and visual racist representations of African Americans and Latinx Americans. The latter provide an illuminating comparison to American Jews because, as with Jews, the people grouped under this descriptor immigrated to the United States from a wide variety of other countries (in addition to being annexed by the United States along with parts of what had previously been Mexico). They have a wide variety of skin colors and vary in appearance from people who look typically American Indian or African to people who are indistinguishable visually from Anglo-Saxon whites. Yet they are frequently racialized in media as having inherent genetic characteristics in common—just as Jews are. Even some African Americans, who remain the ones who define what it means to be nonwhite in America, can pass for white, but because race in America is not (only) a matter of skin color or geographical location of ancestors, no matter how pale their skin may be or how light and straight their hair, Black people are still understood to be black. As Frantz Fanon explains, a significant difference between Jewish people and Black people is that "the Jew can be unknown in his Jewishness. He is not wholly what he is. . . . I am given no chance" (115–16).

VI. Passing

Back to Rosenberg's point, Jews differ from other currently racialized subjects in the United States because while not all Jews can pass for white, all Jews can pass for Gentiles for three main reasons. Since the gradual removal of official anti-Semitism after World War II in such things as college and professional organizations—that is, in the form of Jewish quotas and Jewish exclusion from clubs and social organizations—expressions of anti-Semitism are generally not socially acceptable except by white supremacists and other racial separatists. So, first and rather ironically, a substantial number of people believe that calling someone a Jew is an insult. One needs only to Google the question "Is Jew a racial slur?" to see that anxiety over whether or not to use the word is common. (Some websites recommend, instead, always using the adjective Jewish, as in the phrase "Jewish person" to avoid offense.) Obviously then it would be least offensive not to refer to another person's Jewishness at all and certainly not to attribute Jewishness to someone who denies it. Second, many people, both Jewish and Gentile consider Jewishness exclusively determined by religious belief or practice. And third, Jews come in all colors and have as wide a range of features as there are races, so they cannot be identified—or any claims to a non-Jewish identity contested—on the basis of appearance alone. The result of these views is that to identify as a Jew is a choice in a way that it is not for other racialized subjects in America.

Because Jews who are not Orthodox and thus not recognizable as such by their dress, are most often identified by their surnames, Jews with surnames that are also common among Gentiles can pass most easily. And since legal name changes are always an option, this sort of passing is available to all. Furthermore, while straightening one's hair and nose are also easily available options, many Jews are born with appearances that do not fit the physical stereotypes, while many Gentiles have hooked noses and kinky hair as well as dark tan skin. Really all it takes, then, to pass for Gentile is to refuse to claim Jewish identity. A *Saturday Night Live* skit plays with this reality by offering a fake game show in which a contestant attempts to guess which celebrities are Jewish. Having failed to identify Daniel Day Lewis as a Jew, the contestant remarks that it is a tribute to his acting ability that he can pass for Gentile. The joke is, of course, that many Jews, just like Lewis, are indistinguishable from Gentiles in appearance and behavior, so no acting is required.

It is obvious what one gains by passing in a culture where racism is a feature of everyday life and white Gentiles are the most powerful group. What one loses is also significant. In a review essay of recent books about Black Americans passing as white, Jordan McDonald discusses "the emotional toll" for both those who choose to pass and for their families and friends (71). She calls racial passing "chosen exile" (70). This description also fits the situation of Jews who pass but in a slightly different way. Having the advantage of being in a group with a high rate of economic and professional success in America, Jews can help each other in ways that most other minoritized races cannot.

VII. What Does It Mean to Be Jewish?

If the authors and maintainers of the always witty and often charming website JewOrNotJew.com were the only arbiters of what Jewish identity is, it would all be simple—maybe. As they explain: "We evaluate how Jewish a person is based on three factors. How Jewish they are internally, how Jewish they are externally and how much we want that person to be a Jew in the first place." But then they add this to muddy the waters: "The Jew Score refers to our opinion only and is affected by but not definitive of one's actual Jewishness." The result of this method is that Moishe Rosen, the founder of Jews for Jesus is deemed "barely a Jew." This is consistent with their view, one held by many Jews but almost no Christians, that Jews who convert to Christianity are no longer Jews. Given the centuries of terrible persecution Christians inflicted on Jews, I can see why some Jews feel this way.

However, it seems to me as ridiculous as it would be for Black people to claim that no right-wing politician has a right to claim an African American identity. Despite not practicing Judaism and having an Irish Cherokee Gentile mother, I give myself the Jew score of 100 percent! Why? First, because I have continued through three marriages to use my father's name, which is recognizably Jewish and in fact was assigned to my grandfather at Ellis Island for that reason (he was a Russian Jewish Bolshevik and his real name was Solevev), so that everyone who hears it will know I am a Jew. Second, I am a Jew because I believe and am often told that I "look Jewish" and do nothing to minimize this appearance, instead choosing to leave my hair naturally kinky in hopes that people will recognize me as a Jew. And finally and most importantly, because I understand things about myself—from my being a university professor despite lower-class origins to my love of latkes with apple sauce and sour cream and my commitment to fostering social justice—as being determined by my Jewishness.

There are plenty like me, of course, and even some in my own family. That family is in some ways representative of the many contemporary families formed by a Jew and a Gentile. (Most studies estimate that around 53 percent of Jews marry Gentiles.) I recall being subjected to large amounts of anti-Semitism when we were growing up and being told by our father never to deny our Jewishness because that would be cowardly and when people found out we were trying to pass, they would justly despise us. He told us that the Orthodox would say we were not Jews because our mother was a Gentile, but then he would remind us that anti-Semites would always know we were Jews no matter what we or other Jews said. He didn't say "Gentiles," though; he usually referred to them as "those meshuggeneh goys." Generally my father's view of Jewishness, which I have followed, was that anyone was a Jew who had an ancestral heritage of Jewishness, practiced Judaism as a religion learned in childhood or as a convert, or simply claimed to be a Jew. In other words, Jewish identity was even more inclusive than Christianity because not only was it yours for the taking but also it could belong to you by heritage whether you wanted it or not.

Here are some of the Jews in my family-friend circle: one raised as a red diaper baby by two Jewish atheists, the son and daughter of that person and an African American Christian, their children with Gentiles, another a Peruvian Indian adopted by an agnostic Jewish mother but taken to temple regularly and bar mitzvahed, and another one raised as a Catholic Mexican American who later became an atheist and also found out that his maternal ancestors were Ladinos (Jewish refugees from the Spanish Inquisition). Like my father most of us would consider ourselves damned liars if we denied our Jewishness. Yet for others in our circle, it has been as apparently easy as saying, "Jewishness is a religion. I'm not religious, so I'm not a Jew."

Honestly, I really did not think much about any of this until the 2008 financial crisis. Up to that point, I just enjoyed being a Jew, which has always been both a source of pride for me and a way of connecting to other intellectuals, which can otherwise be difficult for someone from the working class. Working-class Jews, in my experience, tend to think of many things associated by others with high economic status—art museums, symphonies, and serious reading and study for example—as being for everyone and not inappropriate interests for the poor. A large number of the academics I have met from impoverished backgrounds are Jews. And, yes, as Gentiles often complain, we do tend to stick together and give each other support. My Jewish grandparents were my favorites. I have a special love for and pride in many Jewish entertainers and writers, identifying with them and feeling they speak for me. I regularly visit Jewish websites and shout out in triumph pleasant things I learn, such as that chocolate desserts were invented by Jews. So despite having been subjected to lots of anti-Semitism through the years, both casual and scary, I have been able to dismiss those who dished it out the same way my father did: as crazy or stupid or both.

But then the crash came and a very close friend of thirty-five years became an anti-Semite. He was an AIDS survivor who became fascinated by conspiracy theories because they comforted him as he dealt with the terrors and pains of his disease. He felt better, as he often explained, believing that he was the victim of a government plot rather than a person who had made mistakes in managing his sex life. Since he was infected with HIV before any information had been released to the public about the disease, I tried to persuade him to think of his situation as one he could not have been expected to have avoided. His choice not to remain virginal until entering a monogamous union with an equally untouched sex partner was one made by absolutely everyone we knew in the large San Francisco counterculture we inhabited. For me his situation was similar to that of some people who were infected with hepatitis after eating at a popular local restaurant. One might say, accurately enough, that these people's choice to eat in a restaurant instead of cooking at home caused them to contract the disease. But only some sort of fanatic about home cooking who was without any compassion would blame the victim in such a case. It is only the national anti-sex craziness that makes people think it is reasonable to blame AIDS cases on the victims' sexual behavior.

Sadly, though, my friend found no comfort in this idea. He insisted that his disease did not result from his having chosen to have sex with a person who turned out to have HIV; he had been deliberately infected by the US government. Following internet conspiracy theory discussions of the causes of AIDS led him to other websites about conspiracies, and in 2008, he discovered the websites devoted to Holocaust denial and the "international conspiracy of Jews." These websites also blamed the economic crash on Jews, so now he could feel that his considerable loss of retirement income and his home being "under water" due to the real estate market crash in California were not the result of his own choices to any degree at all but entirely due to his victimization by Jews. He turned on me viciously and said things I could not forgive about my parents, who had always loved him, and even my beloved grandparents. As must be apparent from how I have discussed this, I now see in his turn to conspiracy theories a pattern of a desire to avoid any responsibility whatsoever for his life situation. But at the time, I was devastated to see someone I had considered a trusted friend I could always turn to in times of trouble and for whom I would have done anything to help become an enemy who hated my parents and heritage and suspected me of criminal activities.

Because of the racial diversity of America, I do not feel that such people or the philosophies that misinform them will bring about anti-Semitic genocide in the United States. But I feel disturbed to see that anti-Semitism still has such power to reassure Gentiles that their problems are the fault of Jews. And this experience motivated me to go beyond surface pleasure in my heritage and start to think more deeply about what it means to be a Jew. As with the Toledo bookstore, a compromise seems in order. Hence, for the purposes of this book, I will refer to Jews not as a race but as a racialized group. This seems particularly appropriate because this book is about representations. Consequently, because the representations that constitute racialization are embodied and all embodiment of human beings involves the construction of genders and sexualities, this book will explore Jewish racialization in the context of Jewish sexualization. In addition, this focus on intersections of race and sexuality will reveal just how dangerous the anti-Semitic elements of the racialization of Jews are to the progressive goals of sexual and gender freedom.

A couple of years of research on disagreeable websites like Breitbart and Storm Front brought to my attention the propensity of anti-Semites to characterize Jews as major players in a putative destruction of American sexual morality. That Jews are seen as disruptive of sex/gender systems is highly important not only because sex and gender are among the most valorized determinants of human identity and because few humans are free from sexual urges but also because sexual attraction has been for centuries represented narratively as a solution to human problems. One has only to look at the popularity of the love story of two people who begin as enemies, from *Pride and Prejudice* through thousands of other romantic novels and films, to see that in the popular imagination, sex is the answer to the question of how people can get along with each other despite serious differences. In that the only other resolution to interpersonal problems that Western popular culture favors is violence, the place of sex as a force for good might be considered primary. So if Jews are seen as acting to eradicate wholesome/natural sexuality and the good it brings to a culture, we are to be feared.

Many countries have ascribed to this myth; however, the United States is different from other Western nations in its management of its citizens' sexuality, and this difference is reflected in our media. For other Western nations, as Michel Foucault famously discusses in *The History of Sexuality* and his other writings on biopolitics, controlling reproduction was mainly a matter of discouraging births among the poorest and the least able to care for themselves while encouraging births among citizens considered to contribute more to the strength of the country. Prohibitions on sexual activities other than reproductive monogamy were connected closely to religious beliefs. While these motivations for population control were also important in the United States, other considerations were also in play. Up through the nineteenth and even into the twentieth century, white Americans struggled with a huge population of people who would never be allowed to assimilate into mainstream society due to their skin color. There were over four million people of African descent in the United States after the Civil War (according to the 1860 census) and large numbers of Native Americans and people of Mexican descent. Their presence in the United States was seen by many white Americans as threatening for many reasons, prominent among which was the fear of both "illegitimate" mixed-race births and also of births that resulted from racial intermarriage. Since these children could not be easily racially categorized and might well have a white parent who would teach them to insist on their citizenship rights, their existence was considered by many white people to be likely to undermine the racial politics fundamental to the laws, daily practices, and justice system of the United States.

While in the twentieth century eugenics shaped European management of sexuality primarily in fascist countries during World War II, they undergirded US sexual politics much earlier and for much longer. Consequently, the management of sexuality in America has always been and continues to be as much about race as it is about economics and religion. Because conservative Americans want more white, Christian, middle-class babies born but also want to reduce the nonwhite population, which is growing to be a majority, conflicts over the management of sexuality continue to result in some of the most intensely fought battles of our time. No wonder, then, that Jewish advocacy of sexual freedom is often seen as a plot to make white Americans a minority. Consequently, Jewish sexualization cannot be understood as a separate issue from racialization in the United States.

And thus, at last, I return to the subject matter of this book, which will scrutinize the representation of Jews as racialized and sexualized subjects in a selection of films and television series with the aim of exploring how and why this matters. Cinematic treatments of Jewishness obviously matter first of all because the movies are a part of life for almost everyone in America, and most other countries. They teach us about places and people with which we may not be familiar, and they help us place ourselves within a wider world than our circle of friends, family, and coworkers. As countless academics have argued, films play a large role in identity construction not only providing models for spectators but also alerting them to perceptions of the group they are assigned culturally, which they may wish to separate themselves from and resist. I have chosen to discuss television as well as cinema because, despite significant differences in their history and development, they draw on similar tropes in depicting Jews. Television portrayals are also important because this is the media most available and familiar to the majority of people in the United States and worldwide.

The first chapter, "Sexual Perversity and the Jewish Therapist Figure," begins with an overview of the disproportionate presence of Jews in creating therapeutic approaches to sexual problems. This chapter looks at two English language films by foreign directors—*Nymphomaniac* and *A Dangerous Method*—that provide a case study of how Jewish involvement in the treatment of these problems has been understood either as something to be celebrated or as something to be deplored. My discussion of these two art films, made outside the United States, is intended to sketch in the understandings that have developed transnationally of the relationship between Jewishness and sexuality. In the second chapter, "Imaginary Histories of Americanized Jews in Love," my focus narrows to depictions of Jews in the United States, and I turn to the following historical fiction films: *Hester Street, Once Upon a Time in America, Casino*, and *Radio Days*. Here I analyze how they depict the impact of racialization and sexualization on Jews' efforts to maintain community while assimilating into mainstream American culture. Because all four films include corrupt Jews who prioritize wealth above all else, to the detriment of their romantic lives, the chapter contrasts the films that imply that American culture is the corrupting force to the ones that suggest Jews are naturally corrupt. And because all four films center on a love story, I look closely at what they suggest about the exogamous tendency that characterizes Jews in our own times. The third chapter, "Sex and Revenge, Rage and Bliss," turns to two film narratives about World War II that comment on and eroticize Jewish resistance to fascism. Beginning with discussion of the film *Black Book* about a Jewish woman's collaboration with the Nazis, the chapter moves on to focus on *Inglourious Basterds*, a film that explicitly connects the sexual choice of a Jewish woman character to the trauma of World War II while also providing Jewish viewers with a fantasy that meets the requirements of Roland Barthes's "text of bliss." This chapter is meant to shed light on the ways that the impact of the Holocaust on Jewish sexualities are represented in both foreign and domestic films. Chapter 4, "Jews, Sex Crimes, and Holocaust Erasure on Film," looks at ways the acclaimed film *Call Me by Your Name* surprisingly resembles the documentaries *Crazy Love* and *Capturing the Friedmans* and the fictional film *Last Embrace* in omitting from its narrative any consideration of the Holocaust and its effects on the sexual identity formation of Jews after World War II. This chapter shows the unintended results of decontextualization of Jewish sexualities through the erasure of our history: representations that implicitly support the anti-Semitic view that Jews are by nature sexual criminals. With chapter 5, "Two Funerals and a Wedding: Not So Nice Jewish Girls," I leave discussion of art films, which, because of the demands they make on viewers, influence only a limited number of people. I take up discussion of American television, the world's most influential media. This chapter compares the television series *Transparent* and *Broad City*. Here again, as in the first chapter, contrasting visions appear, with one series depicting Jewish sexualities as far more unhappy and dysfunctional than those of Gentiles, while the other provocatively frames identification as Jewish as offering access to pleasure superior to the sexualities represented as characteristic of Gentiles. The sixth chapter, "Monstrous Jewish Sexualities and Minoritarian Cinema," retains the focus of the analysis of *Broad City* on specifically Jewish sexualities as productive of pleasure. Through exploration of double-address narrative strategies that depict sexually attractive and morally flawed Jews, I argue with the frequently made accusation that the films made by the Coen brothers are anti-Semitic. The discussion concentrates on *Miller's Crossing, A Serious Man, Barton Fink*, and *Inside Llewyn Davis*. This chapter looks at the affinities of the Coens' approach to imagining a world of Jewish meanings parallel to what Gilles Deleuze calls minoritarian artistry, a process through which people othered by the mainstream can reimagine their identities when stereotypes are exaggerated to the breaking point. "Our Erasure Is Being Televised," the seventh chapter, turns back to both television and the promulgation of hostile stereotypes that are reinforced rather than broken. It begins with a close look at the historical distortions and omissions in the popular television series *The Marvelous Mrs. Maisel* and goes on to glance at characters with Jewish names but whose Jewishness is not overtly treated as central to the story in recent television series, such as *Oz, The Wire, Breaking Bad, Sons of Anarchy, The Expanse, The Strain, Watchmen*, and *UnREAL*, as well as the Stephen King–adaptation miniseries *Mr. Mercedes*. My aim is to show that no matter the show creators' intentions, they reinforce stereotypes and continue the pernicious racializations the stereotypes support. Thus the discussion places in a context of mostly uncontested received ideas the damage that has been done and continues to be done to American culture and society by the specific type of anti-Semitism that insists on rejecting Jewish thinkers', therapists', and political activists' contributions to sex positivity.

My conclusion comes back to the sometimes vexed relationship of Jews to African Americans that Michael Rogin has shown to be central to the development of a distinctively American cinema. Here I draw from Charles Burnett's *The Glass Shield* and Spike Lee's *Blackkklansman* and the writings of other Black cultural critics ideas about how we might recognize and resist the racing, sexing, and erasing of Jews in visual media that is foundational not just to anti-Semitism but to the relations of Jews to other racialized Americans. This conclusion, like the chapters that precede it, provides new avenues for thought not just about Jewish identities but also about how identifications imposed by hostile others can be reclaimed as foundations of powerful alliances. The entire book, through discussions of visual entertainment texts that offer resistance to anti-Semitic stereotypes, gives us a mapping out and even perhaps an entertainment media studies curriculum for change.

Notes

1. Other Jewish racialized identities are the Sephardi, who are usually understood to be Spanish, although they may also be North African, and the Mizrahi, who are understood to be Middle Eastern or North African but may also be Ethiopian or from other parts of Africa, like some of my ancestors, who came to Russia from Senegal and the Gambia via Morocco, according to a DNA test. Some of these Jews are clearly not white by any definition; others may be light-skinned and have a typically Eastern European appearance, as I do, despite my Moroccan and African blood. More confusion is caused by the Jewish diaspora, which calls into question the place of origin of Jewish families, like my father's.

2. See the Jewish Women's Archive's entry "American Jews, Race, Identity, and the Civil Rights Movement" for an overview of the issues involved.

3. What I would jokingly call volume 1 in this series consists of my writings on the consequences I foresaw of the abstinence-only sex education movement in the United States in the 1990s. But it is a pretty dark joke when one considers just how much damage was done to a generation of young people by a curriculum that promoted homophobia, sexism, racism, and irrational fear of strangers, along with virulent sex-negativity, religiosity, and false information about disease transmission.

4. Micha Danzig's "No, Ashkenazi Jews Are Not 'Functionally White'" and Dani Ishai Behan's "No Such Thing as a 'White European' Ashkenazi Jew," among many other articles on the topic, detail why this classification is not only anti-Israel (in that it emerged as a way to argue that the Ashkenazi have no claim on Israel) but also anti-Semitic. In addition, it seems to me patently ludicrous. Why were my family members, whose parents emigrated from Eastern Europe, forced to use "colored facilities" in the Jim Crow South if they were white? (Maybe this was because they had dark skin, dark eyes, and very kinky black hair.) Why do some of my family members look indistinguishable from Arabs if we are white Europeans? (We are regularly asked if we are Arab or Persian, and when we say, no, we are Jews, we are often told by Gentiles that we *must* be Sephardic.) And why, in my family and many others, are the only ones who can easily pass for white those who have one white Gentile parent? Yes, some Jews classified as Ashkenazi look white, but many do not.

1

SEXUAL PERVERSITY AND THE JEWISH THERAPIST FIGURE

A Case Study of Nymphomaniac and A Dangerous Method

I. Following Freud

Jewish psychotherapists and sex therapists abound in television and film, and the nonprofessional Jewish adviser on sex, sometimes in the form of a concerned friend, is a frequently seen figure. The Internet Movie Database lists seventy-nine films and television programs in which Sigmund Freud, the figure most commonly associated with psychology, appears as a character, and in almost all, he displays his well-known preoccupation with sexuality. This makes sense because, as the father of modern psychology, Freud insisted that libido was at the core of human existence and determined our lives more than any other force. His work changed the general understanding of sexuality throughout the literate world. The sex drive went from being seen as a potential problem that could only be remediated through stern repression or by channeling sexual activities into socially approved reproductive marriages to its being seen as the most important human feeling, the wellspring of all human energies. And just as it became difficult to think of psychological therapy without thinking of sex, so too was it difficult to think of such therapy without also thinking of Jewish counselors.

Dozens more films and television programs feature a therapist, identifiable as Jewish by surname, who in some way impacts the sex lives of his or her patients.[1] This book is primarily a study of Jews in American films; however, because such representations pervade Western visual media, irrespective of genre or intended audience, and thus heavily inform American cinema, I will not make distinctions in this chapter between the national origin of the films under discussion or their status as art or popular entertainment. Instead, this chapter concentrates on how the films either portray Jewish interlocutors to the sexual problems of others in ways that support anti-Semitic views or in ways that combat anti-Semitism. By examining how anti-Semitic theories about both Jewish sexuality and the universal cultural role of Jews as sex counselors impact cinematic representation of Jews as sexual beings, this chapter reveals some ways ancient myths of Jewish conspiracy are maintained, or critiqued, in film narratives. Additionally, it elucidates the effect that imagining Jewish community, rather than conspiracy, has on sexual social justice movements. David Cronenberg's *A Dangerous Method* (2011) and Lars von Trier's *Nymphomaniac* (2013) here serve as the objects of a case study.

My discussion includes consideration of the real-life cultural situations that contextualize these two films' narratives, for although the prevalence of Jewish sex-counselor figures in films can be interpreted in many ways, it also reflects the reality that many of Freud's most famous followers were Jews who, like Freud, concentrated on patients suffering from emotional problems related to their sexuality. The aim of these therapists, consistent with a strong Jewish tradition, was to alleviate the persecution and resultant self-hatred of those minoritized by the dominant culture because of their sexuality. Perhaps for this reason, Jews have been heavily represented in the development of academic theories of sexuality and gender, as exemplified by the leadership roles in gender/sexuality studies taken initially by gay rights pioneers like Magnus Hirschfeld and later developed by Jonathan Katz, Eve Kosofsky Sedgwick, and Judith Butler, among many others.

It is indisputable that Jewish therapists, philosophers, and academic theorists have changed the ways Americans think about gender and sexuality, which has been troubling to many political conservatives. Polls indicate that Donald Trump's strongest area of support was among white baby boomers. Speaking as a baby boomer, but not a Trump supporter, I have seen enormous changes in the way gender and sexuality are understood by the majority of people in America over my lifetime, and Jews took notable roles in all of these changes. It is, for instance, hard to imagine the feminist second wave gaining the popular momentum it did without Betty Friedan and Gloria Steinem or transgender rights being recognized without Kate Bornstein and Jack Halberstam. Perhaps if I believed that women belonged in the home submissively serving their husbands, that homosexuality was evil, and that gender was binary and determined at birth by genitalia, I would see evidence of a Jewish conspiracy in this, as anti-Semites insist, rather than a tradition of which I am proud. But I do see a laudable tradition, which was carried on in popular culture, where Dr. Ruth Westheimer (whose birth name was basically the same as mine, Karola Siegel) and Isadora Alman were among the most notable pioneers of the Progressive "sexpert" pundit role.

An interesting example of how much this figure has become a stereotype across film genres is Barbra Streisand's reprisal, for laughs, of her therapist role as psychologist Susan Lowenstein in *The Prince of Tides* (1991), this time in the form of the rambunctious sex therapist Rozalin Focker in 2004's *Meet the Fockers* and 2010's *Little Fockers*. Much of the humor in these two films comes from the reactions of the conservative and inhibited Gentile parents of her son's wife to Rozalin's sex-positive ideas, but in the end, they acknowledge her superior understanding of sexuality and seek her help. This conclusion adheres to the most common way Jewish sex counselors are represented in Western visual media.

II. Jewish Racialization and the Sex Counselor Role

Looking at the history of Jewish racialization is crucial to understanding not only why Jews appear so often as sex counselors in film narratives but also why they do so in real life. Since its inception, the American film industry has been deeply involved in debates over anti-Semitism. An instructive moment relevant to American cinematic depictions of Jewish identity is recounted in Sylvia Barack Fishman's *The Way into Varieties of Jewish Experience*. In 1954, when asked by Ben Hecht to advocate for Palestinian Jews, David O. Selznick demurred, saying that he was a "non-Jew" (188). But when challenged to find a Gentile friend who considered him not to be Jewish, he failed, and as a result decided to support Hecht's project. Such moments remain as controversial as Hecht's Zionism. Their relevance to the world of filmmaking becomes clear when we understand them in the context of Jewish racialization.

As study of the intersectionality of race, gender, class, and sexuality continues to show, racialization and the attribution of sexualities to specific groups inextricably intertwine. One of the biggest problems in combating anti-Semitism comes from confusion over what exactly Jewish identity is,

because we cannot defend a group of people against bias without deciding who belongs to the group. The issues complicating the construction
of Jewish identities that I discuss in this book's introduction render anti-
Semitism more complex than it initially seems. People who self-identify—
or are identified by others—as Jews are not necessarily recognizable by
physical characteristics, religious practices, or cultural practices. Freud insisted that "being a Jew had little or nothing to do with God. It was a racial
category" (Gilman 22–23). Jewishness for many is racial but sometimes in
weirdly mythologized ways. In some sense it was ever thus, or at least since
the twelfth century, when European "scientific, medical, and theological
treatises argued that the bodies of Jews differed in nature from those of
Christians" (Heng 361).

From the earliest attempts to account scientifically for mental illnesses,
particularly those with sexual components, Jews were deemed especially
susceptible. As Sander L. Gilman exhaustively shows, from Tacitus on, the
racial identity of Jews was inevitably formed in relation to the attribution to
them of sexual perversities that led to disease (136). Susanna Drake's work
on early Christian anti-Semitism establishes that in Origen's writings in
the third century, Jews were characterized as sexually perverse, although
because of their interpretive practices, not race. They were seen as "not only
carnal interpreters but also performers of carnal acts" (44). This understanding of group identity fits Arjun Appadurai's theory that the identifications (or, as he calls them, "names") adopted by or imposed on members of
imagined communities, including Jews, were initially constructed through
a focus on language usage as "philological scholarship [could] shore up the
histories of these names" (163). Jews were considered sexually perverse because their relationship to language, and thus to sacred texts, was deemed
perverse.

Benedict Anderson locates the racialization of Jews later, claiming that
religious communities were united by shared faith and practices and that
this transcended racial and geographically dependent identifications (54).
But with the spread of colonialism and the emergence of a slavery-based
economy in the Americas, imagined religious communities gave way to
communities imagined as national, based on exclusionary definitions of
who belonged to the nation. As a result, earlier attempts to bring about
unification of peoples through forced religious conversions were no longer
seen as valid (59–60). Concepts of race began to dominate construction of
communities. We tend to equate forced conversion of Jews with other types

of anti-Semitic persecution, but Anderson argues that forced conversion, cruel as it was, indicated a belief that Jews could become full members of the dominant group, a belief that ended with the movement into modernity at the beginning of the sixteenth century (60).

In *Unheroic Conduct: The Rise of Heterosexuality and the Invention of the Jewish Man*, Daniel Boyarin explains that another long-standing source of anti-Semitism was the high valuation in rabbinic teachings of values and behaviors that European Gentiles associated with feminine inferiority. The gentle passivity the dominant Gentile cultures considered effeminacy was "a desired trait on the part of the [traditional Orthodox] culture" and "a politically significant form of resistance" to the domineering violence imperialistic cultures associated with virility (81–82, 97–98). While Gentile cultures from the Romans to twentieth-century imperialist nations associated yielding to others with sexual impotence, traditional Jews did not consider forgoing assertions of physical power to result in impotence (Boyarin, *Unheroic Conduct*, 107–12). As a result, Jews were thought to choose perverse and inappropriate forms of sexual expression.

As Jews, along with Gentiles, became less invested in religion, and so reading the sacred texts of Judaism no longer exclusively defined the Jewish community, Jewish physicality became the new focal point. Daniel Boyarin, Daniel Itzkovitz, and Ann Pellegrini describe how, in the nineteenth century, along with "the racial difference of the Jew, the masculine/feminine axis was also being fit to another emerging taxonomy of difference: the modern discourse of sexuality with its 'specification' and 'solidification' of individuals . . . into distinct sexual personages, such as 'the homosexual' or 'the female sexual invert'" (1–18). Negative "racial models of the Jew . . . are present in virtually all discussions of pathology published from 1880 to 1930" (Gilman 4–5). Indeed, "anti-Semitic views became a staple of the substance of medicine itself" (Gilman 12). Jews were despised and feared as a source of contagion because they were considered prone to mental illness caused by "their perverse sexuality" (Gilman 106, 129). They were understood generally as "sexually different" from Gentiles, because they were given to hypersexuality (Gilman 123, 131, 135–37). One way, then, to understand the prominence of Jewish sexual counselors in film is to recognize that in real life, as a defense against their historical characterization as sexually defective due to race, many Jews have been highly motivated to study sexual nonconformity and to advocate for those minoritized as perverts.

III. Anti-Semitic Propaganda and Jewish Responses

As the Anti-Defamation League has documented, since the 2008 economic crash there has been a significant increase in the particular brand of anti-Semitism that focuses on imagined Jewish conspiracies to take over the world through financial trickery.[2] This is one of the most mysterious and illogical forms of anti-Semitism in that it seems predicated on the belief that everyone born to a parent who is identified by others as a Jew is privy to an "international conspiracy of Jews" to impoverish and thus enslave Gentiles. Anti-Semites who subscribe to this conspiracy theory never distinguish between religious and secular Jews. To them Jewish identity is determined by birth and admits one into a strongly coherent, and evil, community.

An interesting intervention into debates about Jewish identity is made by Julia Dahl's first two murder mysteries, which have received considerable critical attention, *Invisible City* (2014) and its 2015 sequel *Run You Down*. Because they are aimed at a popular audience, these novels comment on the general cultural construction of Jews as raced and sexed subjects in a more easily understood manner than Cronenberg's and von Trier's art films do. Dahl depicts her heroine Rebekah as learning the importance of the connection anti-Semitic spokesmen make between what they deem sexual perversity and what they imagine to be "the Jewish agenda." That agenda is to destroy "the white race" through "encourag[ing] pornography, masturbation, bestiality, and all matter of ugly stuff [including homosexuality and women's exercise of sexual freedom] to keep the white race weak and distracted from their evil ways" (Dahl 193). Jonathan Weisman's study of the alt-right details such beliefs (131).

Freud would have easily recognized these twenty-first-century fantasies about Jews, sex, and power since he saw in his own patients the then common delusion that "Jews were at the center of a conspiracy sexually to exploit the world around them for their own power and gain" (Gilman 141). He recognized such discourse as serious theorizing, no matter how ridiculous it seems, because of its deadly influence. In the same spirit, this chapter takes seriously how Jews are portrayed in current films in relation to sexualities that are generally considered perverse in socially disruptive ways. This is not merely an argument for more just consideration of Jewish identity but an argument that attacks on Jewish experts on sex are also attacks on the struggle to free people from oppression due to sexual difference, a struggle increasingly addressed in cinema and television.

IV. Sexual Disease and Healing

Both Cronenberg's fictionalized film about the development of psychoanalytic theory, *A Dangerous Method*, and von Trier's purely fictional film, *Nymphomaniac*, focus on the experiences of a woman whose perverse sexual desires and behavior alienate her from society and cause her great distress. Each of the films contains shockingly transgressive material, although von Trier's film is far more graphic. Both of the central female characters could be described as sexually masochistic, with the caveat that while Cronenberg's heroine prefers to be beaten as a prelude to intercourse, von Trier's only submits to whipping in order to awaken her deadened sexual feelings and later moves on from submission to dominance. In neither film are the sadomasochistic (S/M) encounters presented as healthy in any way. This contrasts the way the S/M scenes in the film *Secretary* (2002), for example, function as unexpected instances of sexual healing.[3] Instead, the beaten heroines in *A Dangerous Method* and *Nymphomaniac* obviously need healing of their sick sexualities and go to Jewish father figures to receive it.

In both *Nymphomaniac* and *A Dangerous Method*, paternalistic characters that identify as secular Jews shape the film's narrative through sessions in which they question the perverse protagonist. Both films present us with a concept of Jewish identity that is developed through these interactions. This is not a question of negative or positive portrayal of Jewish characters. It is a question of how the films portray a worldwide community of Jews, which confers an identity on each individual Jew. It is important to keep in mind that, as Anderson argues, "All communities . . . are imagined. Communities are to be distinguished, not by their falsity/genuineness, but by the style in which they are imagined" (6). Because of how they convey their opposed visions, the two films serve as case studies of possibilities for the representation of Jewish counselors in narratives about sexual perversity. It is through the contextualization of the events they recount that the differences in the two films' depictions of Jews as sexual counselors become apparent.

V. Filmmaker as Freudian Sexologist

The screenplay of Cronenberg's film is an adaptation by Christopher Hampton of his theatrical script for *The Talking Cure* (2002), which he based on John Kerr's 1993 book, *A Most Dangerous Method: The Story of Jung, Freud, and Sabina Spielrein*. Kerr's hostile account of the missed opportunity for collaboration between Freud and Jung, due to what he sees as Freud's attempts to use Jung's affair with Spielrein against him, informed Frederick Crew's notorious essay "The Unknown Freud," which criticizes Freud heavily and contributed to a wave of anti-Freudianism in the early 1990s. However, Hampton represents the trio much differently. Two of the casting choices for the original London stage production suggest the drama's change of emphasis. Jodhi May, the daughter of a French Turkish Jewish mother, brought a delicate vulnerability to Spielrein, while Ralph Fiennes, as Jung, brought to his part associations with the Nazi Amon Goth he memorably played in *Schindler's List* (1993). The audience's attention, consequently, was drawn to Spielrein as a mediating figure whose survival of her affair with a predatory proto-fascist is crucial to the development of the psychoanalytic understanding of the human struggle with the death drive. As Michael Billington writes in his review of the stage production for the *Guardian* online, "Part of Hampton's point is that Spielrein, a patient turned healer, was a highly formative influence . . . the originator of the link between Eros and Thanatos." Cronenberg, whose films frequently represent characters with putatively perverse sexualities as heroic, clearly agrees.

While some film theorists, notably Robin Wood, have seen Cronenberg as sexually conservative, Nick Davis's *The Desiring-Machine: Gilles Deleuze and Contemporary Cinema* provides a fresh, and convincing, perspective. Davis defends Cronenberg against accusations by queer studies critics that his films are conservative sexually by exploring his films' similarities to Deleuze's theoretical writings on sexuality. Davis notes that, as in Deleuze's theory of desire, Cronenberg's films employ "unsettling conjunctions of erotic, organic, and machinic matter, prone to radical transformations" in order to "suggest a fundamental mutability of all desire" (15). In other words, while Freud may be read as positing desire as taking forms and expressions predetermined by fixed "indigenous content: the incest taboo, strict gender polarity, patriarchy, and so forth," Cronenberg joins Deleuze and Félix Guattari in promoting a view of sexuality as productive "in unrestricted ways" (Davis 15–16).

Cronenberg, unlike Deleuze and Guattari, is a Freudian, albeit with a difference from the belief, often associated with Freudianism, that resistance to the binary gender roles that support patriarchy results in sexual dysfunctions. As Ernest Mathijs discusses (90–91), images of and references to Freud pervade Cronenberg's films, starting with *Rabid* (1977). Up until

A Dangerous Method, the culmination of Cronenberg's Freudian interest was his 2002 film, *Spider* (Mathijs 220). This film (adapted from Patrick McGrath's novel) is set in a halfway house for mental patients and presents viewers with a mystery that is finally explained through our recognition of the role played by the protagonist's unresolved Oedipus complex and the matricide it caused. Quintessentially Cronenbergian, the film addresses the question, "Why do men do terrible things to women?" by referring us to Freud not as a theorist who norms patriarchal attitudes but one who diagnoses them as a deadly illness. Cronenberg interprets Freudian theory as compatible with the battle against the concept of gender binary as well as the pernicious patriarchal system it undergirds.

Scott Wilson's extensive commentary on Cronenberg's first feature-length film, *Shivers* (1975), elucidates how important the dream recounted by Nurse Forsythe (Lynn Lowry) is to understanding this horror film's elusive tone. She says she dreamed of making "love beautifully" to an aged and physically decaying Freud after he explained to her "everything is erotic, everything is sexual" (43). Wilson interprets the interplay between Nurse Forsythe, who is infected with a sexually transmitted plague, and Dr. Roger St. Luc (Paul Hampton), who tries, unsuccessfully to stop the spread of the disease, as the film's center of meaning. The "key" point is that "St. Luc has denied his sexuality, his desire and his body in order to maintain the stability of his [patriarchal] identity which, nonetheless is overcome through the medium of sexuality" (45). Consequently, Freud functions here as the conduit through which we recognize the inescapability of desire—everything is indeed libidinal—and as a result, we must consciously work to minimize the potentially destructive impact that gratifying desires in conflict with society's rules may have on our lives by controlling how we actualize them rather than denying them. As Wilson discusses, Cronenberg returns to this theme in *The Brood* (1979), in which a radical therapist's manipulation of his patient's transference precipitates a series of murders as her rage takes on deadly physical forms (Wilson 158).

VI. A Dangerous Method, Indeed

A Dangerous Method comments on more than the dangers posed by how various forms of therapy deal with sexuality. It reflects Cronenberg's increasing dramatization of "questions of Jewish identity and anti-Semitism," which his depiction of Freud in this film places in "the foreground" (Taubin

30). One might scarcely see this in the casting choices for this film, as he not only gives the roles of Spielrein and Freud to Gentiles, Keira Knightly and Viggo Mortensen, but also originally cast Christoph Waltz, best known for playing an especially vicious Nazi in *Inglourious Basterds* (2009), as Freud. Additional associative confusion is generated by his casting Michael Fassbender, who played one of the few Gentile members of the Inglourious Basterds, as Jung. Fassbender appeared in another 2011 film, *X-Men: First Class*, as the Jewish villain Magneto, who was driven murderously insane by his experiences during the Holocaust. Yet despite the problematics of these casting choices, the film goes much further than Hampton's play in its support of Freudian theory and Spielrein's influence on its development and in emphasizing the relevance of Freud's and Spielrein's Jewishness, as Robert Barry writes in a review of the film:

> The standard line on the difference between the respective psychological theories of Sigmund Freud and Carl Jung is that the former was unable to get past his obsessive insistence that everything is reducible to libidinal impulses (probably, as Vincent Cassel's louche Otto Gross suggests here, because his own were left unfulfilled), while his younger apprentice developed a more nuanced, balanced approach to the unconscious. What is made abundantly clear in this new film . . . is that, on the contrary, it is Jung who is blinded by his blinkered Swiss Protestantism and willing to reach out to any form of pathetic mysticism, in avoiding acceptance of the self-evident sexual instincts plaguing him from all sides.

This interpretation of the Jewish historical figures as having healthier relationships to their own sexuality than Jung has makes the casting choices more understandable. As in *A History of Violence* (2005) and *Eastern Promises* (2007), Mortensen plays his character as a sexually self-confident, masculine man. Knightley retains the air of heroic femininity that May brought to the play, enhanced by a lacy white wardrobe. In contrast, Fassbender brings to the role of Jung an aura of repulsively aggressive sexual deviance, as he does to his role as tormented sex addict Brandon Sullivan in *Shame* (2011). This characterization of Jung is consistent with a trend Nathan Abrams attributes to recent work by Jewish filmmakers that reverses anti-Semitic stereotypes through representation of Gentiles as violent, crude sensualists (*New Jew in Film*, 14–15).

Abrams also sees Freud as a force against anti-Semitism, noting that Freud helped his fellow Jews understand the influence on their own identity construction of the stereotype of Jews as so "hysterical" that little difference existed between the sexes (*New Jew in Film*, 20–21). Traditionally in mainstream film, Jewish women were depicted either as monsters or as "tragic, mysterious . . . attainable, sexually conquerable" (46). By positioning Freud and Jung as foils in their psychoanalytic, and also their nonprofessional, treatment of a troubled Jewish woman, Cronenberg not only breaks free of the stereotypes that would ordinarily predetermine the development of each character but also reveals his view of what anti-Semitism had to do with the development of a science of the mind that was focused on sexuality.

In an interview with Nick James, Cronenberg elaborates on his view of Jung as an anti-Semite, saying that at the time in which the film is set, Jung was "slipping away to Aryan mysticism," which generated the basic philosophy of Nazism. The "differentiation" of Aryans from Jews was "very important" to Jung, so much so that he suggested that "Jews should dress differently from other people, so we can tell them apart" (Gilman 32). Jung's defection to an anti-Semitic philosophy was especially problematic for Freud because he had hoped to make Jung his successor and, in so doing, counter the prevalent view in Vienna that psychoanalysis was some kind of sham, a Jewish trick. Cronenberg remarks that the Germans and Austrians of the time, right before World War I, were already obsessed with their negative vision of Jews (James 17–18).

VII. Cronenberg as Historian

While Michael Grant correctly describes Cronenberg's earlier films as "turning away from the immediacies of communal and social existence" and so existing outside chronology, *A Dangerous Method* marks a turn toward historicization (7). In this film, history and place are depicted as crucial to the formation and performance of gender and sexuality for Jews, reminding us that not only Freud but also his patients should be understood in relation to the anti-Semitic atmosphere of Europe in the period before World War II. Patricia Erens praises *The Seven-Per-Cent Solution* (1976) for its depiction of Freud as remaining true to Jewish humanistic values by cleverly devising a way to resist resorting to "physical violence" and yet still defeat an anti-Semitic bully (352). However, in real life, relentless racist harassment drove Freud beyond such model behavior. His fighting spirit was more than just intellectual, as he demonstrated in 1883 when he told one of two anti-Semites who insulted him on a train to keep quiet and invited the other to "step up" as he "was quite ready to kill him" (Gilman 127).

Gilman details what Jews of the time were up against. He notes that "according to a contemporary guidebook, in Vienna the first question one asks about any person one sees on the street is: 'Is he a Jew'?" (44). The answer could carry intense consequences: "Violence against Jews was a common, daily occurrence from the time Freud was at the university and bands of anti-Semitic toughs would drag Jewish students out of classrooms and beat them" (45). In response to "the abuse felt on the streets, in the parks, in the university," Freud developed his persona as a "'big, strong,' heroic Jew" who fought back through his scientific, rather than racist, approach to the intersection of sexuality and mental disease (Gilman 199).[4]

The conclusion of *A Dangerous Method*, with an intertitle informing us that the SS murdered Spielrein in 1942, emphasizes the horrific atmosphere of hatred European Jews faced. As Adam Lowenstein says, "reading that intertitle . . . delivers searing emotional pain" because of the hope represented by the young Spielrein's recovery from Jung's appalling exploitation of her (26). Amy Taubin remarks, "What eventually destroys Spielrein is not Jung's shabby, unethical treatment of her but the anti-Semitism that worries Freud far more than any internal arguments among his heirs over the nature of the libido" (30).

It would be difficult, indeed, for anyone conversant with Freud's writing about his own life not to recognize Spielrein's literally hysterical eroticization of her father's punitive violence toward her in early childhood as a need to see her father as powerful. By beating his little daughter, he confirmed to her his possession of what Jacques Lacan would much later describe as "the phallus," a representation of the penis as the signifier of cultural agency (685–95). By marking her body, he marked himself as a patriarch despite his occupying the debased social position accorded to European Jews during this era. Hearing his father's story of being humiliated by a Gentile who knocked off his hat and forced him into the gutter "provided Freud with a need for a 'big strong' Jewish father" (Gilman 178). As Boyarin explains, Freud's angry reaction to this story led him "to fantasize about becoming Hannibal, whose brave father seeks revenge against the Roman oppressors," noting that "from a traditionalist Jewish point of view," Hannibal was not a Jew, because he was a pagan, but merely "a Semitic warrior" (Boyarin, *Unheroic Conduct*, 273). Boyarin goes on to explain that this is significant because it reflects Freud's discomfort with Judaism as a religion associated with voluntary renunciation of the power gained through willingness to engage in physical battle, the very sort of power Freud obviously valued

Fig. 1.1 *A Dangerous Method*: Spielrein dominated by Jung.

(Boyarin, *Unheroic Conduct*, 273).[5] Within the historical context of modern Jews, like Freud, turning away from the heroism of self-restraint exemplified by the senior Freud, it is easy to understand why Spielrein's response to her father's beating was sexual excitement—because he is proving his power, if only over her.[6] The film strongly suggests she responds the same way to Jung's sadistic beatings, with excitement that she has found a powerful father figure who can protect her in a frightening world.

Spielrein's world *is* frightening, as Cronenberg's historicization of the story constantly reminds the audience. Freud is an atheist, but he is also a Jew because he is assigned that identity by the Gentiles of Vienna, whose anti-Semitism the film repeatedly references. Lowenstein points out that "in a number of key scenes, Freud's keen awareness of social persecution as a Jew contrasts with Jung's blithely privileged Protestantism." These moments in the film move the emphasis from "imagining the powers and consequences of repression" generally to a "special interest in that especially hateful form of repressive blindness known as anti-Semitism" (Lowenstein 29). In reality, Jung went further than just willful blindness to the persecution endured by European Jews. After being rejected by Freud (and Spielrein), he would go on to inveigh against psychoanalysis as a false science springing from "the sexualized disease of the soul" common to Jews (31–32). If this sort of nasty, racist response to being slighted was what Freud thought of as typical of Gentiles, as Gilman shows us he had every reason to think, then it is no wonder that when Spielrein confided in Freud her desire to continue her affair with Jung, he gave her, in a letter, the warning that the film quotes, "We are and remain Jews. The others will only exploit us and will never understand or appreciate us" (34).

VIII. The Rival Therapists

No matter what we may think of their theories—and, as a feminist, I have some deep reservations about Freud's as well as Jung's—Cronenberg does a magnificent job of bringing to life their characters, as they reach the apex of their friendship and then fall away into enmity. At the center is Spielrein, the brilliant masochist and hysteric who overcame her paralyzing neuroses to become a successful psychiatrist, only to be murdered by the Nazis later. The film pays close attention to the meanings of Jewishness in the three main characters' milieu, something Jung seems utterly oblivious to, except in that he is drawn to Jewish women. As Lowenstein observes, when Spielrein compels Jung to admit to Freud what he has been doing with her, this "drives the men further apart and inflames their intellectual, cultural, and class differences" (25). Taubin writes that when Freud "begins to doubt Jung's intellect, talents, and sense of ethics, it weighs on him that the woman Jung has smeared and taken advantage of is a Jew" (30). Freud becomes disgusted with Jung's hypocritical double life: proper bourgeois husband and father in public, fascistic dominant in private. Although Taubin believes the film offers a largely sympathetic vision of Jung, she notes the effect of Jung's last speech (taken from a letter to Spielrein): "'Sometimes you have to do something unforgivable, just to be able to go on living'.... It is an achingly sad, romantic moment, but after I left the theater, I couldn't help thinking about all the unforgivable compromises Jung would make as he sat out World War II by the side of a Swiss lake" (31). Even within the scenes we are actually shown, Jung is presented as dishonest and unethical. His confrontation with Freud, about his opposition to psychoanalytic theory's emphasis on the importance of sexuality, is prefaced by scenes dramatizing Jung's secrecy about his own forbidden sexual obsessions and misery in the respectable marriage he made for economic reasons.

Numerous scenes display Freud's insistence that therapy cannot make people mentally healthy, only more conscious of their own processes and limitations, and so the therapist must avoid being caught up in patients' fantasies lest he contribute to their delusions. The contrast with Jung's self-serving ideas and behavior is clear. To say that Freud offers Spielrein more useful therapy than Jung does is an understatement. Freud's understanding of neurosis provides her with the perspective she needs in order to comprehend not only how her own masochism can be controlled through consciousness of her mental processes but also how eroticism and "the death drive" can intertwine either destructively or productively. In contrast, Jung appears an unprofessional bully. When Freud intervenes to decisively end Spielrein's communications with Jung, the audience can hardly avoid seeing him as a heroic figure who rescues her from a degrading situation that only reinforces her sense that Jews are weak in relation to Gentiles and can have power only in so far as Jews allow Gentiles control over them. In earlier Cronenberg films, such as *Videodrome* (1983) and *Dead Ringers* (1988), the destruction of male protagonists brought about by their being seduced into sexually dominating a masochistic woman is presented as a pitiable fate.[7] However, in *A Dangerous Method*, when Freud casts off his former protégé, Jung, in disgust, the dramatization urges us to feel relief that a bad man has been punished. Spielrein's final rejection of him is strongly coded as heroic.

IX. Out-of-Control Sexuality Reimagined

Somewhat similarly *Nymphomaniac* breaks from von Trier's earlier work, by depicting masochism as a neurosis that is dangerous to women. Von Trier's previous depictions of female masochism in his Golden Heart trilogy (*Breaking the Waves* [1996], *The Idiots* [1998], and *Dancer in the Dark* [2000]) have drawn criticism because, as Linda Badley notes about the first of these films, it "challenges feminism with its conflation of ethics and female masochism," a charge leveled at all three films by numerous critics (85). *Nymphomaniac* is different in that here his female protagonist, like those of the Cronenberg films that depict female masochism, is not a loving, self-sacrificial victim. She vehemently rejects love, and, in fact, loses her ability to feel arousal once she has tamed into domesticity the brute who, much earlier, took her vaginal and anal virginity with eight vicious thrusts. She has no emotional relationship with the professional sadist to whom she later chooses to submit and subsequently emulates his behavior with others.

For supporters of the idea that enjoying sex outside of loving, committed relationships is not necessarily an indication of mental or emotional disturbance, and especially for those who find comical the idea that one can be addicted to sex, *Nymphomaniac* offers many pleasures. The primary one is that the film playfully disputes the view, long promulgated by psychiatry and psychology, of undomesticated female sexuality as an illness. This view was codified in the DSM, as the term *nymphomania* was reclassified first in the 1987 DSM III as "sexual addiction" and later, in the 1994 DSM IV, as "hypersexuality."[8] Joe (Charlotte Gainsbourg), the titular nymphomaniac, embraces her putative disorder and makes hilarious fun of a sexual addiction group to which she is remanded. One sequence, in which she resists being shamed by an angry, jealous wife, is particularly humorous in its depiction of a confrontation between two completely incompatible value systems. Whereas contemporary sexual therapy promotes the idea that we must strive to control what is seen as excessive sexuality and domesticate it, the film insists, as "The Voice of the Devil" does in William Blake's *The Marriage of Heaven and Hell*, that "those who restrain desire do so because theirs is weak enough to be restrained."

Joe explains that her whole life must be understood as a refusal to experience sex as anything other than physical intensity unconnected to emotional attachments. The extreme nature of her encounters with the professional dominator she calls K (Jamie Bell) provides some of the film's most transgressive images. Yet she is not represented as his victim, nor is he hers. Instead, she learns from submission to his sexual torment how to torment others and puts that knowledge to work in her later job as a debt collector, a role that gives her apparent sadistic pleasure and brings her financial success. This sort of mocking of conventional ethical judgments enlivens most of the film.

The film reaches a conclusion that is not at all pleasurable, however, in its depiction of the failure of talk therapy to help those made unhappy by the mismatch between their sexuality and their world's expectations. This is hardly surprising considering that much of von Trier's work has taken as its subject the misery wrought by sexual desire and the failure of psychology to help the unhappy. This is especially notable in the first two films in his Depression trilogy, *Antichrist* (2009) and *Melancholia* (2011). As Peter Schepelern discusses, these films strongly foreground von Trier's rebellion against his upbringing in a family that embraced Danish cultural radicalism and its high valuation of love as the basis of a happy sex life and, by extension, a happy society: "*Nymphomaniac* can be understood as a challenge to Cultural Radicalism's concept of sex. The rather complex and ambiguous lesson of *Nymphomaniac* could be that sexuality is not a natural biological circumstance, but a kind of destiny, a condemnation that defines your personality—a cruel and irrational force that controls your life. And the option of thoughtful, humanistic culture as a cure against it is discarded." But in *Nymphomaniac* a new theme appears: the linkage of Jewishness to the failure of a humanistic sex therapy to help the victims of destructive desires. What is most shocking about *Nymphomaniac* is not its graphic sexual images but its all too traditional representation of a Jew as a dangerous, sexually perverse trickster.

X. Von Trier's Jewish Identity Issues

Jewishness was not a central issue in Cronenberg's films until his contribution to the 2007 collection of short films called *To Each His Own Cinema*, "At the Suicide of the Last Jew in the World in the Last Cinema in the World."[9] In this short, he plays himself holding a gun to his head as he listens to a television panel of experts discuss Jews and film. Von Trier's relationship to Jewish identity construction seems far more complicated but equally dramatic. He has often commented on the effect on him of his mother's 1989 deathbed revelation that he was not the son of her secular Jewish husband, Ulf Trier, but of Fritz Michael Hartmann, with whom she had an affair. Since both men were Danes and members of the Danish resistance during World War II, it is not clear why this knowledge led von Trier to begin characterizing himself as a Nazi. While this self-description is obviously part of his general behavior as a provocateur, and not meant to be taken seriously as a declaration of fascist political beliefs, it remains disturbing. Beginning with his joking claim to sympathize with Hitler at the Cannes Film Festival in 2011, his contradictory remarks about this pronouncement and the reactions to it have led to considerable debate about von Trier's attitudes about Jews. His public persona makes it impossible to make definitive claims about von Trier's true attitude about his own or others' identification as Jews. However, while we cannot know his motivation for depicting Jews the way he does in his films, we can examine whether or not these portrayals support specific anti-Semitic stereotypes.

XI. An Anti-Historical Perspective

Cronenberg's *A Dangerous Method* is deeply concerned with creating an alternative history of the development of psychoanalysis by placing that history in relation to a realistically rendered Europe. Von Trier does not work this way. Caroline Bainbridge praises him for "repeatedly show[ing] that cinema is important precisely because it does not deal with 'reality' and because of its extraordinary links to unconscious processes of fantasy and identification" (ix–x). While I have no argument with this assessment of the value of cinema, some of the interventions of von Trier's films into that process of identity construction may well give pause to those concerned about anti-Semitism. *Europa* (released as *Zentropa* in North America, 1991) provides a pertinent example.

As Bainbridge says, in one of the "most memorable" scenes in *Europa*, von Trier plays a Jew who, for his own benefit, gives false testimony that exonerates a Nazi (54–55), perpetuating the popular anti-Semitic belief that Jews' lack of honor is instrumental in causing their persecution. Because the film focuses on the postwar love affair between an American and a Nazi who involves him in her group of German terrorists, the film drew criticism at Cannes as sympathetic to fascism. (Defiance of this criticism may have been part of the motivation behind von Trier's offensive Hitler joke at the later Cannes film festival.) It is possible to read *Europa* otherwise, as a critique of American idealization of fascistic values. We might also interpret the film's vile Jew as a self-referential reflection of von Trier's own conflicts regarding his German Jewish heritage. Still this portrayal fits well with the vein of harsh criticism of the humanistic values generally associated with Jews that runs through von Trier's work.

Bainbridge rightly points out, "For von Trier, 'humanist pieties' are closely bound up with prescribed social and ideological values," which he not only rejects but also connects to social decline (45). Indeed the "failed idealism and its function in prompting greater evils" that Bainbridge sees as a major trope in his films makes a startling appearance in *Nymphomaniac* (51), where humanism is explicitly connected to a Jewish worldview. If this connection were contextualized through references to real places and events, the film would have the philosophical gravitas of *A Dangerous Method*.

However, in contrast to *A Dangerous Method*, despite its references to some recognizable cultural moments and locations, *Nymphomaniac* is mainly set in an indeterminate place and time. Schepelern assumes, based on von Trier's unpublished manuscript for the film script, that "Joe is 'about 50 years old' . . . therefore, when Seligman finds her in the alley, we can assume that she was born in 1962 or 1963. Her youth then takes place from the late '70s through the 1980s." However, "There are no references to contemporary events, or other markers of that era" (Schepelern). In addition to this problem with placing the film's events is that Gainsbourg was in her early

Fig. 1.2 *Nymphomaniac*: Cruising the train in hot pants.

forties when the film was made and looks barely forty at the conclusion. In addition, the styles of clothing and hairstyles Joe and her contemporaries wear in her youth—for example, the hot pants Joe wears to seduce men on a train—are typical of the fashions of the mid-1960s to early 1970s. This was a style, along with the miniskirt, launched by famous 1960s designer Mary Quant.

As a consequence of the lack of specificity about the time and place, Joe's Jewish interlocutor, Seligman, represents the sort of decontextualized, transhistorical, and transgeographical sexual dysfunctionality traditionally assigned to Jewish characters throughout film history, as amply documented in such studies as Erens's classic *The Jew in American Cinema*, Omer Bartov's *The "Jew" in Cinema*, and Eric A. Goldman's *The American Jewish Story through Cinema*.

Casting here, as in Cronenberg's film, is interesting in its undermining of the view that Jewishness is physically recognizable. Stellan Skarsgård, a Swedish Gentile who appears in many von Trier films, plays Seligman. His lack of a stereotypical Jewish appearance is countered, though, by the character's name, which evokes the Jewish American founder of positive psychology, Martin Seligman, and as Sean Erickson remarks, "It's certainly not a coincidence." Unlike Martin Seligman, who presents as masculine and has seven children, von Trier's Seligman takes the feminized weakness often attributed to Jewish men to a comical extreme.[10] Joe laughs at his daintily eating rugelach with a dessert fork. While she boasts of her many conquests, he timidly confesses his virginity. Thus, he is racialized Jewish through behavior rather than appearance.

Seligman has much in common with those male intellectuals in von Trier's earlier work, who seem meant to represent the failure of a Western patriarchal approach to life based on rational humanism. Bill Houston (David Morse) in *Dancer in the Dark*, Tom Edison (Paul Bettany) in *Dogville* (2003), He (Willem Dafoe) in *Antichrist*, and John (Kiefer Sutherland) in *Melancholia* all win the trust of the female protagonist and the audience with what seems to be gentle, encouraging counsel, based in reason, only to shock us with later cruel betrayal. The differences are that the others are not called on to give counsel on sexual matters, nor are the others Jews. Tom Paulus poses the question: "Why have critics been so coy about stating the obvious? That Seligman—an allegorical Everyman name, for sure, but also echoing famous self-help guru Marty Seligman . . . —is a Jew, the only man in the story who tries to rape Joe, and the only one who gets killed at the end."[11]

That Seligman's victim and killer, Joe, is played by Charlotte Gainsbourg (another von Trier favorite) will remind some audience members of the sexual scandal the actress was involved in as a girl.[12] She is the daughter of the notorious Jewish musician Serge Gainsbourg (born Lucien Ginsberg), whose sexually provocative hit song "Je T'aime . . . Moi Non Plus" (1967) was followed in 1984 by "Lemon Incest," a pedophilic duet sung with then twelve-year-old Charlotte. Therefore, we have a sort of confusing inversion in which Jewish sexual perversity is evoked by a casting choice that involves a Jew playing a Gentile while a Gentile plays a Jew who seems at first to be sexually pure and generally virtuous before being revealed to be a sexual danger to others. Through Gainsbourg's presence bringing to mind her family history, the film nudges the audience to think about Jews as predatory sexual perverts (and of her as the victim of one), just as Cronenberg's film pushes us to think about Gentiles in that way and of Jews as potentially subject to the predation because of their historical/cultural vulnerability.

Von Trier's film, which is basically a series of stories about the sex life of the self-declared nymphomaniac Joe, is structured around flashbacks to the tales she tells Seligman during a long night that begins with his finding her lying beaten in an alley and bringing her home with him to recover. Numerous reviews have referred to her as a Scheherazade figure, but they are off the mark because, unlike Scheherazade, Joe is not afraid of her interlocutor, nor is she in any apparent way trying to seduce him in order to keep him from killing her. Instead, they quickly fall into a companionable rhythm, the only tension between them coming from their opposed views of life, which schematically structure the metanarrative containing Joe's story. As Judy Berman observes, "Although they get along just fine, their conversation as she recovers sets them up as two opposing archetypes. . . . The relationship between Joe and Seligman is the relationship between nature—brash, destructive, uncontrollable—and civilization. He very literally brings her out of the wild, attempts to domesticate her and intellectualize her wild proclivities." What results is "a conversation between a woman trying to explain herself as dispassionately as possible and the eager intellectual who keeps interrupting her with questions and analogies, trying to fit everything she says into a form he can analyze—and thus understand" (Berman). The power dynamic between the captive Scheherazade and the murderous Shahryar does not exist here. If anything, Seligman seems less powerful, the one who is struggling to help and reassure his somewhat irritable guest.

As Jonathan Romney describes it, "Joe's unreliable first-person narrative is seemingly improvised off the cuff triggered by the cues she finds scattered around Seligman's flat" ("Review," 86). The tales themselves are so absurdly unrealistic that most reviewers assume we are meant to imagine Joe makes them up as she goes along. For example, in the hot pants scene mentioned above, she and a friend have a contest to see who can have sex with the most strangers they encounter on a train. Very unrealistically, none of the men they approach assumes they are prostitutes, although both the women's tawdry outfits and their crude advances and offers of fellatio would certainly suggest that. Along the same lines, Joe has trouble holding down a job but never considers sex work, although she will have sex with any man who is willing. Joe refuses to use condoms and never gets an STD, although she does have two unplanned pregnancies. When she visits the sadist K, he inflicts what looks like crippling damage on her, but she swaggers away, barely visibly marked. Later, Joe's vagina bleeds not just once but chronically because she masturbates too much, and this condition persists so that she cannot have sex with men anymore. Yet sex with a female partner presents no apparent problem.

These and many more inexplicable happenings are more than matched by the unrealistic mise en scène. Although filmed in Belgium and Germany, the film seems meant to be understood as taking place in Britain, since all the characters speak English and all visible signage and writing is in that language. Yet it certainly does not look like the United Kingdom because we see respectably dressed and carefully made-up women with bushy unshaven underarm hair. Moreover, Joe's name is spelled in the masculine form in English rather than the British feminine form "Jo," and the name of her main—and only named—sex partner, Jerôme, is distinctly European. We can conclude, as many reviewers do, that this is an allegory, meant to be taken as timeless and universal, in which Joe represents raw, unrestrained sexuality and Seligman represents (Jewish) liberal humanism.

XII. Seligman's Jewish Secular Humanism

At first Seligman seems appealing enough, and his appeal is strongly connected to his identification as a secular Jew. True to stereotype, he is open-minded and humanistic. He accepts Joe without judgment, even when the actions she recounts, such as abandonment of her child, seem to him tragic. He tries to inspire her to love herself as a person, not just a vagina, and to embrace love and kindness. And as Liel Leibovitz points out in a fascinating defense of the film in *Tablet Magazine*,

> A perfect embodiment of Jewish eschatology, [Seligman] believes, like the sages of old, that there aren't any fundamental differences between our own time and the days of the Messiah to come and that all attempts at redemption must focus not on some desperate thrust heavenward but on a series of small and incremental earthly steps. If you believe this—if you believe that everything you do is an important step toward salvation—interpretation becomes your steeliest sword. If you are your own savior, and if every one of your acts facilitates the saving, you are likely to read a lot into everything. That's how we got the Talmud, the ultimate book of ordering the world, and that's how we got a grinning Seligman, alone in his apartment with his books, trying to do the same.

If the film ended with Joe going peacefully to bed, resolved to try in the future to better manage her sexuality and avoid further antisocial, self-destructive sex practices, I would agree with Leibovitz that this is a spiritual film that affirms core values traditional to Jews, secular and religious. However, the film does not end that way. Instead, it ends with Seligman attempting to rape Joe and her shooting him dead.

Thus, the humanism the film presents as typical of Jews is shown as a facade that conceals their desire to prey on others. The banality of this depiction is nicely contextualized by Henry Kellerman's angry comment in his polemical indictment of mainstream American film portrayals of

Jews, *Greedy, Cowardly, and Weak*: "And of course, in Hollywood movies, it's always the case that the Jewish character invariably, and inexorably [sexually] pursues the Gentile character" (158). The sweetness Seligman exudes as he explains that he has been virginal all his life due to his greater interest in the mystical deep meanings of life than in sexual pleasure is revealed as a sham by his pouncing on Joe when she is most vulnerable, a sham just as fake as the impossible tales Joe spins.

This depiction belongs to a tradition that began long before film but has continued as a recurrent feature of cinema. As Omer Bartov discusses, *Jew Süss* (1940) encapsulates traditional anti-Semitic stereotypes including that "the 'Jew' is a lecherous male who pollutes the blood of innocent maidens and thus their entire race" as part of the Jewish "secret cult intent on taking over the world" (13). According to this vision secular and "assimilated Jews were in fact the most dangerous, because hiding under the mask of civilized conduct lurked the very same mythical Jew of yore," the determined destroyer of Christian civilization (Bartov 14). Throughout Bartov's study, the term he most frequently uses to describe the constructed figures of Jewishness in cinema is *protean*. Anderson offers a persuasive explanation for this type of anti-Semitism when he says that in contrast to nationalism, which "thinks in terms of historical destinies . . . racism dreams of eternal contaminations . . . outside history" so that Jews are "forever Jews" and never can be true citizens of any nation outside Israel. He goes on to say, "Thus for the Nazi, the *Jewish* German was always an imposter" (149, original emphasis). Since the film provides not even a hint of an explanation of Seligman's sudden transformation from a kindly counselor to a coldhearted sexual assaulter, we have little recourse but to conclude that this shocking development reveals his true, racialized nature.

XIII. Conclusion

In terms of their depiction of Jews, *A Dangerous Method* and *Nymphomaniac* are mirror images of each other, near perfect reversals of each other's definitions and valuations. Each engages in an opposite way the question posed in popular dramas about motherless and abandoned Jews, such as the film *Ida* (2013). For those outside a religious community and outside any Jewish social organizations, what does it mean to be a Jew? Cronenberg tells us that accepting a Jewish identity brings with it a responsibility to take action to increase human awareness of the need to treat one another fairly. Like Jung, Freud sees that Spielrein is beautiful, young, impression-able, and submissive, but this does not inspire Freud to take sexual advantage of her. Quite the contrary, it inspires him to act as a true father figure and protect her from Jung's predation. He also inspires her to take power on her own behalf, to become the psychoanalytic theorist she has the potential to be. Cronenberg's film conveys the message that because the Jews function as scapegoats in an anti-Semitic world, it behooves us to fight systematic oppression not just for ourselves but also for others. His Freud behaves the way he does because he is a Jew in Vienna at a specific place and time, and he rises to the challenge to act with honor while being tempted to do evil.[13] Ultimately, the film suggests that the community imagined by secular Jews offers benefits to the world due to its high valuation of social justice.

While von Trier may not have intended this effect, his film implies that the commitment to humanism and social justice that has historically helped secular Jews identify as members of a Jewish community, despite lacking a common religion, is simply empty rhetoric. Underneath all their good talk and good works, the film strongly suggests, Jews are deceivers without the desire or ability to help others. Because Seligman is the only character in the film identified as Jewish, whether or not von Trier intended his behavior to reflect on all Jews, his dangerous duplicity and his attempt at rape naturalizes sexual perversity as a defining attribute of Jews. Cronenberg's film belongs to a tradition of Jewish resistance both to this slander and to the vilification of Jews' historical role in expanding knowledge of sexuality and the psyche.

These differences are important not because they would then lead us to say that Cronenberg's film is superior to von Trier's or that one director is a better person than the other. They are important because, for centuries, Jews have taken leading roles in bringing about social change, in promulgating humanism as a philosophy while interpreting it to mean caring about social justice and working to alleviate unnecessary suffering. Jews have been especially prominent in applying that principle to the treatment of sexuality. To dismiss this motivation as a lie and this work as a "Jewish trick" is not just an attack on Jews; it is an attack on the very idea that humans can form any sort of community that supports sexual health and happiness. What comparison of these two films, as case studies of contrasting depictions of Jewish interlocutors for the sexually troubled, discloses is that racialized identifications and the sexualities attached to them matter in more ways than films—or film theories—ordinarily acknowledge.

Notes

1. Two recent examples are Alana Bloom, a member of the erotic triangle linking the two main characters in the television series *Hannibal*, and Olive Goldberg, the psychiatrist mother of Rachel Goldberg, the protagonist of the television series *UnREAL*.

2. For statistics see Anti-Defamation League, "ADL Audit: Anti-Semitic Assaults Rise Dramatically across the Country in 2015."

3. Although the actress playing the heroine, Maggie Gyllenhaal, is Jewish, the masochistic secretary she plays is not identified as a Jew.

4. See also Daniel Boyarin's "Homophobia and the Postcoloniality of the 'Jewish Science'" for a detailed discussion of Freud's "complex and conflicted" response "to the racism directed against Jews . . . by recoding race *as* gender" leading to an apparent acceptance of "the characterization of Jews as differently gendered" and effeminized (173). Cronenberg's Freud is not afflicted, as the real Freud was, with the "Janus-like doubleness" that leads to his theorizing race and gender in ways that are "radical and reactionary at the same time," as Boyarin shows (198). Instead, he is simply a heroic defender of the embattled Jewish woman.

5. In fact, Boyarin points out many affinities between Freud's view of healthy masculinity and the nineteenth-century Zionist concept of Muscle-Jews, who are "the very antithesis of the [traditional] Jewish ideal" ("Goyim Naches, or Modernity and the Manliness of the Mentsh," 76–77).

6. In *Sex vs. Survival: The Life and Ideas of Sabina Spielrein*, John Launer offers evidence from Spielrein's diaries to support his claim that her father not only was extremely physically abusive toward his children but also sexually molested Sabina (22). However, this information was unavailable to any of the authors or filmmakers under discussion here. They uniformly depict Sabina as referring to one isolated beating not inconsistent with the ordinary child-rearing behavior of her times.

7. As in *Secretary*, the masochistic heroine in this film, Nikki Brand, is played by a Jew (Debbie Harry) while the character is not marked as Jewish.

8. While it does represent some progress that high sex drives are no longer understood through official gender bias—because the terms *sexual addiction* and *hypersexuality*, unlike *nymphomania*, are gender-neutral—the idea persists that a high sex drive is pathological. Given the gender biases of most societies, women who want undomesticated sex will still be considered cases for treatment.

9. This is not to say Jews and Jewishness have been entirely absent from Cronenberg's films. *The Fly*, for example, his 1986 remake and reimagining of Kurt Nuemann's 1958 horror film of the same title, clearly alludes to Kafka's short story "The Metamorphosis" (which numerous critics have seen as inspired by Kafka's sense of alienation due to his racialization as a Jew) and stars Jeff Goldblum.

10. See Abrams's "Passivity" chapter in *New Jew*, 91–198, for discussion of the history of cinematic portrayals of Jewish men as effeminate, weak, and timid.

11. Psychologist Martin Seligman created the positive psychology method and is the director of the University of Pennsylvania's Positive Psychology Center. He served as president of the American Psychological Association in 1998 and is the founding editor in chief of *Prevention and Treatment* (the APA electronic journal). All of these accomplishments make him a prime target for those who, like von Trier, disapprove of the idea that psychological methods can cure pessimism and mitigate melancholy.

12. The younger Joe is played by the Gentile French actress Stacy Martin.

13. This might be said of Cronenberg himself. See Ira Robinson's *A History of Antisemitism in Canada* for detailed discussion of the persecution and exclusion of Jews not only in that country's past but in the present. Cronenberg's turn away from supernatural horror stories and toward exposure of real life horrors with this film could be seen as heroic in the same way that he sees Freud's choice to help rather than exploit the emotionally ill.

2

IMAGINARY HISTORIES OF
AMERICANIZED JEWS IN LOVE

I. Making History

The previous chapter examines traditional representations of Jews as a racialized group defined in large part by our relationship to sexuality. As that chapter's case study reflects, this relationship can be seen in terms of the threat that the perceived otherness or difference from the Gentile majority that Jews are assumed to pose. Or the outsider status of Jews caused by racialization can be seen as providing Jews with a deeper understanding of how sexual codes and behaviors work as part of the culture on which we, as members of a marginalized minority, have a unique perspective. As I have shown, the representation of Jews as sexually different from Gentiles is deeply rooted in European cultures and persists today. This representation, initially in written texts and theater, formed part of the heritage that came with the Jews to America. The identities that had been assigned to Jews in Europe, however, were complicated in the United States by specific racial tensions when those Jews began to arrive in America in great numbers at the turn of the twentieth century.

Jews lived in America from colonial times onward but were not part of a massive wave of immigration until the 1880s, when almost three million European Jews came to the United States, most fleeing anti-Semitic violence in Eastern Europe. The world they entered when they arrived was one largely defined by racial conflict. Of course, the most well-known racial conflict of the 1800s was the Civil War. But from the 1800s on, America was faced with two other situations concerning race that many found threatening. Westward expansion contributed to a heightening of the battles over territory that had been fought between white colonists and the Native

Americans since the colonization of America began. In the West, despite more than a century of attempted genocide, Native Americans continued to fight sporadically against the invading whites throughout the 1800s, while the expansion of the southern border brought westerners also into conflict with Mexicans, culminating in the Mexican-American War of 1846–48. While these open conflicts were pretty much a thing of the past by the time the great wave of Jewish refugees from Europe began in the late 1800s, Anglo-Americans in the West still had to contend with a population of Latinx and Indigenous people most of whose land had been stolen from them and who, consequently, were residents of the country but not truly citizens, if citizenship means having the same legal rights as the majority.

After the Civil War, large numbers of African Americans, many of whom had been enslaved, lived in the southern states where they were seen by the white majority as a social and political problem. Because of their disenfranchisement, due to voter suppression, it was impossible for them to demand just treatment as citizens or even protection from racist violence, so many migrated to the North hoping for a better life. But in neither the South nor the North were the majority of white Americans willing to accept people of African heritage as full citizens. In fact, the view that the very idea was outrageous was reflected in several states' antimiscegenation laws. The Chinese who came in large numbers to the United States during the gold rush of the mid-1800s and to work on the transcontinental railroad were also subjected to these laws. The justification was that children born of racially mixed marriages or more casual sexual activities across racial lines could not be true Americans.

Due to endless racial conflict in the United States, race has been seen far less as a matter of the geographic location of one's forebears than it was in Europe. Rather than a cultural heritage linked to a particular ancestry, physical characteristics were understood to be what defined people as nonwhite. While many groups of people now considered white were racialized in America because of their ancestry, just as they had been in Europe, a provisional status of whiteness was legally and socially granted to some groups of people if they not only could successfully adopt the behaviors common to the mainstream but were also light-skinned enough to pass for white. In Europe, while assimilation was valued, those who assimilated into an adopted culture were not considered to belong to it in the same way as those born into it. The difference in the way race was understood in Britain is very marked in fictional texts, as shown, for example, in the 1859 novel *The*

Woman in White by the popular British author Wilkie Collins. This text presents two Italian characters who stand for two types of refugees from political turmoil in Italy. Both are racialized as naturally overly emotional and childlike, but they are sharply contrasted as well due to their behavior. One is a criminal who frighteningly pursues a white English woman who is repulsed by him. The other assimilates into English culture, behaves virtuously, and helps the hero rescue his beloved from the criminals who plot against her for financial gain. So while one is seen as a threat because of his racialized characteristics, the other is understood to be still Italian, which is seen to be racially different, but a good Italian. That is, he is an Italian who does not behave like one.

Thus, in nineteenth-century Western Europe, people who were racialized because of the country they or their forebears had come from were often seen and treated as potential full citizens if they were personally capable of behavior deemed proper. This was the case even if, because of their supposed natural greater libidinousness, they were assumed to have to exercise greater self-control than those not racialized. Generally, throughout Europe, religious Jews were seen as a threat to cultural unity, but that happened primarily when they stayed apart from Christian society by choice. Jeffrey Jerome Cohen makes the following argument about religious Jews: "Scattered throughout Europe by the Diaspora and steadfastly refusing assimilation into Christian society, Jews have been perennial favorites for misrepresentation, for here was an alien culture living, working, and even prospering within vast communities dedicated to becoming homogeneous and monolithic." But the extent to which this was the case for secular or Christian-convert Jews varied from location to location. While Jews were definitely racialized and considered sexually Other in Western Europe, they were more than merely tolerated in England. And this is important because England was the country with which the majority of racially unmarked white Americans identified themselves due to the shared language among many other cultural heritages. The Jewish-by-racialization but Christian-by-religion prime minister of England, Benjamin Disraeli, is the best example of the way England accepted as full citizens Jews who assimilated even while continuing to regard them as racialized and thus nonwhite people.

In the United States things were quite different for those who were racialized. Hostile racialization and the attitude that one could never become a proper citizen was not a matter of appropriate or inappropriate behavior, self-discipline or its lack, or a desire or refusal to try to assimilate. The primary mode of racialization was through attention to skin color and the shape of mouths and noses, physical aspects that marked Native Americans, African Americans, and Asian Americans as Other. The very presence of physically different people, whether belligerent or peaceful would-be assimilationists, was seen as threatening to the new nation. For this reason, sexual relations, and especially intermarriage, between those considered white and those racialized as Other by their physical characteristics were deemed dangerous to the cultural integrity of America. Because Jews generally could pass for white physically and thus, if not openly practitioners of Judaism, could assimilate into mainstream culture, such attitudes about Jews were not yet common in Western Europe, whence most of the heritage with which white Americans identified came, and would not become so until the rise of fascism in the 1930s. And in America the ability to pass for white became a tremendous advantage, separating Jews from most other racialized subjects. Part of the evidence for this is that Jews were not subject to miscegenation laws, and so were never legally forbidden to have sexual relations with, marry, or have children with Gentiles in any of the United States.

Still, Jewish sexualities were seen differently in the United States than they had typically been in Western Europe, not just by Gentiles, but also by the frequently marginalized and excluded Jews themselves. While Jews were racialized and sexualized in America, the sexualities attributed to them were not seen as necessarily disruptive of national unity, even when the Jews retained Judaism. The threat Jews posed was understood less in terms of the possibility of intermarriage or sexual relations that could produce children with a mixed heritage, than in the way Jews might influence Christians to adopt a life centered more on sexual pleasure than on familial duty. The rise of a motion picture industry understood, not without reason, to be controlled by Jews contributed to the construction of a stereotype of Jewishness as more concerned with sexual activities, either more immoral or more free-spirited, depending on one's value system, than that of Gentiles (Garber 204). The effects were either to look to Jews to see how to enjoy sexuality more freely or to call for restraints on their contributions to American popular culture. Both effects have significance because they shaped and continue to shape relations between Jews and Gentiles, as explored in the previous chapter, and because they necessarily impact filmmaking and how audiences receive films. This chapter looks at how a collection of representative American films reflect Jewish identity construction in America's particular atmosphere of race-based sexualization.

As Tony Michels discusses, since the 1940s, American Jews have debated the relation of our collective history to our individual self-definition, seeking to avoid an unquestioning acceptance of the dominant narrative of our experience as "a steady process of voluntary [and successful] adaptation to a free, democratic, and prosperous society" (22). Jews in America today stand in even more urgent need of a useable history as we attempt to deal with persistent Holocaust denial, external and internal battles over Israel, and continuing debates among ourselves and with Gentiles over whether or not Jewishness is racialized in this country. As long-standing American arguments about immigration, and the 2016 presidential election, have highlighted, America demands assimilation from its citizens and awards or denies social status on that basis. So, looking at Jewish assimilation is crucial to how we understand the place of Jews in America.

However, we cannot create a useful history from our personal experiences alone because age, family income, and regional cultures in the past created vast differences in how much assimilation was possible for American Jews. Looking instead at how audiovisual texts participate in the construction of our history allows examination of how memories are made that to some extent erase the actual lived history of Jews through fictionalization meant to appeal to both Jewish and Gentile audiences but also continue a national story of what our presence in America means.

Part of placing Jews in America involves understanding how our sexuality is understood because, as the previous chapter discusses, in anti-Semitic propaganda, and the entertainment media it informs, we are consistently demonized as people who discourage heteronormative sexual practices and encourage those that undermine traditional marriage. Our own sexual relationships come under frequently hostile scrutiny since not only is marriage, leading to the creation of a family, generally seen as the foundation of any society, but intermarriage with Gentiles constitutes a major form of assimilation for Jews, and so it is seen by anti-Semites as an intrusion into white racial purity. Consequently, analyzing cinematic depictions of Jewish assimilation must begin with consideration of how that assimilation is affected by various understandings of Jews as sexual subjects.

There are many films about American Jews in love. I have chosen to center this chapter on *Hester Street* (1975), directed by Joan Micklin Silver; *Once Upon a Time in America* (1984), directed by Sergio Leone; *Casino* (1995), directed by Martin Scorsese; and *Radio Days* (1987), directed by Woody Allen, because they represent a range of cinematic attempts to create a fictionalized history in which Jewish sexualities are treated as formative of specifically American Jewish identities. All four films focus on significant times in American history when these identities were forged, and all four films deeply engage with the relationship between Jewish sexualities and the corruption often associated with American capitalism, a system in which moral values are seen to be undermined by the pursuit of wealth. Rather than looking at the films in chronological order, I have ordered my discussions of them according to how approvingly or disapprovingly they portray the interplay of Jewish sexualities and Jewish attempts at assimilation into American mainstream society.

Stereotypes are not absent from the four films. They include corrupt Jews who prioritize wealth above all else to the detriment of their romantic lives. Consequently in this chapter, I contrast the film plots and characterizations that imply that American culture is the corrupting force to those that suggest Jews are naturally corrupt. And because all four films center on a love story that is linked to problems with assimilation into mainstream white culture and two include the stereotype of the shiksa, the Jewish term for a Gentile woman who is considered desirable because of her high status as a love object in mainstream culture, I look closely at what they suggest about the exogamous tendency that characterizes Jews in our own times. To possess her becomes a sign of attainment of the American Dream. Yet all four films suggest that this dream is corrupt at the core. In one of the films, Judaism is treated as the antidote to a toxic dream, but the other three films are decidedly secular.

Scholarly consideration of cinematic representations of American Jews often conflate secular Jewish identifications with Jewish identifications determined by religious practice, resulting in the false impression that identifying as Jewish is primarily a religious choice. This chapter deals, instead, with films that construct Jewishness as a racial identity in relation to American sex and gender systems. Through comparison of these films' widely varying representations of the impact of racialization and sexualization on Jews' efforts to maintain community while assimilating into mainstream culture, a picture emerges of how a specifically American process of racialization works to affirm the Jewishness of even the most secular Jews in ways either hostile or friendly.

Hester Street depicts the marriages and romantic relationships of Jewish immigrants to New York City in the late 1800s, emphasizing the resistance of heroic Jews from the Old Country to America's corrupting influence. *Once Upon a Time in America* continues the theme of America as a corrupting force by depicting the lives of two hoodlums in the period between 1920 and 1968, when Jewish gangsters rose to prominence in organized crime. And *Casino* provides a surprisingly sympathetic look at the role of one such Jewish gangster in creating the notoriously corrupt atmosphere that characterized Las Vegas in the 1970s and '80s. *Radio Days* looks at a Jewish American family in Rockaway Beach during the crucial period between the late 1930s and 1944, when American understandings of Jewishness were deeply influenced by revelations about the Holocaust. This is the period when, due to the eugenics theories central to Nazism, Jews themselves began to resist their common designation as "Hebrews," which was "as much a racial label as a religious one" (Sen 6). The nostalgia about majority Jewish neighborhoods that structures both *Hester Street* and *Radio Days* makes an instructive contrast to Leone's film, which sensationalizes the Jewish ghetto as a lawless space where forming community can only mean fighting against the American mainstream and success can only be achieved through subjugating the weak, especially Jewish women. *Casino* paints a Jewish man's choice of a Gentile as his wife as an unmitigated disaster for everyone even remotely involved in his life, suggesting that Jews cannot and should not use intermarriage as a means of assimilation—an important idea because, according to sources such as the Pew Research Foundation, in the 1990s (when the film was made) the majority of Jews in America who married chose Gentile spouses.[1]

Part of the United States' anti-immigration rhetoric has always been the argument that the immigrants come from cultures that violently oppress women and lack Western Christian concepts of chivalry, making the male immigrants dangerous potential rapists. While this argument has been made repeatedly about Mexican Americans during Donald Trump's presidential campaign and presidency, the main focus of the early twenty-first-century panic over an invasion of sex criminals has been on Muslims, with the hijab standing for extreme misogyny. As Sharmila Sen argues, the "uniquely American concept of race" has always "racialize[d] religion" and now increasingly centers on a narrative about "the clash of civilizations," which makes "explicit the intertwining of race and religion in the West" (xxiv–xxv). This atmosphere of intense suspicion of any religion other than Protestantism creates tremendous pressure on the immigrants to assimilate and show that they have done so by abandoning the religion common to their group of origin and all the matters of dress and behavior that symbolize it to the citizens of their new country.

II. Love in Old New York

As Eric A. Goldman's excellent comparison of the stage and film adaptations of Samson Raphaelson's 1922 short story "The Day of Atonement" into *The Jazz Singer* shows, the seminal story of Jewish American identity construction pits assimilation for the purpose of individual success against "the bonds of neighborhood, family, friends, and religion" (23). Goldman calls the 1927 first film version "the classic story of Jewish assimilation," which, although based on the life of its star Al Jolson, "told the story of a whole generation of immigrants who wanted better lives" (19, 18). In the short story, Jakie Rabinowitz reinvents himself as jazz singer Jack Robin, rejecting his father's desire that he take his place as the eleventh cantor in the family line. This religious role is very important not just to the Rabinowitz family but to the community because a canter sings the liturgical music and leads the synagogue in prayer. When his father, who has disowned him, dies and so cannot fulfill that role, Jack gives up his Broadway opening to return to the Hester Street Synagogue and sing Kol Nidre, the prayer for Yom Kippur, the Day of Atonement and the holiest day of Judaism.

As Goldman points out, the film versions of the story shift the conflict from "career versus religion" to "career versus family" (39). The film version accomplishes this shift by showing Jack taking his sick father's place, with his blessing, in temple on Yom Kippur but then returning to the theater where his mother applauds his blackface rendition of "My Mammy." Since Jack continues his career as a jazz singer and will not permanently replace his father as cantor, this change conveys a "strongly assimilationist message" that Jews can ultimately reject the traditions and roles of the past and yet still retain family ties. And the message remains a feature of all the remakes that follow (40, 45–49). In this vision, pursuit of American success, consisting of fame and wealth, does not demand adopting a corrupt value system so long as one still honors one's parents. If Jews do that, they can have it all, even, in the earlier adaptations, the pleasures afforded by marriage to a Gentile whose guilt-free upbringing contrasts Jewish unhappiness, as does Jack's tourist-like self-racialization through performing in blackface (24). While for some of those involved in the entertainment industry assimilation of this sort was attainable and became "a goal for many" (49), as Goldman argues, by the 1970s, when Joan Micklin Silver was working on her film *Hester Street*, the dream of assimilation had soured for many of us. So, looking back to our past was not an exercise in understanding how we became as culturally influential as anti-Semites often accuse us of being. Instead, it meant experiencing the pangs and pleasures of nostalgia for a time when Jewish community and cultural heritage stood powerfully against the American valuation of individual monetary success with which many had become disenchanted.

Silver's film's turn-of-the-century Jewish immigrants have left any parents that they might still have alive back in the old country, and they are never mentioned (so much for honoring one's parents). There are no opportunities to black up and entertain Gentiles to attain celebrity while still holding on to some simulation of racial difference. And there are no discernable Gentiles at all in the Hester Street neighborhood, let alone candidates for happy assimilationist marriages. The film's treatment of assimilation occurs in an all-Jewish world, taking away the issue of racial mixing. However, the issue of particularly Jewish sexualities is foregrounded.

Hester Street concerns the battle of an assimilated husband, who has changed his name to Jake (Steven Keats) and his newly emigrated wife, Gitl (Carol Kane), who immediately realizes and resents the pressure on her to abandon everything that has given her identity as a Jew. They first fight over her sheitel (a wig traditionally worn by Orthodox women to cover their hair in accordance with religion), which here carries the symbolic weight of American Jewish resistance to assimilation. Jake cannot love her or make love to her so long as he sees any bonded relationship to her as symbolic of a return to the old country he wants to leave behind.

The most violent moment we see in their relationship occurs when she gives in to his pressure and comes to him with her big mass of curly hair uncovered. He grabs her by the hair, thinking it is a new wig, and tries to tear it from her head. One might guess that this would discourage any future attempts on her part to depart from Eastern European Jewish traditions. However, after their divorce, while she returns to tradition by running a store to support her second husband, a Talmudic scholar, she does not return to covering her hair. Perhaps her partial assimilation is meant to calm Gentile fears that the post–World War II relaxation of Jewish quotas and Jewish exclusions that allowed more of America's Jews to move out of inner-city ghettos and into suburbs that included Gentiles would result

In America they don't wear wigs.

Fig. 2.1 *Hester Street*: Jake explains Jewish assimilation to Gitl.

in an undermining of mainstream American gender codes. Her ultimate blend of old practices and new ones also seems aimed at a 1970s Jewish audience, who valued sexuality and romance and could see both suggested in Carol Kane's luminous beauty as she gazes amorously at her new husband, her excessive and lovely hair (which, of course, was traditionally covered because it might arouse lust) proudly on display.

Shaina Hammerman focuses on the symbolic meanings of the wig in her analysis of how the film works both to reassure those audience members who believe Jewish women should "adopt a bourgeois brand of femininity, the American ideal" (122) while still "offering Jewish feminists the elusive 'roots' that so many sought at the time. . . . The film makes Jewish tradition more palatable to a 1970s American audience by couching Jewish traditionalism within a feminist plotline" (120). Following the rallying cry in the title of the popular self-help health guide for feminists of the time, *Our Bodies, Ourselves*, Gitl takes control of her own sexuality by rejecting the husband to whom she was probably given through a parental arrangement and remarrying for love. In addition, Gitl's choice of a second husband helps the film construct a history that has it both ways, although in very different terms than the happy ending of *The Jazz Singer*. *Hester Street*'s conclusion allows the film's heroine happiness because her second marital choice strengthens her connection to a Jewish past and community through her defiant rejection of American Gentile masculinity standards she, along with the audience, finds repulsive, as reflected in Jake's ludicrous and undignified athletic posturing.

In an essay in the *New Yorker*, on Shakespeare's depiction of Shylock, Stephen Greenblatt discusses what he calls his ethnic heritage from his grandparents: "Theirs was an insular community in which sexual selection . . . had for centuries favored slender, nearsighted, stoop-shouldered young men rocking back and forth as they pondered . . . tractates of Jewish law." He goes on to say that this Jewish concept of ideal masculinity was abandoned after they came to the United States. Yet I would argue that the shadows of that vision of a masculinity so opposite to the muscular Christianity inherited from the British Victorians and favored by Americans, especially anti-Semitic conservatives, fell heavily on many American Jews. As I will discuss, it is resignified as valuable in *Hester Street*, along with another Jewish gender stereotype that some Jewish immigrants tried in vain to escape: the stereotype of the slender scholar's female complement, a strong, assertive maternal woman who could take care of the family's worldly needs—in other words, what most Gentiles and many Jews derided as the shrewish Jewish mother. As many Jewish film critics have observed, these stereotypes have frequently been reinscribed cinematically and are part of the way American film in particular presents us with immediately recognizable ethnic—or as I find a more accurate descriptor—racialized characters.

Were Jews really sexually different from Gentiles? In the United States, as in Western Europe, the majority of the population identified as Christian either by belief or by heritage. Christianity profoundly differs from Judaism in its view of celibacy as the ideal human condition, as is famously discussed by St. Paul in Corinthians. If Christians cannot maintain celibacy, they are urged to marry and procreate. But for Jews celibacy is seen as undesirable and marriage as the ideal state for all adults. Noah Benjamin Bickart advises that "if we want to understand the power dynamics the Rabbis [in ancient times] wished to create in visions of the utopian society we would do well to focus on sex and sexuality," keeping in mind that "all modes of copulation are permitted" between spouses (505–6). Christians have traditionally focused on sex and sexuality only to emphasize the restrictions religion demands. Married Jews, like married Christians, are urged to procreate by members of their community, and many Jews consider this an important method of ensuring the group's survival of attempted genocides. Again the situation is different for the Christian community because, unlike Jews, they have traditionally depended on proselytizing to expand their numbers. For many religious Christians, rather than those for whom a Christian identity is merely a heritage, not only proselytizing but, in defiance of the American constitutional separation between church and state, keeping the entire country in line with Christian values is seen as a vital mission. It is vital because establishing Christian values as the national norm helps the effort to convert others to active Christianity. The way this has played out is generally in terms of regulating the sexuality of others. Here Jews differ strongly.

Many religious Jews disapprove of sexual activity outside heterosexual marriage, but they do not concern themselves with the sexual behavior of Gentiles, only that of other Jews. In contrast, religious Christians have organized in the United States to fight against sex education, premarital sex, birth control, abortion, open homosexuality, gay marriage, and transgender identification. That even the most religious Jews do not show any interest in making Gentiles obey Judaic religious restrictions on sexual behavior makes Jews seem distinctly Other and, in the view of many Christians, sexually immoral.

Furthermore, in the United States there were valid reasons to think of all Jewish sexualities, even those contained within heterosexual marriage, as different from those of mainstream Americans after the wave of Jewish immigration from Eastern Europe began because of the prevalence of arranged marriages among the immigrant Jews. My paternal grandparents, who came to America at the end of the nineteenth century, were typical in that they claimed to have met on their wedding day, with their first face-to-face encounter occurring when my grandfather lifted my grandmother's wedding veil. Despite, by their own admission, not liking each other from that moment on, they went ahead and had nine children, and their marriage only ended when my grandmother's death freed Grandpa Siegel to marry a woman of his choice, my beloved Grandma Lena. Jews often jokingly refer to ourselves as "the tribe," but to many of their fellow Americans, these immigrants' marriage customs must have seemed atavistically tribal.

For generations in Western European countries, love-match marriages had been the norm, while in the United States from the country's beginning almost all marriages between white people of European heritage were arranged by the marital couple themselves following a romantic courtship. Marriage was, therefore, seen as the proper outcome of falling in love. The only notable exceptions were "mail-order" brides, whose marital arrangements were generally the result of a shortage of women in frontier communities. Such marriages were never the American norm but rather seen as responses to emergency situations. Since marriage is the only institution within which socially sanctioned and legitimized sexual experiences could occur in America, Jewish sexualities must have seemed primitive as well as alien due to the nineteenth-century Eastern European Jews' preference for marriages arranged by parents with the help of the communities' matchmakers.

In cultures where romantic love is assumed to be the basis for marriage, arranged marriages are seen as loveless and the cultures that prefer them as violating the natural(ized) connection between sex and love in favor of materialistic concerns. Moreover, because the main purpose of arranged marriages is to benefit the extended families of the couple, it has traditionally been seen by most Americans as anti-individualistic. Consequently, American Jews are often depicted as people who marry for the wrong reasons because they fail to properly value romantic love.

In contrast, *Hester Street* celebrates Jewish romantic love. This may be because it seems aimed primarily at Jewish audiences. Beth Wenger points out that "within the physical boundaries of the Lower East Side, American Jews expressed the conflicts and contradictions embedded in the dual quest to become successful, acculturated Americans while preserving Jewish community and culture." This quest provides the theme of the film. And the film depicts the history of assimilation correctly according to critics like Joyce Antler, who claims it "provides an accurate template for the stresses of Americanization at the turn of the century" ("Hester Street," 178). The depiction includes the paradox of this situation, described insightfully by Sen, an East Indian, about her own assimilation, which ended when she realized that "to be *Americanized* is precisely not to be American." Instead, she "became American by becoming Not White," because for Southeast Asians, as for Jews, the United States will never validate a complete identification with racially unmarked whiteness (184–85, original emphasis). Patricia Erens claims of this film that "more than in any other work in recent times, it is a genuine attempt to deal with the experience of immigration and assimilation" (325). And part of what makes it genuine is that it shows the limits of possible assimilation for a virtuous Jew.

Gitl, the Orthodox wife, is an endearing figure who for many of the viewers will be reminiscent of those immigrant grandmothers who fled European genocides and had as their primary goal in life the survival of the Jews, a group the grandmothers implicitly racialized because of their belief that converts were not true Jews. Gitl is treated emotionally abusively by her husband who wants to divorce her so he can marry his assimilated girlfriend, Mamie (Dorrie Kavanaugh), because she has considerable savings and he has accepted the American view that money matters more than anything else. Gitl agrees to a *get* (Jewish divorce) contingent on receiving a large bribe from Mamie, which depletes her savings, leaving her future as Jake's second wife uncertain. Gitl's marriage to their Talmudic scholar boarder, Bernstein (Mel Howard), whom Shaina Hammerman succinctly describes as "the religious, scholarly, visibly Jewish man" (125), seems more promising since he is a kindly man who respects and admires Gitl and is affectionate to her son, who we see also likes him. He is the sort of scholar that Greenblatt describes and so is not at all athletic like big, strong Jake. But he is a virile heterosexual, who explains to Gitl that he came to America because back in the old country his continual sexual thoughts about women interrupted his studies and made him unfit to be a rabbi. While he and Gitl behave with perfect propriety until the divorce frees her, the camera pans in on their lovestruck faces and uses shot–reverse shots to emphasize the shy but longing glances they exchange. At the conclusion, as they promenade, arm in arm, down Hester Street, we see none of the awkwardness that characterized physical contacts between Jake and Gitl. Their harmonious movements promise the success their physical union will have.

Their marriage is also promising because Bernstein, while certainly moved and fascinated by Gitl's physical beauty, behaves honorably toward her and in all things acts as a force against American corruption. When Gitl praises him for his love of God, demonstrated through his Torah study, he bitterly tells her that coming to America means saying, "Goodbye, Oh Lord." Yet their marriage suggests that love can overcome the United States' opposition to specifically Jewish family values. While Abraham Cahan's 1896 novella *Yekl*, on which the film is based, depicts both the retention of Orthodox Jewish traditions and the abandonment of these values for the pursuit of wealth as faulty and advocates the embrace of socialism instead, audiences likely came away from the film feeling happy that the sweet Orthodox couple found happiness together. Wenger notes that as "Jews moved farther from the immigrant experience, it became possible to reimagine the Lower East Side in terms that transformed poverty, crime, and poor living conditions into a narrative of Jewish struggle, perseverance, and self-congratulation" (27). And this is exactly what the film, with reference to the iconic, Lower East Side central street in its title, gives us.

III. America the Ugly

Once Upon a Time in America lacks such sweetness, to say the least. Loosely based on the 1953 novel *The Hoods* by Harry Grey (Herschel Goldberg), it follows the relationship of two Jewish gangsters, Noodles (Robert DeNiro) and Max (James Woods), who meet as youths in 1920 and remain friends until 1933, when Max fakes his own death to get Noodles out of the way so he can assume a new identity and enter politics as a representative of criminal interests in a union modeled on the Teamsters. The narrative is provided primarily through flashbacks but is divided into three segments. In the first we see Noodles as a teen (played by Scott Tiler) who adores Deborah (played as a teen by Jennifer Connelly), the beautiful daughter of the neighborhood's Jewish delicatessen owner.

Deborah aspires to become a ballerina. For some viewers, this may bring to mind the parody ballet dancing Fanny Brice performed in the *Ziegfeld Follies* and Barbra Streisand reprised in *Funny Girl*. But whereas, as Hannah Schwadron discusses, these performances were intended as an earthy and specifically Jewish "deliberate contrast to white women's famous fragility" (55), Deborah is serious about her dancing and through it her ability to exhibit a fairytale loveliness. And the cinematography agrees, spotlighting her in white on white as she poses on a long white table, in a filmy, translucent white dress, in front of rows of white flour bags, under an enormous arched ceiling lined with radiant skylights. It is the most ethereal delicatessen backroom in film history. Still a touch of earthiness remains as she practices her ballet dancing in as provocative a manner as possible and then takes off her ballet costume exposing her nakedness to Noodles, who she knows is spying on her through a hole in the bathroom wall.

She sexually teases him constantly, presumably because she finds him attractive, but is also very dismissive and critical due to his criminality and lack of interest in even a show of propriety to conceal it. While everyone else is at the temple on Pesach/Passover, she seduces him with readings from the Song of Songs, but they exchange only a kiss before Max calls him away. Deborah seems intent on wresting Noodles's attention away from Max and using her sexual appeal to reform him. But reform him into what? A scene in which he pursues her through a crowd of Orthodox men in their black hats, side curls, and prayer shawls makes us realize how grating and frustrating he finds her efforts to shame him into virtue, for what are its rewards? Owning a pushcart? Working as a lowly clerk in the diamond trade?

Fig. 2.2 *Once Upon a Time in America*: Deborah's seductive dance.

Being scorned by the Gentiles who rule the country and being relegated to a rat's hole ghetto existence?

Unlike *Hester Street*, this film's depiction of American Jewish ghetto life is not predominantly nostalgic. Although the early sequences are shot with golden lighting, as is typical of cinematic evocations of protagonists' childhood and adolescent adventures, many gritty and unpleasant details continually remind us that this, like the Hester Street of *The Jazz Singer*, is an impoverished place that any sensible person would want to escape from. Noodles despises the cramped apartments and pedestrian-clogged streets and wants to live large. When he meets Max, a really clever and charismatic young crook, they put together a gang as a way to make that happen. But Noodles gets sidetracked into jail when he kills the hoodlum who is trying to wipe out his little gang and has just murdered its youngest member, a merry little child criminal.

The second segment begins toward the end of Prohibition when an adult Noodles is released from jail and is welcomed back by a slick, grown-up Max, who has developed the gang into a real power and turned the old deli into a speakeasy. Part of the film's evocation of the slide from a poor but honest Jewish society to a corrupt one comes in the form of Noodles's troubled and conflicted sexuality. Although Noodles heavily identifies as heterosexual, the chemistry between him and Max is intense. Numerous shot–reverse shots emphasize their rapt attention to each other. Noodles, however, is distracted by Deborah (now played as an adult by Elizabeth McGovern), who is still hanging around, leading him on and admonishing him. Finally, he takes her out on an extravagant dream date with all the trimmings—an elegant restaurant in a little hotel by the sea, deserted except for the charmed couple, a huge staff of formally dressed waiters, and a band that plays just for them as they dance in the magical moonlight. But on the way home in the limousine, when she taunts him with her plan to leave for Hollywood the next day, because he is still unworthy of her, he assaults her in one of the most harrowing date rape scenes ever filmed. She is an unpleasant, manipulative person, but like the limo driver and Leone, who provides close-ups of her face that reveal her shattered response, we feel sorry for her helplessness, her physical pain, and her disillusionment as her most wonderful memory turns so quickly into her worst nightmare.

After she leaves, Noodles descends into Max's world of total cynicism, and life becomes meaningless to him, as he becomes a powerful gangster embroiled in Teamster-like union politics. When Max confides in him an illogical plan to rob the Federal Reserve Bank but first do a liquor run the night the repeal of Prohibition is announced, Noodles believes it all. He informs the police of Max's intention of making the liquor run, at the behest of Max's girlfriend, Carol (Tuesday Weld), so that he will be arrested for a very minor crime in order to stop him from completely destroying himself with the bank robbery, which can only fail. Unfortunately, this plan goes awry: Noodles is knocked out in a struggle with Max, and while he is unconscious the rest of the old gang is killed in a gun battle with police. Max dies along with the rest, or so Noodles believes. Noodles, awakened by this news while he relaxes at his favorite opium den, tries to run with the million dollars they have kept hidden for emergencies; however, the money is gone, and he has only enough to shuffle off to Buffalo.

The last segment, set in the 1960s, shows us Noodles summoned by a world-weary Max, now a politician facing imminent exposure of his past in which he tricked and robbed Noodles and committed far worse crimes. It seems that Max wanted to get out of the life of crime and staged his own death so he could start a new life, posing as an Irish politician called Bailey. Despite the revelation that Max has also made Deborah his mistress and had a child with her, Noodles refuses to acknowledge that Max deceived him and stole from him. This man who calls himself Bailey is not his old friend Max. Nothing can convince him otherwise!

The director's cut puts the film back into its original fragmented narrative order, which strongly suggests, as Leone did when questioned by Noël Simsolo, that the whole 1960s segment of this saga could be understood as merely Noodles's opium dream after he inadvertently destroyed the man he idolized. The film makes better sense that way, and then the huge span of time between the second segment that occurs at the end of Prohibition and the final segment need not be accounted for—which is a good thing because how could we possibly believe that Noodles was living as a contract killer in Buffalo for decades without attracting any attention and that Max was active in politics under an assumed name for over thirty years before his past was exposed? It is also much more poetic to imagine Noodles dreaming away until Max's remaining soldiers come to kill him in retribution for all his sins, with the purity of his love for Max indestructible.

But the film as originally released takes away even that one note of purity. We are shown scenes of great brutality as the enforcers seek Noodles, who has betrayed their gang. Jews have a special word for someone who informs to the police on other Jews, a moser, and this despised person is what Noodles has become. World War II heightened the infamy of mosers as the term now fit Jews who betrayed others to the Nazis. Over and over, what we are shown is loss and death. When the film cuts back to the old ghetto in Segment Three, Ennio Morricone's lush musical score romanticizes it but in an elegiac tone. Noodles, returning from his exile, observes with obvious distaste many Blacks and Latinos in what was formerly an almost exclusively Jewish neighborhood. He watches as a coffin is lifted out of a Jewish cemetery that is being dug up. As Jonathan Freedman remarks, the "shot of earthmovers digging up gravestones with Hebrew inscriptions and tossing them around like so much detritus [makes the point that] not just memorialization but memory itself comes to be uprooted, contingent, variable" (124).

The film's excavation of Jewish memories brings up dead and rotting things. And the ugliness is mainly figured through sexual behaviors and remarks. In the first part of the film, Noodles is initiated sexually by Peggy (Julie Cohen), a coarse, fat girl who prostitutes herself for sweets, is defined by her gluttony and public defecation, and later, as an adult (Amy Ryder), becomes the madam of a whorehouse. Max takes as his first girlfriend Carol, a nasty Jewish girl Noodles raped when they were robbing her diamond dealer husband's store and whom the husband later sends to

Peggy's whorehouse so he can watch her have sex with other men. When Noodles finds Carol in the whorehouse, she rejects him in favor of Max after inspecting the penises of both men. The men in the gang seem turned on by her masochism (she begs Noodles to hit her during the rape and abases herself to Max). She suggests a "threesome" with Max and Noodles, but Noodles leaves contemptuously. Later Max cruelly kicks Carol out of their home to demonstrate to his pals that he won't let "broads" get between them. The gang members all laugh. The connection between sexuality and death is emphasized when Max comes to meet Noodles after his release from prison in a hearse with a prostitute in the back and Noodles has sex with her in the coffin.

Women are not the only ones whose putative weakness and inferiority mark them as deathly. Vicious homophobia haunts the entire film. Noodles and his boyhood buddies make many homophobic jokes: for example, when asked by a cop, "What are you boys doing here?" they reply, "Taking it up the ass," which we hear them say frequently about others. They also seem obsessed with "trannies," mentioning them contemptuously at every possible opportunity. Yet Max acts so flirtatious with Noodles, as when they are helping out bootleggers on the river and Max spits water provocatively at Noodles, that it is hard to tell whether Noodles's fatal love object is Deborah or Max. Max plays Mercutio to Noodles's Romeo, always admonishing him for having romantic feelings about women, not just using them for sexual relief as Max himself does first with Peggy, later with Carol, and finally with Deborah.

Still Noodles typically responds to Max as if he were a romantic love object, and Max reciprocates. At one point, as they argue over whether to rob the Federal Reserve Bank, which Noodles feels would be literally suicidal, he says, "You know, Maxie, wherever you go, I go," and Max replies teasingly, "Maybe I should just dump you." The scene at the climax when Max, now passing for "Secretary Bailey," begs Noodles to kill him because his being under investigation has caused the crooked union to put a contract on him comes across as extremely homoerotic. Max makes it clear that he can only accept death at the hands of the person he cares most about. Noodles not only refuses to kill him but also refuses to acknowledge that this man is his beloved Max. We then see Noodles's memory montage of his love for Max and the gang, but mostly for Max. As he leaves, Noodles says, seemingly sincerely, that he hopes "the investigation will come to nothing." But we see Max being taken away and apparently ground up in a garbage truck.

The film idealizes Jews as paragons of tough, defiant masculinity throughout, somewhat as Clint Eastwood's Man with No Name is romanticized in Leone's westerns, but unlike Eastwood's character, the characters in *Once Upon a Time in America* lack his sympathy for weak, victimized women and his adherence to a rough code of honor. They are rapists and dishonorable in pretty much every way. Noodles is at least as much human garbage as Max. As this brief summary may suggest, the film depicts Jews as utterly corrupted by America's idolization of wealth and lack of sexual morality. The men establish their masculinity through contemptuous abuse of women and constant expressions of homophobia. The women, like Deborah and Noodles's other rape victim, Carol, are graspingly materialistic, cold, vain, and disgustingly masochistic.

Yet there are some surprising similarities between *Hester Street* and *Once Upon a Time in America*: in both films, assimilating into the American culture that surrounds them corrupts the Jews. *Once Upon a Time* begins, ironically, with "God Bless America," sounding diegetically via a radio as we see a street in New York's old Jewish ghetto on Manhattan's Lower East Side. The song's repetition at the film's conclusion, together with the scene in which Noodles rejects the Passover observance as being for losers, conveys the message that if Jews are criminals and rapists in America, it is because they have accepted American values, their spirituality is dead, they care only for money, and they despise the weak, which includes women. So traditional Jewish culture appears not as misogynistic or materialistic but rather as a lost purity, which we glimpse in those nostalgic moments from Noodles's impoverished but still love-filled childhood memories, which are bathed in golden light and which futilely beckon Noodles when he observes the teenaged Deborah dancing in a world of pure whiteness. If only he could care more about love than money, the film suggests, he could enjoy those spiritualized beautiful moments unambivalently. But Max and the American greed he represents always call Noodles away.

Obviously, the use of the adulterous assimilated couple in *Hester Street* as foils to the newly emigrated wife and the Talmudic scholar, while not going so far as to imply that Jews who assimilate will become criminals and rapists, also makes the point that if American Jews are corrupt, it is America that corrupts them.

Freedman argues:

> In Leone's hands, the mythos of Jewish upward mobility—especially that wrought via the powers of the entertainment industries that his film is constantly referencing, reanimating, and deconstructing—becomes not a way that Jews negotiate new identities for themselves in an ambivalent America, but rather a way that America used its Jews to construct enabling fictions about itself. At the end of the film, we return to Noodles's memory of the opium den where he goes to forget his own presumed betrayal. He takes a long drag from the pipe and grins—the very last image of the film, over which the credits appear. All we have just seen, it might appear, has been his dream—certainly, some critics have taken it as such. But Leone's ambitions are more pointed still. Via his incessant reference to mechanisms of image and performance, to narratives both cinematic and literary, Leone has been telling us that Noodles's is the dream America dreams about itself—a dream of upward class and ethnic mobility, default whiteness, endless opportunity for self-making—and that it is not just false but self-alienating, soul-destroying, corrupt and corrupting—affixing on our collective faces the stupid, opiated grin of boundless possibility and endless abundance. (132–33)

One might well recall Lauren Berlant's exploration of the poisonous effects of the American Dream throughout *Cruel Optimism*. And, of course, Jews have been producing scholarly commentary on the failed promise of America's premier ideology, capitalism, since Karl Marx.

Casino even more extremely depicts the corruption of a Jew by life in America. The film is based on the nonfiction book *Casino: Love and Honor in Las Vegas*, by Nicholas Pileggi, who also cowrote the screenplay for the film with Martin Scorsese. Carrying associations with many other gangster tales, this film gives us two generally complementary alternating voice-over narratives by the two protagonists to relate how Sam "Ace" Rothstein (Robert DeNiro), the "golden Jew," a careful, scientific gambling handicapper, built up the prototype of today's casinos and then Nicky Santoro (Joe Pesci), a violent, psychopathic enforcer without any impulse control, destroyed the casino culture Ace created. On the side, we have the tragic tale of Ace's obsession with the beautiful prostitute Ginger (Sharon Stone), who can only love her sleazy pimp Lester (James Woods) but marries Ace for his money and has an affair with Nicky to persuade him to kill Ace.

It does not become evident that the narratives of Ace's and Nicky's rises and falls present opposing visions of what it means to be an American until the conclusion when we realize that all along up until his horrible death (beaten into immobility and then buried alive in a hole with his brother's dead body), Nicky has imagined he inhabited a world of Italian American racial alliance and honor while Ace thought he was living the American Dream where hard work and reliability make others admire and reward you. Yet really all that governed their fates was the fact that Ace was a consistent source of income for the mob. Consequently, he survives to be a sad little bookie on the periphery of the kingdom he inspired.

Corruption is central to every aspect of the film. The Chicago mob sends Nicky to Las Vegas to skim money from the profits of the Tangiers casino, which they have sent Ace to manage. Although Nicky is charged with protecting Ace, who has doubled the casino's profits, he soon causes trouble by assembling a team of hoodlums who begin to demand protection money from other casinos and even to burglarize them. His wild, unrestrained corruption is mirrored by the bland, smirking, institutionalized corruption represented by Pat Webb (L. Q. Jones). Webb uses his position as county commissioner to pressure Ace into hiring his nearly moronic brother-in-law, Don Ward (John Bloom). Unable to train Ward, who is incapable of catching the most obvious cheaters, Ace fires him. When he refuses Webb's demand that he rehire Ward, Webb retaliates by making sure Ace does not get a gaming license. As Joel Samberg observes, Ace is represented as an ethical person who "even talks of commandments and morality like a one arm bandit rabbi" (179). Ace's obvious contempt for "Goyim naches" (what Daniel Boyarin translates from the Yiddish as "games Gentiles play") encompasses not only the gambling Ace facilitates but also the nepotism that keeps power and control in the hands of a privileged few.[2] To Ace, this nepotism is part of the Gentile cult of masculinity based on raw physicality and bonding in order to violently defend the privileges afforded to one's own group. Nathan Abrams sees this show of contempt as exacerbating the anti-Semitism of the local authorities who subject Ace to racist insults such as "crazy Jew fuck" and "kike" (*New Jew in Film*, 120–21). Unable to accept that this is how things work in Nevada, and as is implied in the United States generally, Ace attributes the denial of the license to Nicky's shenanigans, which causes a breach between them.

What compounds Ace's problems, however, is his inextinguishable passion for Ginger, who is the very personification of golden American corruption, emphasized by numerous shots in which we see her at the gaming tables, lit from above, her blondness gilded with light. Despite his adoration of her, willingness to shower her with money and gifts, and their having a daughter together, Ginger clearly thinks of him only as a source of income for herself and, worse, for Lester. When Ace gets Nicky to try to drive Lester away with a beating, she falls into alcoholic despair and neglects their little daughter, Amy (Erika von Tagen). When Ace initiates divorce proceedings, Ginger runs away with Amy and Lester, hoping to escape to Europe. He is able to persuade her to come back to him, but she is angered by his objection to her having taken Amy away. After he overhears Ginger on the phone trying to talk Nicky into killing him, Ace kicks her out of the house; however, his desire quickly overcomes his common sense, and he lets her return. Ginger then begins an affair with Nicky. Ace learns about it when he finds Amy tied to her bed by Ginger so that she can meet with Nicky. Finally both men reject Ginger, but it is too late to keep her from stealing all of Ace's secret emergency savings, which he kept in a safe deposit box. She continues deeper into substance abuse and prostitution until she overdoses in a motel and dies. But not before furnishing the FBI with the information it needs to shut down the casino. Ultimately, though, the casino is reopened as a corporate venture that has no room for people like Ace, who have criminal pasts. Ace becomes another Jew ruined by both his unmanageable sexual obsession with the woman who represents successful assimilation to him, because she is white and blond, and the pervasive corruption that, in this film, defines life in America.

IV. Nostalgia and the Self-Hating Jew

Radio Days avoids the depiction of America as a corrupting force in Jewish lives, and particularly Jewish sex lives, that structures the other three films. The parable-like opening comically emphasizes the change of fortune Jews experience in America and attributes it, jocularly, to the assimilationist force of popular entertainment, in this case radio, which compels Jewish attention. The adult Joe (Woody Allen), as narrator, tells us "radio stories" and gives us vignettes of his childhood memories of his Jewish family and neighbors during the late 1930s and into the 1940s. The film cleverly takes us back to the time when entertainment narratives that told us what it meant to be an American would nightly be brought into American homes through the radio. It does so, not with words and sounds alone, as the radio did, but in lavishly colored sets and comically exaggerated period props and costumes, with a visual extravagance that foregrounds the artificiality of visual entertainment. The very term *radio stories* emphasizes the contrast between a past that can never really be seen as it was but only re-created through the unreliable, because romanticizing, medium of memory.

The opening story is of the Needlemans, whose house was broken into by burglars who could not resist tuning in to *Name That Tune* during the robbery and calling in to guess correctly and win the grand prize. While in the Europe of this period whatever luck the Jews had is horrifically running out, the Needlemans' loss of fifty dollars and a few household items is soon recompensed when trucks full of prizes arrive the next day. Although the narrator tells us that the radio shows and their stars and the inhabitants of his neighborhood occupied "two completely different worlds," what we see is considerable overlap to the benefit of both groups. The beginning of the story during the Great Depression shows no poverty or even financial anxiety among either group.

These Rockaway Beach Jews are shown assimilating rapidly into mainstream American life. They live in small but comfortable-looking row houses and enjoy the usual pleasures available to the lower middle class, including evenings spent listening to the radio. Young Joe (Seth Green) hero-worships the radio character the Masked Avenger, blissfully unaware that he is voiced by a short, bald Jew (Wallace Shawn) who would fit right into the neighborhood. Joe's uncle Abe (Josh Mostel) is converted to communism when he goes next door to demand the Jewish "Reds" stop playing loud radio music on Yom Kippur. He ends up joining them in a meal of forbidden foods, including pork chops and clams, and comes home an hour later declaring his family's prayers and food laws nonsense.

Abe seems reasonable in his rejection of Jewish traditions because they do nothing to bring peace or harmony to the family's daily life. Vincent Brook says the film light-heartedly "pokes fun at Jewish pettiness, tribalism, and superficial religiosity" (9); however, the disagreeable characteristics of the family go beyond good fun. All the adults bicker constantly, Joe's aunt Bea (Dianne Wiest) fruitlessly pursues potential Jewish husbands who deceive and betray her; Abe and his wife, Ceil (Renée Lippin), appear to despise each other; and the parents show Joe no affection and argue repeatedly over who will get to hit Joe in the head. No one has any discernible values except to long for the wealth and prestige they lack.

They are aware of American anti-Semitism, as is demonstrated by Abe's telling Ceil that they could never go to the Stork Club, even if they had the money to patronize such fashionable places, because "they don't take Jews in the Stork Club, no Jews, no color." But whatever the Gentiles think, these

Jews refuse to consider themselves racialized as people of color, as is shown by the comical story of the catatonic state of shock induced in their neighbor Mrs. Silverman when she sees the daughter of the communist family kiss a Black man. Their view of themselves as racially unmarked Americans rather than as racialized Jews, like those in Germany, is perhaps most evident in their reactions to World War II, which indicate their obliviousness to the ongoing Holocaust.

When Joe steals the money, he and his friends are asked by the rabbi to collect for a Jewish homeland in Palestine, no one mentions any reason this homeland might be important, despite the fact that Jews are being refused refugee status all over the free world and so must return to Germany to be tortured to death; he is only punished for disrespecting the rabbi. No one finds in bad taste or upsetting his aunt and uncle's frequent punctuation of their bickering with the suggestion that their spouse "take the gas pipe." While enjoying the view of the stars afforded by a blackout, his mother does mention that the activities of "certain people" are ruining her pleasure in the world, but who exactly is doing this and what exactly they are doing gets no elaboration, although we know, of course, that it is Hitler and the Nazis. Joe gets caught up in the excitement of his favorite radio show focusing on the threat of a Nazi invasion of New York and imagines he sees a U-boat in the harbor. But quickly thereafter with his friends, as the narrator tells us in voice-over, "the talk has shifted away from Nazis to something more important." That more important something is pretty Gentile women they find desirable.

And what adult Joe focuses on when he remembers New Year's Eve 1944 is the romance developing between the Masked Avenger voice actor and the former cigarette girl and now rising radio star Sally White (Mia Farrow). The film repeatedly suggests that acquiring a blond Gentile girlfriend is what spells success for a Jewish man. And who could be whiter than the hostess of the show *Sally White and Her Great White Way?* As Erens remarks about Allen's films, "for Woody, survival means the warm acceptance of a compassionate woman, who is always Gentile" (310). This is such an obsession with him, in her view, because a blond Gentile woman represents America and so "will provide him with a sense of identity and a place of refuge" (332). One sees somewhat the same attitude in the tragic love Ace, in *Casino*, has for Ginger. The many scenes where he triumphantly parades her around Las Vegas emphasize her symbolic value to him. He can demonstrate his equality or even superiority to his anti-Semitic persecutors by showing that he possesses the kind of woman they value most, an undeniably white one. That she is completely corrupt does not matter because she is blond and beautiful and so signifies American desirability and his ability to attain the object of cinematic dreams. However, Scorsese's vision differs from Allen's in treatment of the Gentile dream girl in that we see nothing corrupt about Sally: she is earnest and good. This stands in contrast to the grotesque corruption represented by the Jewish community in Rockaway Beach, especially its female members, such as greedy, status-obsessed Ceil and racist Mrs. Silverman, and a host of other horrible Jewish women throughout Allen's cinematic oeuvre, as Ehrens discusses (310–11).

V. Conclusion

Dismal as we may find all of this, especially in light of subsequent events between Woody Allen and Mia Farrow, all four films do provide a useable history of Jewishness in America. In all four films, we can see the response to intense pressure to assimilate taking the form of a rejection of values and virtues associated with European Jewish life. Even in *Hester Street* a happy and equitable marriage between two Jews is depicted as something that only exists in a romanticized past. As Jon Stratton observes, later American films often feature a heroine who, like Roberta Glass in *Desperately Seeking Susan* or Judy Benjamin in *Private Benjamin*, must "leav[e] behind an apparently morally bankrupt Jewishness" represented by the men in their lives (159). It is sobering that *Once Upon a Time in America* and *Casino*, each of which was directed by a Gentile, posit America as corrupting, whereas Allen's *Radio Days* presents the Jews as already completely corrupt. But then Jews ourselves are often our harshest critics. All four films are consistent with the statistical history of Jews in America in reflecting that the majority of us are no longer traditional, or Orthodox, in the way of our ancestors but, instead, embrace American ways even when we are not embraced back. What emerges for me as most useful in the histories these films sketch is that the only glimmer of hope for an escape from a life empty of all value is the idea that if we can reject the racist stereotypes of us as failures in the proper performance of gender, love each other despite how we are seen, and adopt a vision of gender that is based on complementarity, not competition and domination, we might be able to achieve more solidarity among ourselves—and with others who are racialized—and so find happiness in this often inhospitable land. In the next chapter, I continue my examination of how films participate in the construction of Jewish identities by, as in the first chapter, looking at two films with comparable characters and narrative foci. These films contrast with each other in that one continues European traditions of representing Jewish sexualities as inherently corrupt and as a source of corruption of Gentiles, while the other foregrounds and promotes solidarity among Jews and people of color as subjects of unjust, hostile racialization.

Notes

1. Based on my own experience, observation, and common sense, I assume that most of the over 50 percent of American Jews who marry Gentiles do not choose their partners in an attempt to assimilate into mainstream WASP culture. We choose them because we are in love with them. However, we are often seen this way by both Gentiles and our fellow Jews. And to anti-Semites, intermarriage between Gentiles and racialized (rather than merely religious) Jews is seen as a dangerous situation, as was reflected by the very detailed prohibitions against this putative miscegenation in Nazi Germany.

2. See Daniel Boyarin, "Goyim Naches, or Modernity and the Manliness of the Mentsh," for a full description of the derivation of this term and how it relates to constructions of male power.

3

SEX AND REVENGE, RAGE AND BLISS

I. Audience Appeal Matters

The previous chapter mainly concentrates on a selection of filmmakers' serious attempts to represent the experiences of Jews in a new world to which they came in order to escape racialization, and the prejudicial treatment it enabled, but where they had to struggle with a national ideology that many found corrupting because of its prioritization of monetary success. In addition, the American emphasis on individualism brought their efforts to assimilate and take the privileged place America ostensibly offers good citizens into conflict with their need to belong to a Jewish community that might offer them some protection from persecution. While in that chapter I look at the messages these films convey to Jews and Gentiles alike about how much assimilation was possible in twentieth-century America for anyone identified as a Jew, here I look primarily at audience responses to a different type of films, ones in which serious historicization is frequently set aside in favor of popular entertainment value.

It has always seemed odd to me that films about the Holocaust can be marketed as entertainment, probably because it touched my family directly through my parents' friends and relatives. Certainly no one watches a film like *Shoah* (1985, directed by Claude Lanzmann) for a good time. But as historical events become more distant, tragedies that once seemed personal and terrifying can become merely good yarns. We experience this in cinematic historical fictions all the time. And as attitudes about Jews have changed from postwar pity to the current views prevalent in the United States, that either we are just privileged white people like any other successful group or noxious elites who interfere in others' sex lives, the representation of the most important Jewish experience of the twentieth century has changed, too. Jews are now assumed by many Americans to be aggressive people who know how to get what they want from life, and as this book extensively explores, we are portrayed that way in a wide variety of entertainment media. So, it seems only natural that, as Naomi Bloomer notes, in the past, films made about the Holocaust tended to depict Jews as martyred victims, whereas "cinema in the new millennium has seen a new wave of resistance and revenge narratives" (2).

In the earlier films, Jews who maintain a strongly Jewish identification are generally portrayed as "weak and ineffectual" outsiders who survive only through the intervention of "benevolent" Gentiles, including "good" Nazis, like Oskar Schindler (Bloomer 6). And as Bloomer observes: "In *Schindler's List*, the Jewish characters are barely more than two-dimensional, they conform to stereotypes—Stern is an accountant, cooking books, and the women are sexualised playthings—and they usually react only to non-Jewish characters and have little of their own subjective stories" (17–18). She attributes this in large part to the cinematic tradition of depicting conflicts as taking place between "goodies" whose virtue means they must prevail and "baddies" whose immorality predestines them to be vanquished. Because the Jewish resistance to the Holocaust was not successful, Jews could not be depicted as the good guys, and so the result is often a sort of "victim blaming in extremis" through plotlines that insist that due to their own weakness Jews can only be martyred or saved by Gentiles (34–35). However, a new trend has emerged in which Jews are represented as action heroes capable of fighting back.

This chapter is about two films that court audiences by providing them with exciting action sequences and suspense and change history whenever it gets in the way of that project. And for that reason, I concentrate here on audience reactions to the racializations, sexualizations, and erasures seemingly made to appeal to audiences that include both Gentiles and Jews. In this chapter, I reverse the clichéd journey from the sublime to the ridiculous and travel instead form the ridiculous to the sublime. I add a further twist, by beginning with a film that critics have mostly praised and respected but that, while entertaining me, ultimately seemed historically and psychologically ridiculous and the more so with repeated viewings. I will finish the chapter with consideration of a film dismissed by some as ridiculous but one that I, and many other Jews, experience as sublime. Both films, although set during World War II, are fictional to the point that they effectively erase the roles of real Jews in resisting the Holocaust and replace those true stories with tales of beautiful Jewish women who use their sex appeal to fight Nazis and avenge the deaths they caused.

As Lawrence Baron observes in an essay on cinematic representation of the Holocaust, "Over the past decade, nearly 190 feature films employing the Holocaust as their primary or secondary plotline were produced, and we are still nowhere near fatigue with these depictions, as the continued production of such films shows" (1). But, as he goes on to argue, "Commercial demands and genre conventions of motion pictures as popular entertainment restrain filmmakers from treating the subject as complexly, depressingly, and graphically as it merits. Consequently, the annihilation of the majority of the targeted population usually serves as the backdrop for uplifting stories about potential bystanders and persecutors who mustered the courage to resist the transgressions of their peers" (4). As a result, Jews may end up as secondary characters in their own story. One strategy to give us center stage is to use an attractive young woman, a standard appealing main character in artworks of all kinds, as the representative Jew. Thus, this chapter turns to film narratives about World War II that comment on, and surprisingly eroticize, Jewish resistance to fascism through the use of an attractive young woman protagonist. I look closely at the deployment of this sort of figure in Paul Verhoeven's 2007 film, *Black Book*, and Quentin Tarantino's 2009 film, *Inglourious Basterds*.

These two films have a large number of plot similarities. Both are set during World War II in an occupied country (the Netherlands and France, respectively) rather than in Germany, the country that voted Hitler into power. So, both are set in areas that include an active resistance movement whose participants believe, with good reason, that they represent the feelings of their countrymen. Both have a beautiful young Jewish woman protagonist, and in both, she is protected for part of the war by a Gentile farmer and his family. In both films, she sees her entire family slaughtered by Nazis. Both feature a sadistic Nazi villain who gloats over the killings of Jews, including the heroine's family. She saves her life by passing for Gentile in both films, and she takes a position where she must provide Nazis with entertainment. This particular plot device hints at the role of Jews in the entertainment industry, a conspiracy often brought up by anti-Semites who think we control the world, or seek to, in this way. And the films evoke this slander in a context that suggests that we entertain Gentiles not to gain pernicious power over them but as a means of survival. However, any good effects of this theme are somewhat undermined by each film's emphasis on the old European trope of the Jew whose exotic beauty empowers her to entrance Gentiles to their destruction. In both films, the Jewish heroine attracts the sexual attention of a powerful Nazi, and that Nazi is later shot dead. And both include a parallel story of resistance fighters. It is the differences between the two films that give one affinities with conventional anti-Semitic myths and the other a refreshingly direct opposition to such libels.

One striking difference is that in *Black Book* all the Jewish characters except the heroine are wealthy but weak people who must depend on rescue by altruistic Gentiles to survive, while in *Inglorious Basterds* strong and aggressive Jews are helped by some sympathetic Gentiles but clearly do not need protection or even help to kill large numbers of Nazis. (The goal of the Basterds is for each one of the group to kill and collect the scalp of one hundred Nazis.) Both films are ahistorical fantasies. They are compared by Scott Foundas, who discusses them both in relation to *Defiance* (2008, directed by Ed Zwick). This film shows and celebrates the heroic actions of three Jews who, in 1941, organized a group of other Jews hiding out in the Belarussian woods into an armed force to fight German soldiers and collaborators. At the end of the war, the camp was still there, and 1,200 Jews had saved their own lives. Foundas observes that while Zwick's film is deadly serious, "based on a true story," and attentive to historical realities, including that Jewish resistance to the Nazis ultimately failed, "Tarantino, who has never been shy about depicting the cathartic power of violence, gives *Inglourious Basterds* an exultant, burlesque flavor closer to Paul Verhoeven's *Black Book* (another film accused by some of vulgarizing sacrosanct history)" (31). Verhoeven's film is closer to Tarantino's film in its substitution of fantasy for fact, but it is not in any significant way identical.

II. All about the Benjamins

If, as Jewish composer and comic songster Randy Newman, who has contributed to many film soundtracks, sang, "It's money that matters / In the U.S.A.," *Black Book* makes the obvious point that this is not only true of America. In every country of the world money determines who is seen as valuable, who is admired or resented, and who is denigrated or not seen at all. And in almost every country of the world ambivalence about this fact informs dislike of Jews. Anti-Semites the world over regularly promulgate the myth that all Jews are wealthy and those of us who do not appear so are simply craftily hiding our ill-gotten gains.[1]

The fantastical departures from history in Verhoeven's film depict Jews in this sort of anti-Semitic light. The film returns repeatedly to the idea that Jews are hated throughout Europe because they are rich and consequently not only anti-Semitism but most resistance to it centrally involves a sordid battle over money. The cynicism of the film, frequently commented on admiringly by critics, would not work without its facile and ahistorical equation of making casual anti-Semitic remarks with carrying out the horrors of the Holocaust. While microaggressions are a matter taken seriously today, no one would argue that they are equivalent in impact to murder. But when one treats the murders of Jews as being primarily financial in motivation, with the existence of cultural anti-Semitism simply serving to make Jews the easiest victims of thieves, then the Holocaust seems less horrific and inhuman and more like any other property crime that includes a violent attack on the affluent people being robbed, rationalized by the perpetrators as deserved because the victims are also oppressors of the poor.

As Stuart Klawans notes, *Black Book* suggests, through its depiction of the murder and robbery of the corpses of Jews attempting escape, that the motive for killing Jews was financial rather than racist with a pervasive anti-Semitism acting as the excuse for this money grab: "Verhoeven fixes one idea indelibly in your mind: The murder of Europe's Jews was a profit-making enterprise" (Klawans 35). This only makes sense if we ignore the historical fact that a large number—and perhaps even the majority—of the Jews who were killed were those who lacked the money to buy their way into a safe country. And as a Jew, I must ask, If Gentiles are so immune to the allure of money, why was it necessary for Jews to bribe their way to freedom? The film's single scene of Jewish deaths shows only wealthy Jews, not the impoverished ones who died by the millions. Moreover, it ignores the reality that it was not Jewish greed and focus on money that led to the deaths of the Jews who did not escape the Nazis but rather the way the rest of the world refused sanctuary to so many refugees. Ultimately the film's obsession with Jewish money looks very like the age-old message that Jews are cursed by their disproportionate wealth, which causes ordinary folk to resent them. And, as we know, this has been a common way of blaming Jewish victims at least since the Crusades.

The film title is particularly offensive in respect to this apparent message because a real-life text entitled *Black Book* was written by Ilya Ehrenburg and Vasily Grossman to record the anti-Semitic crimes committed against Russian Jews during World War II and to memorialize the work of Jewish resistance fighters.[2] In Verhoeven's film, the eponymous book, is a record kept by the lawyer Smaal (Dolf De Vries) documenting his financial dealings with wealthy Jews he ultimately betrayed. So, in the film, a record of financial transactions in which Jews were cheated becomes a substitute for a book that established their much greater victimization by torturers and murderers. The Black Book was also a name used for the *Sonderfahndungsliste G.B.*, a Nazi list of British citizens to be arrested if England was conquered by Germany. The use of the term for Smaal's record book hammers home the film's point that fascism was, as some of its defenders claimed then and continue to do today, an understandable, if perhaps excessive, response to economic injustices often attributed to an international conspiracy of Jews.

III. The (Jewish) Girl Can't Help It

But the most disturbing and ahistorical difference between *Black Book* and *Inglourious Basterds* is that while both explicitly connect the sexual behavior of Jewish women characters to the trauma of World War II, they do so in highly contrastive ways: one portrays the woman protagonist as naturally inclined to seize every opportunity to exploit her sexuality while the other admiringly depicts a woman victim of fascism as a virtuous heroine, which accounts for different audience responses from Jews. Although to be fair, I must concede that some Jews do like *Black Book*, as evidenced by its inclusion in the *Tablet Magazine* "Best of 2007" round up, in which Lawrence Levi says, presumably as a joke, that it gives us the "Best Nazi-Loving Role Model." And he provides this capsule review:

> The Hague, 1944: A frisky young singer joins the Resistance after narrowly escaping the Nazis' massacre of her family. To help free a Resistance leader's captured son, she seduces the handsome local head of the Gestapo. Do they fall in love? Of course! But in *Black Book*, the wild, violent, sexy thriller by the Dutch provocateur Paul Verhoeven, that's mere plot. Verhoeven is also out to expose his countrymen's anti-Semitism and barbarity. He does it with typically outlandish wit and cinematic dynamism—and by putting an awe-inspiring Jewish superheroine (Carice van Houten, in the performance of the year) front and center.

Yet one might ask if Verhoeven wanted to make a film about a sexy Dutch superheroine resistance fighter, why not dramatize the exploits of

Freddie Oversteegen or her sister Truus or the famous "girl with the red hair," Hannie Schaft, who all used their sex appeal to get close to Nazis whom they then killed? While all three were Gentiles, they were devoted not only to resisting the Nazis' control of the Netherlands but also to helping Jews resist and escape. None of them fell in love with Nazis, casually brushed off any idea that these men might be bad people because of their murderous acts in support of the Third Reich, or tried to save them from punishment for war crimes, as Verhoeven's heroine does. Anyone with a strong interest in Dutch World War II resistance fighters would know about these women. So, the choice to make this extremely flawed heroine a Jew suggests the view that while Gentiles might have a clear sense of right and wrong and so only use their sexuality as a weapon of war, Jews are too morally deficient to be able to function effectively in resistance to fascism due to their slavish idolization of violent strongmen.[3]

Black Book's Rachel Rosenthal is a Jewish girl who enjoys sex and sexual attention without any inhibition, as we see initially when, while riding on the handlebars of her new boyfriend's bicycle, she sees Nazi soldiers looking at her bare legs and wiggles them seductively. She smiles widely and seemingly spontaneously when they react with enthusiasm. Her lack of any repugnance toward these agents of war crimes strains credulity. She has been in hiding with a Gentile family. Could she possibly not know about the Holocaust that is taking place? Why else would she and her family be in hiding, if not to escape being beaten to death by Nazis in the streets or being sent to a death camp? She dislikes her Gentile protectors who are unpleasant to her and refuse to feed her unless she memorizes texts from the Christian Bible. So why the flirtatious joy at being admired by the very German soldiers from whom she has been hiding? In this early introduction, then, the character already seems rather demented. She appears to be an exaggerated version of the sort of nymphomaniac featured in some pornographic films who simply cannot resist being aroused by any male sexual attention no matter the circumstances or the men giving it. It is worth noting that in contrast to Rachel, von Trier's nymphomaniac, Joe, seems sensible and sane, since despite her willingness to have sex with almost anyone who is interested, she apparently draws the line at people who would murder her as a matter of policy. But Rachel's eroticism has no such boundaries. And so things quickly get worse.

The SS murder her family, along with many other Jews, in front of her eyes, as they try to escape in a boat to the unoccupied south of the

Fig. 3.1 *Black Book*: Rachel flirting with the Nazis.

Netherlands, yet she still succumbs to the dubious charms of the local Gestapo officer, Ludwig Müntze (Sebastian Koch), whom she is sent to spy on when, after her family's murder, she joins the Dutch resistance. A big, beefy blond who exemplifies the Aryan type celebrated by Hitler, Müntze initially accepts her assumed identity as a Gentile cabaret entertainer and uses his power to get her to have sex with him. But when he sees the dark roots at her hairline, he roughly accuses her of the crime of being Jewish. She seems so grateful that he does not despise her for being a Jew that she is eager to please him sexually and otherwise. We might initially assume she is simply acting so disgustingly in order to trick him, but as the film continues, we see that she has immediately fallen in love with him. She even helps him escape punishment when the Allied forces take over, and the two of them enjoy an idyllic interlude in the countryside before he is captured and executed. Is such a love plausible as anything other than a variation of Stockholm syndrome? It is not presented this way but instead naturalized by close-ups of her radiant face as she looks adoringly at him.

This aspect of the film can be particularly annoying to those familiar with Verhoeven's cinema, as we are accustomed to seeing his heroines seek revenge against men who dominate women and use them sexually. While such revenge plots allow him to create exploitative sex scenes, they still convey the feminist message that having their sexual vulnerability exploited enrages women. His most infamous film, *Basic Instinct* (1992), features a female serial killer who loves and protects women who killed their abusers. In another of his reviled exploitation films, *Showgirls* (1995), the heroine violently punishes a powerful celebrity who has beaten and raped one of her fellow showgirls, leading to reconciliation between these two women who were formerly rivals. These sorts of plot structures are characteristic of his work. Yet in *Black Book*, the poetic justice formula is replaced by a more morally ambiguous depiction of a woman's response to sex she cannot refuse.

As Linda Ruth Williams observes, *Black Book* is set "in morally questionable times" and "it is around the issue of sex that the film's ambivalence about taking sides opens up" (18, 19). Jews might see World War II as a time when morality was not in question but rather was completely absent in the supporters of fascism. And this view is not limited to Jews. In the majority of films that depict World War II, it is treated as the only modern war in which there was a clear distinction between good and evil behavior. Nonetheless, Williams seemingly approvingly quotes Verhoeven's assertion that there were some good Nazis and his film dramatizes this view through Müntze's opposition to the murder of Jews for the wrong reasons, that is, in order to rob them rather than merely to exterminate them. Sane Jews strongly prefer not to be slaughtered for any reason at all and most believe, as I do, that being a Nazi and being a good person are mutually exclusive. The film's gestures toward depicting Rachel's love for Müntze sympathetically do little to address this offensive subtext. Additionally, most Jews do expect others to "take sides" with us against those who would murder us, no matter their motivation.

The first and last scenes, which bookend the narrative as Rachel's memory, sympathetically depict her once again in harm's way as the October 1956 Suez Crisis begins and air raid sirens sound outside the kibbutz where she lives. Given that many remain hostile to the very existence of Israel, it is nice that the film acknowledges that Jews have reasons to feel that the defense of Israel is synonymous with survival. But the film's World War II content, over 95 percent of the screen time, by omitting any direct reference to the concentration camps and Eastern European killing fields of the Holocaust, undermines this point.

The film's dual foci are Rachel's love affair with Müntze and the struggles of the Dutch resistance. While we do see Rachel's family along with other Jews being shot, all the people whom we see being detained by the SS, tortured, and subsequently killed are Gentile resistance members. The killing of the Jews is quickly over and all the stomach-churning horrors the film lingers over are inflicted on Gentiles. It is their agonized screams we hear. And we are pushed to feel for them because they are developed as characters. We see their youth, courage, and idealism. They represent the best and brightest of the Netherlands, as young men who sacrifice their lives in the name of decency and freedom. In contrast, the Jews we see are not developed as characters, wealth and cowering cowardice seem to be their only distinguishing characteristics. Because Rachel is living with the Gentile farmers, apart from her family, when the film opens, we see almost no interaction with them. And the camera spends more time on them as part of a pile of corpses than it does on them as living people.

We are also shown that the resistance members themselves, just like the Gentile farm family that hides Rachel in the beginning, have some anti-Semitic beliefs and seem comfortable expressing them. This is obviously unpleasant, but in comparison to the Holocaust, it does seem like microaggression. If we accept this weirdly twisted context as historical fact, Rachel's irrepressible joie de vivre and enthusiastic sex life with a high-ranking Nazi can be attributed to a youthful apolitical attitude. Since in the fictional world Verhoeven creates for her Nazis are hardest on their fellow Gentiles, it makes some sense that she seems to have little fear of them and that she refuses to take personally or feel any apparent animosity about the Nazi ideological position that Jews are vermin of which it is a service to rid the world.

Rachel's ebullient personality allows her to remain surprisingly cheerful under what might be terrifying circumstances to most people, so she does not seem to suffer emotionally. The only time we see her suffer physically is when, after the German surrender, partisans pour a bucket of excrement on her as punishment for her collaboration. However, the Jewish viewer might not find this particularly cruel because she has just come from her pleasant time on the run with Müntze. And in spite of her membership in the resistance, she was a collaborator, not only enjoying the luxuries her Gestapo boyfriend provided, but also doting on him. By this point in the film, I was thinking of her as a shithead, so having my view actualized by the subsequent events did not upset me. Fortunately for her, she is able to convince the occupying Canadian military authority that in all she did, she was working for the resistance, although, of course, we know that she was also trying (albeit unsuccessfully) to protect Müntze from punishment for his war crimes. Ultimately then, the image that emerges is the old European theme (memorable in texts like *Ivanhoe* and *The Merchant of Venice*) of the Jewish girl who cannot resist the allure of the master race but is saved by the good, compassionate Gentiles from any deadly consequences of her oversexed folly.[4]

Would she be such a sympathetic heroine if the film focused instead on what Müntze was doing for the majority of the war, not just in the final days that we see here? We would then have visual confirmation of what common sense tells us: that the vicious interrogations and reprisals the Dutch partisans—and many others—endured happened under his command if not explicitly at his direction. And would the character development of her as a pretty, young girl who just wants to have fun even be possible if the film were accurately historicized? As Klawans says, the film's conclusion suggests that there will be "no salvation for Rachel Stein [her married name], beyond [her] sheer animal resilience" (36). Nathan Lee goes further, calling Rachel "the most sympathetic embodiment of the prostitute-protagonist" in Verhoeven's oeuvre (30). As a fan of Verhoeven's *Keetje Tipple* (1975), I think not.

Keetje is a character based on the memoirs of the working-class Socialist writer Neel Doff. Keetje turns to prostitution as her only option for controlling the amount of sexual violence to which she is subjected due to the poverty that makes her vulnerable to the cruelty of the men she refers to as "rich bastards." But she remains proud despite continual humiliations and in the end becomes a committed Socialist. At the conclusion, this sentence appears as an intertitle: "Her indomitable spirit lives on in this film." Of course, not all Jewish women abused by the Nazis were as heroic as Gentile Keetje, but surely those who survived often did so due to their indomitable spirit rather than their willingness, like Rachel's, to be sexually exploited and enjoy it.

IV. Glorious Shoshanna

We see such an indomitable Jewish heroine in Quentin Tarantino's *Inglourious Basterds*. The film begins, as he himself explains in *Sight & Sound*, as a "spaghetti western" transposed to World War II Nazi-occupied rural France, where a frightened peasant betrays his Jewish neighbors hidden under his farmhouse floor to Colonel Landa (Christoph Waltz), a sneering "Jew hunter" and his vicious band of murderers (Gilbey 6). The only survivor is the daughter Shoshanna Dreyfus (Jewish actress Mélanie Laurent), who runs away and escapes into the woods because Landa wants the fun of hunting her down like the vermin he says she is. Heidi Schlipphacke claims that despite the many techniques that Tarantino uses to draw our attention to Shoshanna, such as her character name being the one mentioned in the opening credits, pauses and slow motion emphasizing her actions, and her final appearance as "the face of Jewish revenge," critics and reviewers have treated her as "a side note" in their analyses of the film (114). Yet as Schlipphacke compellingly argues, this "tough as nails" figure of female vengeance is the most transgressive feature of the film, in that she demonstrates the transcendent excess of *Inglourious Basterds'* revisionism, moving it beyond a fantasy of correcting a historical outrage and into a critique of the masculin(ized) violence whence the Holocaust came (129).

Shoshanna's part of the story quickly moves to thriller territory as she takes over a Parisian theater, passing for a Gentile, and, with the help of her West African Black lover, Marcel (Jacky Ido), develops a plot to use its stock of highly explosive 35mm nitrate film to burn up the leaders of the Third Reich, including Hitler, during the screening of a film celebrating the exploits of a sniper, Frederick Zoller (Daniel Bruhl). Zoller's fame comes from his shooting a large number of American GIs. Shoshanna is, as Roger Ebert says, "a curvy siren with red lipstick and, at the film's end, a slinky red dress. Tarantino photographs her with the absorption of a fetishist, with closeups of shoes, lips, a facial veil and details of body and dress. You can't tell me he hasn't seen the work of the Scottish artist Jack Vettriano, and his noir paintings of the cigarette-smoking ladies in red." And you can't tell *me* that this is not a corrective to Spielberg's use of the girl in the red coat in *Schindler's List* (1993) as a representative innocent Jewish victim. Spielberg's film conveys the message that these poor, pathetic Jews depended on the mercy decent Gentiles provided, and by doing so, it supports the view that people who collaborated with the Nazis were not necessarily cowardly or immoral. Of course, it is true that some Gentiles saved the lives of Jews, including the historical figure Schindler, who saved over a thousand. But whereas the camera's focus on the body of the little girl in the red coat, who stands out from the other corpses, is meant to shame those who knew what was happening and did nothing and to bring the rest of us to pitying tears, no one needs weep for Shoshanna.

Shoshanna is neither a victim we must pity, nor is she marked as deserving our sympathy because she is innocent. This stunning beauty coolly and cleverly flirts with Zoller, causing him to talk Joseph Goebbels into using the theater Shoshanna has taken over for the premiere of the film. But unlike Verhoeven's heroine, Tarantino's is not attracted to the Nazi and, instead, shares with the audience looks of disgust at the need to keep Zoller's sexual interest so that she can accomplish her revenge and prevent the killing of more of her people. Their "romantic" moments may bring to mind Judith's with Holofernes. Shoshanna, too, is a Jewish heroine for the ages. And we might also think of her name's both biblical and contemporary Hebrew meanings, as she is pure as the lily and lovely as the rose.

V. Basterds of Bliss

Meanwhile, in a parallel story, the Inglorious Basterds, an American Jewish guerrilla military unit led by part Apache Lieutenant Aldo Raines (Brad Pitt) roams the countryside terrorizing German soldiers until his unit is ordered to Paris to make sure Shoshanna's plan to take out the entire Nazi command is executed. In the end, they quite ahistorically succeed, and we are treated to various realizations of vengeful fantasies, including Hitler being shot to pieces by Jews and Landa having a swastika carved into his forehead so that he can never hide his shameful past.

Roland Barthes's *The Pleasure of the Text* provides an ideal approach to analysis of the intersections of wish-fulfillment fantasy, reconstruction of Jewish identity, and politicization of cinema in this controversial film. I approach the bliss generated by the film through what I experience as its direct address of Jews via double coding. As Henry Bial argues, Jews, like all members of minoritized groups, read texts in ways different from the interpretations they are given by audience members who belong to the majority (Gentile) group, and so we may find in performances of Jewishness messages to decode that seem meant specifically for us (60–61). Still, different Jews, coming from different experiences of Jewishness, as we all do, will decode differently. My Jewishness is secular and racial rather than religious, as is the case for a large number of self-identified Jews. My paternal grandfather was an atheist Bolshevik Jew escapee from Russia and his second wife, my grandma Lena, was a Polish Jewish concentration camp survivor. I think they would have enjoyed seeing the Nazis killed by Jews in this film. My father was a street gang leader in the Cleveland ghetto, boxed Golden Gloves, and joined the army as a paratrooper as soon as the United States entered World War II. I know he would have loved *Inglourious Basterds*. I wish I could have screened this film for all of them because, like the creators of JewOrNotJew.com, they would likely have said, "When we first heard of Quentin Tarantino's *Inglourious Basterds*, a movie about Nazi-killing(!) Jews(!), we thought . . . great! We can never have enough of those!" Obviously, Jews like us are different from those devout people of whom Patricia Erens writes, "Despite centuries of suffering, the Jews have never condoned the use of physical violence" (352).

I have chosen to start discussion of Tarantino's film not with this high-minded—and excellent—study but instead with psychoanalyst Henry Kellerman's 2009 book *Greedy, Cowardly, and Weak: Hollywood's Jewish Stereotypes*. This nonacademic study of the portrayal of Jewish characters in twenty representative films nicely illustrates what I have experienced to be the responses of many Jewish audience members to standard depictions of Jews on the screen. Like me, Kellerman was outraged by the vision of Jews promulgated by *Schindler's List*: pathetic weaklings who cannot defend themselves (100–101).[5] This fits well, as he shows, with the convention of having any Jews in films who do fight back die as a result (75). Although it does not seem intentional, Hollywood films relentlessly convey the message that Jews cannot expect to defend themselves or others and live. And although Erens's far more comprehensive book does show more variety in the depiction of Jews, especially in independent films, she also gives numerous examples of irritating depictions of Jews, highlighting cinema's frequent recourse to "the Jew as symbolic figure—outsider, wanderer, scapegoat, and ultimately martyr" (215) and "the Jew . . . as Comic Soldier" who can be rendered serious only through his death (220). Erens also points out the infuriating tendency of World War II films made since the 1970s to emphasize "the contribution of non-Jews to the fight against fascism" (346), culminating in depictions of Nazis as men of conscience who break ranks to protect Jews (358).

Truly, as Kellerman's lively, conversational book observes, it is amazing that Jews like the movies as much as we do, but this is a reader-response issue often covered in feminist studies of women's fondness for reading misogynistic novels against their grain. Dominique G. Ruggieri and Elizabeth J. Leebron chart similar territory in a recent essay on the representation of Italian and Jewish women on television. Jewish viewers consistently "saw Jewish female characters . . . being portrayed as pushy, controlling, selfish, materialistic, high-maintenance, shallow, domineering, and cheap bargain-hunters," but Ruggieri and Leebron conclude that despite the intense negativity of such portrayals, Jewish viewers tended to like these characters and enjoy the shows in which they were presented, focusing on laudable aspects of the depictions of Jewish life such as the sense of humor and the "strong family orientation" (1269–70). Perhaps any representation, no matter how anti-Semitic, is better for these viewers than no representation at all.

I had my own moment of this when watching the Safdie brothers' 2019 film *Uncut Gems* about the misadventures of compulsive gambler and Diamond District jeweler Howard Ratner (Adam Sandler). When, in someone else's bathroom, despite being in terrible trouble and fighting for his life, he cannot resist stepping on the scale to see how he is doing at managing his weight, I burst into delighted laughter at how very Jewish I felt that action to be. It is not that I want films to portray Jews as hypervigilant, as my doctor kindly puts it, about our health. I just sometimes love to see depictions of us that feel real, even when they also seem to support our stereotyping as neurotic. Certainly, one can see this desire for something we can recognize as veracity in representing Jews in popular entertainments as a reason that so many Jews have been grateful for any film treatments of the Holocaust that do not support its denial or its persistent representation by anti-Semites as justified. To be depicted as pathetic because your race is incapable of self-defense is better than being erased entirely—I suppose.

But Tarantino's film does something new. As Stella Setka notes, "The film unsettles received representations of America as the liberator of Europe's Jews from their Nazi oppressors and . . . prompts us to question the reliability of films as instruments of public memory by calling attention to the cinematic strategies by which they represent the Holocaust" (144). According to his friend Jeffrey Goldberg, who helped with the script, Tarantino, through bits of allusion, pastiche, and parody, "managed to create out of these parts something that seems entirely new: a story of emotionally uncomplicated, physically threatening, non-morally-anguished Jews dealing out spaghetti-Western justice to their would-be exterminators."

This new vision was not welcomed by all Jews. In *Film Quarterly*, Ben Walters quotes Jonathan Rosenbaum's film blog pronouncement that the film is "deeply offensive as well as profoundly stupid . . . morally akin to Holocaust denial" and then responds with some ambivalence, noting that the film revises not only the historical facts of World War II but also film conventions for its representation in which "piety and sentimentality have become the dominant registers" (19). Ultimately, Walters finds the film troubling in its celebration of violence, which to him shows that the Jewish avenger Basterds are essentially no different from the Nazis. His support for this claim is that Zoller, the German sniper honored for killing over a hundred GIs, carves a swastika into the floor of his machine-gun nest, while Raines, the Basterds' leader, carves swastikas into the foreheads of German soldiers (21).

This seems to me as weird a decontextualized misreading as Thomas Doherty's claim that Private Zoller is meant to be seen by the audience as "the German Sergeant York," as the Nazis claim he is (60). The film within a film about Zoller's exploits, *Stolz der Nation* (*Nation's Pride*), shows us Zoller safely ensconced in an inaccessible balcony picking off people below like the proverbial fish in a barrel. Sergeant York risked his life in hand-to-hand combat as he took over thirty-two machine gun nests. Even the film-within-a-film highlights the distinction through high angle shots that make clear how safe Zoller's position was. Similarly, it distinguishes, through its meta-awareness of the audience, the distinction between the German audience gleefully laughing over this slaughter and our own laughter at the deaths of these soul-less monsters. For Doherty "the basterd squad" comes across as a "tribe of psycho killers" (60), whereas for me they are angry men with an obvious motivation, despite the film's avoidance of "serious evidence of the Final Solution," which Doherty laments (61).

Holocaust deniers typically demand to know what evidence we have for claiming that any Jews were deliberately and systematically killed simply because of their identification as Jews. Yet a mountain of evidence, including piles of bodies of people, among them children, who could not possibly all have been actively working against the fascist war effort never convinces them. Because the film does not dramatize anything that would fuel an argument that the Holocaust really happened and instead focuses on cinema as a force for vengeance and does so with ample dark humor, Doherty decides that it lacks seriousness and so precludes emotional response. Tarantino "builds a Wall of Irony so thick that no sensation penetrates," he claims (61).

Once again, my view differs. I agree with Holocaust survivor and national director of the Anti-Defamation League Abraham H. Foxman that *Inglourious Basterds* is a deeply satisfying film that should have won best picture at the Academy Awards because it gives us the revenge fantasy Jews have been waiting for all these years. In doing so, it becomes a veritable text of bliss. Consequently, in what follows, I apply Roland Barthes's theory of the text of bliss to the film to explain why, in opposition to how many reviewers said they expected Jews to respond to Tarantino's film, the majority of Jewish critics wrote about it in nearly ecstatic terms.

The most blissful moment for me comes, appropriately enough, with the climactic scene, in which a close-up of Shoshanna's face suddenly fills the film-within-a-film's screen from an inserted clip and dwarfs the burning theater in which the trapped Nazis are no longer guffawing about the deaths of their victims but facing their own. She says, "This is the face of Jewish vengeance," laughing as the flames rise to engulf the image.

This recalled for me the conclusion of the film *Exodus* (1960), in which, as Erens observes, "Flames rise from the bottom of the screen and the film ends" (219). Like most American Jews of my generation, I am not pleased by the State of Israel's treatment of the Palestinians and do not think of them as enemies to be purged from the earth by fire, but I am very happy to see Nazis meet that fate. So, since there is no such thing as an objective account of history, the question becomes, if we are imagining alternative pasts, shall we rewrite history to justify ourselves, as *Exodus* does, or shall we rewrite it to reimagine ourselves as winners whose subsequent behavior needs no justification to anyone who believes genocide is wrong?

Barthes's discussion of textual pleasure offers, if not an answer, a way of thinking about what values are entailed in the responses we have and takes us beyond simple condemnation of vengeful violence or celebration of it. Although Barthes's *The Pleasure of the Text* ends with an assertion of its greater relevance to cinema than to written texts, some of its central ideas have been neglected by film studies. Applying them to Tarantino's *Inglourious Basterds* provides a new approach to both the controversies about the morality of the film's reimagining of history and also those over the significance of the film's pervasive allusions and self-referentiality. Although Barthes warns against analyzing texts to explain their production of such a response lest it spoil the intensity of our pleasure in them, I have risked that loss to explore how, by rewriting what have come to be cinematic conventions of the representation of the Jewish victims of World War II, this film takes at least some of its viewers beyond what Barthes designates as the pleasures of historicization, and into the disintegration of identity and the new becoming that he calls textual bliss. The text of pleasure consolidates identification within a cultural history; the text of bliss shatters historically fixed identity. *Hester Street* is a good example of a text of pleasure, while *Inglourious Basterds* exemplifies the text of bliss.

As all commentaries on the film have noted, *Inglourious Basterds* references many other films, especially ones about World War II, with *The Dirty Dozen* (1967) seen by many as providing its model. Yet this 1967 film serves mainly as a departure point, for whereas the earlier film privileges ethical questions such as whether soldiers should disobey immoral orders, Tarantino's film concentrates on providing intensities that far exceed philosophical

Fig. 3.2 *Inglourious Basterds*: Shoshana's face of Jewish vengeance.

conclusions, moments of bliss that undermine what Barthes deems "the *moral unity* that society demands of every human product" (31). Apparently, Shoshanna immolates the Nazi audience because she profoundly resents their dehumanization and subsequent murder of her family; she exterminates them as they would exterminate her. Likewise, we can assume that Donny Donowitz (Eli Roth), the "Bear Jew," a big, muscular soldier who bashes in Nazis' heads with a baseball bat, is similarly motivated.

Setka's exegesis of this motif is worth quoting in full, as it is a return to the iconic baseball playing scene in *Hester Street*. Setka discusses the way the game of baseball was first appropriated from Native Americans and then used as an acculturation technique in the notorious Indian schools where boys were forced to learn and play the new version of the game:

> For Jewish immigrants to America, baseball also acted as an avenue for acculturation and assimilation and therefore played a role in the "transformation" of young Jewish men from "*Yidn* to Yankee." By rendering the bat, an instrument of the American melting-pot theory, an execution device, the film would seem at first to suggest that the film's minority heroes—the Apache and his platoon of Jewish Basterds—have fully assimilated into American culture. However, our knowledge of the US government's exclusionary stance toward both Native Americans and Jewish Americans at the time of World War II helps us to understand the film's underlying emphasis on the status of these men as they would have been regarded by a 1940s America—that is, as unwanted minorities—and requires us to consider the histories of oppression and disenfranchisement that both groups experienced at the hands of the American public and the US government. (Setka 151)

In *Hester Street* both Gitl and Bernstein argue with Jake that not only can Jews not assimilate into the American mainstream because Gentiles will not allow it but also Jews should not want to. Jake ends the discussion by insisting on trying, comically unsuccessfully, to teach his small son to play baseball. Because Gitl and Bernstein provide the film's moral center, we see their rejection of baseball as proper for political reasons. Why wear yourself out trying to assimilate into a culture that will always reject you? It seems better to sit under a tree and study philosophy as Bernstein does during this scene. One might make the same argument about the unconventional use of the baseball bat in *Inglourious Basterds*. It is an ethical act to appropriate the symbol of a melting-pot America that never existed and employ it as your defense against those who would eradicate your people.

However, the film never discusses the ethics of the Bear Jew's and Shoshanna's vengeful activities. In fact, Tarantino deleted from the final version of the film a scene from the original script (and available on the DVD) showing Donny in flashback buying a heavy baseball bat and asking his friends and neighbors to write on it the names of their loved ones in Europe. We can see that one of the names is Anne Frank. The violent acts are presented not as behavior needing this sad justification but instead for our enjoyment. Charles Burnetts says that "the Basterds replicate the inhuman ruthlessness of the Nazis, intent on immediate, bodily violence and torture without compassion, forgiveness, or rationalization" (10). He continues, "Because it seeks to dismantle received images of a persecuted Holocaust Jewry, the film makes a political statement that runs against the amoral grain of Tarantino's own corpus, its characters inevitably standing in for historical victims who still carry the weight of trauma and loss. Negotiating a racial politics in this way, the film takes on a moral and political position in many ways despite itself, a sincerity not of style, to be sure, but a sincerity nonetheless, which speaks to its inevitable and unflappable engagement with truly existing ethnic groups and identities" (12). Thus, we are not urged to think about motivations but instead to feel the bliss of for once seeing something different than pathetic victims of prejudice being killed or being rescued by virtuous members of the dominant group.

Some might say that the film retains some of the latter in the form of Raines, as the Basterds' leader, nicknamed Aldo the Apache, both for his racial heritage and for his demand that his soldiers each take the scalps of a hundred Nazis, because he is a Gentile. I would argue that his role says more about the affinity that has developed between the majority of American Jews, who are political Progressives, and many Gentiles who are members of other minoritized groups. In an interview Tarantino explains:

"I had a whole history with Pitt's character, Aldo. Aldo has been fighting racism in the South; he was fighting the Klan before he ever got into World War II. And the fact that Aldo is part Indian is a very important part of my whole conception, even of turning Jews into American Indians fighting the unfightable, losing cause. So that lead guy is legitimately an Indian" (E. Taylor). It matters that we are told that he identifies as an Apache because, like the Jews, American Indians have had to fight back against attempted genocide and have been forced into diaspora. And whatever other Indian tribes were like and whether some of them were as gentle and peace-loving as the violence-avoiding Jews Erens praises, the Apache were famously intensely violent against those who would destroy them. Tarantino sees the film as concerned with "the tragedy of genocide. I'm dealing with the Jewish genocide in Europe, but my Jews are going native and taking the roles of American Indians—another genocide" (Huddleston). As Baron discusses, Holocaust films evoke thoughts about other genocides (3). And of course, as in much of this blackly comic film, there is an inside joke for Jewish viewers in that we often refer to ourselves as "the tribe," thus the leadership provided by an American Indian makes some sense. Additionally, Aldo Raines's passionate alliance with the Jewish resistance certainly brings bliss for many of us. But not, perhaps, as much as the antics of the Bear Jew.

That Eli Roth, the director of the horror film *Hostel* (2005), plays Donny Donowitz, the Bear Jew, adds to the emotional impact for many Jewish film buffs, like me, who are descended from pogrom escapees. For us, the shock, horror, and torture-porn aspects of the film *Hostel* symbolically depict the Eastern Europe of our grandparents' stories, in which, as I was often told, meshuggeneh goys would kill you for fun. We have seen Roth's retelling; now *Inglorious Basterds* shows us him striking back directly at the fascists who enacted newer anti-Semitic atrocities. Raines's remark that "watchin' Donny beat Nazis to death is the closest we ever get to goin' to the movies" is not only funny; it insists that World War II movies can have functions outside the realm of delivering redeeming social messages. They can be about seeing what we have never seen before and viscerally reacting to those sights. Baron, among many others, praises the originality of the film, saying, "This alternate history is more than the sum of its parts, comprising an irreverent hybrid of campy humor, gory violence, and musical, verbal, and visual references to American war movies, Weimar and Nazi cinema, Hitchcock films, and spaghetti westerns" (3). As Barthes writes, "The New is not a fashion, it is a value" (40); it takes us away from the certainty of being at a specific location within culture—of having a fixed identity that explains our place within history and justifies our constructions of a self that claims pleasures appropriate to it—and takes us, instead, into the bliss of becoming, of experiencing our truths within our own bodies.

A text of pleasure, like *Hester Street*, is satisfying on many levels, it touches our hearts and minds. But a text of bliss, like *Inglourious Basterds*, goes straight for the gut reaction. In "Film Bodies: Gender, Genre, and Excess," Linda Williams points out that pornography, women's romance, and horror films are all scorned for being what she calls body genres—that is, genres that stimulate physical responses (2–5). Although not usually seen as so low on the cultural value scale as the genres she discusses, comedies and thrillers also rely on causing physical responses and as a result are considered less artistic than "serious" dramas. Tarantino plays with this view here as we laugh at the Basterds' cruel witticisms and Tarantino's inside jokes but also feel heart-pounding fear for Shoshanna.

And this leads to the equation Tarantino suggests between Jewish identity construction and cinema, along with his disquieting vision of the triumph of cinema being realized through the destruction of films' material artifacts, the archival treasures, the movie theater, and its audience. Setka argues, "In the act of writing a fictional Holocaust history that empowers Jews—and particularly American Jews—as avengers of Nazi crimes, *Inglourious Basterds* also points to the ways that Jewish Americans were historically disempowered, both by the public and the American government" (151). And in so doing it attacks and, for some audience members, destroys the conventional representations of Jews as victims in need of rescue by Gentiles, for which we must be eternally grateful. "Handsome, muscular, and quite tall—or so he seems from the angle at which the audience views him—the Bear Jew defies Hollywood stereotypes of the passive, weak, and feminized victim" (Setka 150) and literally bats such representations away.

Once again, I turn back to Barthes for elucidation. One of the sources of bliss in art is what is "unexpected, succulent in its newness . . . what explodes, detonates" (42). As Erens and Kellerman both show, the literal explosions in World War II films have always been all too familiar, and all too often, they serve to destroy those sacrificial victims the Jews. Although the Bear Jew is himself blown up in the attack on the movie theater, he is hardly a sacrificial victim, as he has just finished shooting Hitler's face off with his machine gun when the building explodes. In most films, Jews who survive must go away to Israel to assert themselves against the Palestinians, the only arena in which the movies routinely let Jews win. And this is a good time to emphasize that Palestinians, too, are mostly Semites and as such, and also as mostly non-Christian, dark skinned people, are stereotyped even more perniciously than Jews in popular entertainment. Bliss, according to Barthes, comes out of abandoning stereotypes (43), leaving behind ideology (50), and giving up moral certainty to the "unpredictable extreme" (52). He notes that "art seems compromised, historically, socially. Whence the effort on the part of the artist himself to destroy it" (54), an idea Tarantino echoes in defense of his making the destruction of the Third Reich contingent on the destruction of (the) cinema. He claims that whether we imagine the films being burned as those banned by the Nazis or as those made as Nazi propaganda, the metaphors still work the same way: in his film, movies themselves end fascism by reaching a fiery conclusion (quoted in Gilbey 6–7).

Goldberg quotes Tarantino as saying, "Holocaust movies always have Jews as victims. . . . We've seen that story before. I want to see something different. Let's see Germans that are scared of Jews. Let's not have everything build up to a big misery, let's actually take the fun of action-movie cinema and apply it to this situation." And that is precisely how the operations of the text of bliss fit Tarantino's self-proclaimed masterpiece. While Setka makes many important points about the film, I cannot agree with her central claim that it functions primarily to expose the way the Holocaust has become a "screen memory" that serves to obscure from Americans our own history of genocide and racism. Nor do I feel that we should recognize that the film does not have as its main purpose the glorification of "violent revenge fantasies" or the mocking of "conventional Hollywood film representations of the Holocaust" but instead aims to "reveal the danger of appropriating Holocaust memory as a means of distracting attention from other historical tragedies" (162). Instead, in my view, the destruction of the theater and the movie screen metaphorically stand for the destruction of a particular form of didacticism in cinematic Holocaust representations and their replacement with the antifascist violence many of us long to see.

The film blows up the old, refuses to be ideological, and rather lets the audience have the fun of seeing what Barthes defines as "the corporeal exteriorization of discourse" (66). The pleasure of this destruction is heightened for the Jewish audience by our awareness that movies were a primary vehicle for Nazi propaganda, especially in its dehumanization of Jews. A friend remarked, "It would be nice to think that the nitrate going up in flames is Leni Riefenstahl's films, Hippler's *The Eternal Jew*, and Harlan's *Jud Süß*."

But Tarantino does not stop at a wild celebration of the burning away of the images that limit our thinking about the history of Jewish identity construction. As Tarantino claims, "The entire film is about language" (Gilbey 10). Through his polylingual facility Landa holds control through most of the film. He uses English in the first scene to make fools of the hidden Jews before making corpses of them. His knowledge of Italian thwarts the plot of the Basterds. He talks rings around all his opponents, dramatizing what Barthes declares, that language belongs to the dominant group (32). But in the end, he is defeated by the marking of his face with a silent symbol. As Barthes also argues, those who are under the rule of a hostile ideology can only create a rival form of signification through introducing new images, presenting us with new faces for which we have not yet any words. And although we have seen the face of Jewish vengeance, alas, rising up in flames over the Middle East, we have never before seen the defaced visage of German culpability, the Nazi with the insignia he chose to wear imposed forever on his forehead. And of the way seeing this made me feel, I can only quote Barthes one last time: "Pleasure can be expressed in words, bliss cannot" (21).

Notes

1. In contrast to this vision, it seems worth noting that Newman's song "It's Money That Matters" begins with attention to "all of the people" who "never adjusted to the great big world" because they couldn't take in this message. Instead they spend their energy "lurking in bookstores' and "working for Public Radio," and although, "in any fair system they would flourish and thrive," as a result of their high social conscience, they "eke out a living and they barely survive." We very rarely see celebrated in cinema such Jews impoverished by their altruistic concern for truth and human welfare, although some of us see them every day in real life.

2. Another famous *Black Book* is the 1974 collage collection of images and clippings edited by Toni Morrison. It covers the experience of African Americans from 1619 to the 1940s.

3. The 1988 documentary *Hannah's War* (dir., Menahem Golan) and the 2008 documentary *Blessed Is the Match: The Life and Death of Hannah Senesh* (dir., Roberta Grossman) offer powerful correctives to this grotesque misrepresentation of Jewish women resistance fighters.

4. William Shakespeare's *The Merchant of Venice*, first performed in in 1605, dramatizes the successful efforts of the heroine, Portia, disguised as a male lawyer, to save the titular character, Antonio, best friend of her fiancé, from being killed for defaulting on a loan from the vicious Jewish moneylender Shylock. A subplot concerns Jessica, Shylock's daughter, who elopes with the Christian Lorenzo. Shylock's anger about her rejection of him and conversion

to Christianity motivates him to decide to exact a deadly penalty from Antonio as revenge against all Christians. Shylock's penalties for losing the lawsuit include forced conversion and the loss of his fortune to his rebellious daughter, who has proved her worth by turning against Judaism and her family. For this betrayal, she is rewarded by the Gentile judge. In Sir Walter Scott's 1819 historical novel, *Ivanhoe*, the eponymous hero is a devoted follower of England's King Richard and exemplifies knightly honor and virtue. He engages in a trial by combat to save the beautiful Jewess, Rebecca, from execution by the Knights Templars, who believe she has enchanted one of them into loving her. Ivanhoe, recognizing that she is a virtuous Jew with no designs on Gentiles, almost loses his life defending her. She falls in love with Ivanhoe but must renounce him so that he can marry the Christian queen Rowena. Despite remaining loyal to her father, Isaac of York, Rebecca is allowed to depart with him to Grenada, where Jews are tolerated. A sympathetic and tragic character, Rebecca, like Jessica, represents the stereotypical good Jewish woman who knows her place. As Michael Ragussis argues, *Ivanhoe* put "the 'Jewish question' at the heart of English national identity" (12). The answer the novel gives seems similar to that given much later by E. M. Forster in *A Passage to India* to the desire some have for a union between the English and those they racialize: "No, not yet" (322).

5. See also Jason Epstein's film review in which he objects to the film's lack of interest in "the others" whom Schindler did not save. He asks, "Did they die by the millions simply because they weren't clever enough themselves or lucky enough to find a Schindler of their own? Does the film mean to suggest that if only there had been enough Schindlers, the problem of evil which the Holocaust raises would have been solved, that it was merely for lack of cleverness or luck on the part of the victims that they died?"

4

JEWS, SEX CRIMES, AND HOLOCAUST ERASURE ON FILM

I. From Bliss to Disgust

In the previous chapter, I ended by looking at what made one film what Roland Barthes calls a text of bliss for me and many other Jews. In this chapter, I will look at films that create anything but bliss for many Jewish and philo-Semitic viewers with their depictions of Jewish sexual outlaws. One might hope that such films would at least reference the impact of the Holocaust on the psyches of post–World War II Jews, but if so, one hopes in vain. For contrast I begin with one film that is sympathetic to a Jew who, although acting as a pimp and a gangster's helper as well as sex object, is also clearly identified as a victim not only of his gangster boyfriend but also of the psychological impact of the Holocaust on later generations of Jews. This discussion is followed by two quick glances at documentaries about Jewish sex criminality in real life. And then I closely examine a film about a criminally insane Jew whose madness manifests in her sexuality. I conclude by looking at *Call Me by Your Name* (dir., Luca Guadagnino, 2017), a film that has been heralded as a beautiful fantasy, uplifting for Jews, and satisfying the need for affirming images of love between Jews, with the added bonus of being also gay positive. To many reviewers this film is a text of bliss. However, my view will depart from the predominant praise of the film for reasons that the rest of this chapter will contextualize as I argue that the film should be understood in relation to earlier depictions of Jews as sex criminals.

Why do I want to ruin such a potentially pleasant viewing experience? Because I am what Sara Ahmed has famously called a "feminist killjoy"—that is "an affect alien [who is] not made happy by the right things" but instead opposes the pleasures others take in representations that include sexual and/or gender oppression (57). In addition I am a spoilsport, spoiling the fun that others may find in watching the sexual exploitation of others depicted as a sort of sport. (As you may have surmised from the previous chapter, my idea of cinematic sport lies more along the lines of watching the Bear Jew bash Nazis' heads in with a Louisville slugger.) And if this were not enough opposition to specific types of texts of bliss, I also oppose the trend of providing a racialized rather than a historical context for the sex crimes committed by some of my fellow Jews.

Sadly the first two decades of the 2000s presented us with the most egregious sexual misbehavior of some Jews that the United States has ever seen. I am referring to the cases of Jeffrey Epstein and Harvey Weinstein. Epstein suicided in his jail cell in 2019 after being arrested for sex trafficking teenage girls to wealthy and powerful men. Harvey Weinstein, the cofounder of Miramax and the Weinstein Company and an Academy Award winner, was convicted, in 2020, of rape and criminal sexual assault and sentenced to twenty-three years in prison. Both men's arrests were to a large extent brought about by the #MeToo movement and have been rightly praised by feminists as signaling women's refusal to tolerate subjection to sexual abuse as a requirement for employment.

While the removal of these men from the positions of power they abused seems to me a very good thing, it was not so good that the exposure of the crimes of these men and other Jews revived the ancient image of the sexually predatory Jew discussed in chapter 1. And it was not only Jewish men who were involved in highly publicized scandals. While not involving forced sex acts, the relationship between Avital Ronell and her graduate student, Nimrod Reitman, both of whom are Israelis, resulted in a lawsuit against her for sexual harassment and New York University for failing to address it adequately. Reitman claimed he was subjected to unwanted fondling and that he was forced, through threats that she would withdraw support for his work, to express affection for her that he did not feel.

This case, as well as those of Weinstein, Epstein, and others, were followed by a flurry of attempts to explain this behavior as somehow specifically Jewish. Louis Farrakhan published a video claiming that Judaism itself was to blame "because Talmudic, Satanic Jews are the ones that feel nobody has a right to punish them for what the Talmud has made lawful to them" (*Jerusalem Post* staff). But, as always, racialization accompanies religious prejudice in the attacks. As Sam Kestenbaum discusses, the former

Ku Klux Klan leader, David Duke, who consistently refers to Jews as a racially constituted, nonwhite group, called the Weinstein case "a case study in the corrosive nature of Jewish domination of our media and cultural industries" and released two podcasts detailing what he called Weinstein's "assault on American culture." Kestenbaum also notes that on "white nationalist Richard Spencer's website Altright.com, a blogger known as Vincent Law speculated why it was that the expose on Weinstein was only coming out now, given that the allegations stretch back decades. Perhaps, he wrote, Weinstein was simply being used by other Jews as a distraction" from "the massive hive of degenerate Jews at the heart of Hollywood." The insect metaphor beloved of Nazis should not be ignored here. The Nazi connection was made even stronger by Andrew Anglin, editor of the infamous neo-Nazi website the Daily Stormer, writing that "the Jews have made our nation into the global center of filth that they made Germany into in the 20s. . . . And I just want you to remember this: back then, a bunch of guys got really . . . pissed off about it. And I am just going to tell you this: that didn't end well for the Jews," which he followed with the threat that "it isn't going to end well for them this time either" (Kestenbaum).

Surprisingly, the depressing trend of connecting sexual abuse to Jewishness included Ronell's claim that she had behaved toward Reitman in a campy way because such behavior is typical not only of queer culture (she is lesbian and he is gay) but also of the culture of queer Israelis. Several famous scholars, including Judith Butler, came to Ronell's defense in a letter protesting the decision of NYU to suspend her employment while the case was being examined. Numerous furious responses from contributors to the #MeToo movement followed, and threads in internet discussions of the case frequently mentioned Jewishness as intrinsic to the case and usually in anti-Semitic terms. I found these writings so disturbing that this was the first thing I thought of when I had one of those dark Jewish humor moments at the Association for Jewish Studies conference. I came running back into the hotel after a meeting with a colleague and realized that I had missed a panel I wanted to attend. I exclaimed, "Oh, no, I missed 'Anti-Semitism in America'!" only to be reassured by a laughing attendee, "Don't worry, Carol, you'll get plenty more of it." I also laughed but could not avoid thinking of the internet attacks on Judith Butler—a lifetime of progressive activism in support of sexual minorities wiped out for some people who will now think of her only as a "bad Jew," because of her defense of Ronell. However, the worst of this for me was that anti-Semites were not the only ones who attributed unethical sexual attitudes to Jews.

In an ill-advised essay in *Tablet Magazine*, for which he subsequently apologized, Mark Oppenheimer discusses Weinstein as "a deeply Jewish kind of pervert." His explanation is that, like Philip Roth's Portnoy, Weinstein must have suffered from "the particular anxiety of the Jewish American man in the twentieth century, finally coming into power but, having not grown up with it, unsure of what he's supposed to do now. All those years craving unattainable Gentiles, but never before [having] the means to entice them." When he finally can get one "shiksa goddess" after another, he forces them into private sexual performances designed to humiliate them and demonstrate his power. As Oppenheimer later wrote in the *New Republic*, his article "was praised by white nationalist Richard Spencer and David Duke, whose website ran a piece titled, "Major Jewish Mag Admits Weinstein Is a Jewish Racist Who Wants to Defile White People and White Women.""[1]

Andrew Silow-Carroll, writing for the *Jerusalem Post* about the problem of how Jews ourselves should respond to these and other recent incidents of Jewish sexual misconduct,[2] said, "When Jews do something bad, it is not our role to ignore it or justify it. [Philip] Roth, after being urged to stop writing about 'bad Jews,' invoked Jewish tradition itself: '[T]o indicate that moral crisis is something to be hushed up is not, of course, to take the prophetic line,' he wrote, 'nor is it a rabbinical point of view that Jewish life is of no significance to the rest of mankind.'" And I concur.

As I have discussed in detail up to this point, there is a long history of defamation of Jews based on the idea that we are sexually different from Gentiles and in pernicious ways. While these broad allegations are clearly anti-Semitic because of the attribution of vicious sexual deviance to all Jews, it would be a mistake not to take into consideration the impact of specific types of persecution Jews have endured on the behavior of Jews who are sexually criminal. This sort of contextualizing approach is common in critical race studies, so if we consider Jewishness as a racialized identity looking at the social and cultural history of Jews is important. Because of its major impact on people living today, I will do that here by analyzing what happens in both fictional and documentary representations of Jewish sexual criminals when the Holocaust is ignored.

My bringing together the Holocaust and shameful and criminal sexual behaviors on the part of Jews is not an attempt to justify these behaviors but is meant to raise questions about what sexual actions mean in the context of a racialized group, always fighting genocide, who have no uncontested homeplace on earth. The Ronell case additionally raises the question of whether if the conventions of sexual expression are different for self-defined queers, might they also be different for Jews? We might even ask whether Jews take sex as seriously as Gentiles and perhaps answer, no, in that we typically do not seem to take any aspect of life as seriously. We joke about everything, even the darkest subjects. And because we do not come from a religious tradition, like Christianity, that deems sexual expression intrinsically sinful and in need of redemption through a procreative purpose, we are likely to regard it more as a means of working through problems, including the problem of how to continue to live, love, and hope in a world that includes a significant number of people who continue to call for our extinction. So, confronting the fact that some Jews today act sexually in horribly unethical ways can reasonably be considered related to the Holocaust. And films can either make this connection or deny it.

II. Facts and Fictions

While the previous chapter deals with fictional Jewish heroines' resistance to fascism, I now turn to a real-life courageous Jewish woman fighter against fascism, historian Deborah E. Lipstadt, author of *Denying the Holocaust* (1993), who came to worldwide attention when David Irving sued her for libel, a lawsuit he lost due to ample evidence that he is in fact a Holocaust denier, just as she claimed in the book. In her 2019 book, *Antisemitism Here and Now*, Lipstadt continues her efforts to educate people about the Holocaust, pointing out that denial of its occurrence "is, quite plainly, a form of antisemitism. It's not about history. It's about attacking, discrediting, and demonizing Jews" (143). She provides a nearly overwhelming amount of evidence that the denial movement is growing as we move further from the revelation of the Nazi death camps to the world. And she asserts that the current trend among political Progressives and leftists, intent on criticizing the policies of Israel, of dismissing the Holocaust as now so far away as to be irrelevant to any discussion of Jews as deserving the same rights and respect given to other racialized and minoritized subjects is a form of anti-Semitism that should be seen as dangerous not only to Jews but to other racialized subjects.[3] It is dangerous because denying that the Holocaust still matters opens the door to denying that any racial injustice matters beyond the immediate period in which it occurred. As Timothy Snyder says, "The Holocaust is not only history, but warning" (xv).

Snyder objects to "the grotesque claim that Germans did not know about the mass murder of the European Jews while it was taking place" (207). Instead, as he shows, "long before Auschwitz became a death facility . . . in the East, where tens of thousands of Germans shot millions of Jews over hundreds of death pits, most people knew what was happening. Hundreds of thousands of Germans witnessed the killings, and millions of Germans on the eastern front knew about them. During the war, wives and even children visited the killing sites" (207–8).

His account of people taking photographs and souvenirs should not surprise anyone who has seen the photographs of merry white families enjoying picnics in the American South as they watched Black people being mutilated, lynched, and burned alive. Isabel Wilkerson powerfully makes this connection in her analysis of America's caste system.[4] And we should not consider this sort of festive cruelty, as Nietzsche called it, no longer possible in our current world (48).

I agree with Lipstadt that there are many things that might be called Holocaust denial, depending on what exactly about the Holocaust is being denied. For neo-Nazis and other active anti-Semites—that is, people who are not simply biased against Jews but take action to promulgate anti-Jewish lies—the denial concerns the intentions of the World War II fascists and the number of Jewish dead. They use websites, videos, and written "educational" materials to attempt to prove that the Germans did not intend genocide and that those who died in concentration camps were prisoners of war whose demise was caused by wartime food shortages. They maintain that there were no death camps or gas chambers and no executions of noncombatants on the eastern front. They claim that an international conspiracy of Jews falsified history in order to make Gentiles pity them and as a result be vulnerable to their tricks. This is the most extreme form of Holocaust denial.

As Aryeh Tuchman shows, "The 1980s and 1990s were the golden age of Holocaust denial in the United States," as the Institute for Historical Review began to broadly disseminate its message that the Holocaust was a Jewish lie, and "repeated references to Holocaust denial in U.S. media . . . exposed average Americans of the first, second, and third generations born after World War II" to the idea that this was a topic of legitimate debate (356, 358). Tuchman points out that the result was that "by the year 2000 and continuing to the present we have seen the [Holocaust denial] movement expand to include . . . conspiracy theorists and anti-Zionists not affiliated with the extreme right" (350).

Less extreme, not to mention less insane, but still troublesome, denials include the claims of various groups, currently including a sizable contingent in Poland, that Jews did not suffer more than any other of Nazi Germany's designated state enemies. And even when they do agree that Jews were targeted for extermination, they often argue that only a small number of Germans committed war crimes against Jews. Nationalists in Poland insisted on the passage of a law in 2018 that imposes criminal penalties on anyone who claims that country was complicit in the genocide, despite a long history of violent anti-Semitism in Poland before and after World War II.[5] Related to this stance is the denial by many individuals and organized political groups that the Holocaust belongs to a continual history of persecution and attempted genocide of the Jews throughout the world. This denies the significance given to the Holocaust by the majority of people in the world, who have treated it as one of the most important events in modern history. And that particular denial, along with the claim that the Holocaust was an isolated incident that the Jews should by now have gotten over, feeds into a specific sort of criticism of the State of Israel. One may disagree with many of the policies of the Israeli government, including its treatment of the Palestinians, as do I and as do the members of the Jewish Voice for Peace, among many other groups, but still understand why the founders of modern Israel felt that a Jewish state was necessary to Jewish survival, in light of the turning away of thousands of World War II refugees by the Allied nations.

Cinema definitely increased this sort of understanding generally. As Alvin H. Rosenfeld argues, "It is not primarily from the work of historians that most people gain whatever knowledge they may acquire of the Third Reich and the Nazi crimes against the Jews but rather from that of novelists, filmmakers" and other creators of popular culture (14). Two very popular films deserve mention in this regard. *Exodus*, although propagandistic, made clear that Jews were justified in their fears of being wiped out completely as a race due to the Holocaust. *Fiddler on the Roof* (1971), although it deals with Russian pogroms prior to World War II, suggests a history of murderous persecution and also that the emigration of Jews from Europe has long been necessary to our survival.

Outright Holocaust denial or explicit minimization of the Holocaust's place in history are so rare in cinema as to be almost nonexistent. One can see some such amateur videos on neo-Nazi and white supremacist websites such as Jew Watch and Stormfront. Films that oppose Holocaust denial, such as *Denial* (2016) and *I Do Not Care If We Go Down in History as Barbarians* (2018), powerfully refute these right-wing fringe efforts. But tacit minimization in popular visual media of the Holocaust's ongoing impact on Jewish lives is far more common. And you do not have to go to Nazi websites to see surprising erasures of the ongoing effects of the Holocaust on Jews. As with all things to do with Jewish identity issues, sexuality often figures largely in these erasures, and that is important to note for reasons this chapter will explore.

III. The Damage Done

When Helen Epstein's *Children of the Holocaust: Conversations with Sons and Daughters of Survivors* was published in 1979, scholarly, as well as popular, interest was sparked about the effects of parental trauma on Jews born after World War II. Numerous subsequent studies have shown the persistence of the trauma and PTSD, not only in the next generation but in the one that followed. Currently psychologists are recognizing the ongoing effects of the Holocaust on the descendants of American Jews who were never in any danger of being sent to concentration camps. And why should this surprise us? As Susan A. Glenn observes in "The Jewish Cold War: Anxiety and Identity in the Aftermath of the Holocaust," American Jews experienced intense "anxiety about the loss of six million European Jews and the future survival of a distinctive Jewish community in the United States . . . the physical loss of almost 40 percent of the world's Jews made the terms 'Jewish survival' and 'Jewish survivalism' into common 'household words.'" This anxiety contributed to what many saw as "the fragile psychological state of American Jewry" (Glenn). That this fragile psychological state resulted for some in a loss of ordinary sexual inhibitions should also not be surprising. Rachel Gordan argues, in "Alfred Kinsey and the Remaking of Jewish Sexuality in the Wake of the Holocaust," that Jewish sexualities were reimagined by Jews themselves in order to address both fully justified fears about the dangers of more genocidal attacks and anxieties about reproducing enough Jews to ensure survival of the race.

Additionally, while many post-Holocaust Jews felt pressured to reproduce and so replace the ones lost to fascist violence, they were often also cognizant of the role sexual abuse took in the genocide and, thus, perhaps disinclined to join those Americans who began, in the mid-century, to romanticize sex as naturally wholesome and good, so long as its expression was lawful. After all, rape and sexual torture of Jews had only recently been not only lawful but encouraged in Nazi-controlled countries.[6] While mainstream white Americans focused increasingly on the reproductive family as a protected private haven from political problems and fears, Jews could hardly avoid recognizing, as did most African Americans, that being allowed to maintain family values and sexual propriety were privileges reserved for the racially dominant group.

Regina Mülhäuser's study of the use of rape and sexual violence by the Nazis as "a weapon and strategy of war" reveals how ordinary soldiers came to understand the Blood Protection Law that forbade sexual contact between "Aryans" and Jews as only prohibiting "affectionate relations," not sexual abuse and torture (366, 396). This sexual terrorism was amply documented by survivors "immediately after and even during the war" (Timm 353–54). Currently, as Annette F. Timm notes, historians "have provided irrefutable evidence that sexual violence was ubiquitous in every phase of the Holocaust" (355). Surely the awareness, which many Jews had from the beginnings of Nazism's rise, of such a history would impact the way Jews thought about sexual morality. In fact, for many of us this is foundational to what Henry Bial refers to as "a Jewish reading position" (71). Jews can decode the behavior of vicious or merely self-absorbed and casually cruel sexual outlaws among us as a response to being denied legitimacy as sexual subjects, instead being persistently cast in the roles either of natural sexual victims righteously used by others or as natural sex criminals, or both.

As I note in the previous chapter, there is no shortage of films made about the Holocaust (let alone World War II generally). Yet any explicit consideration of the sexual pressures on Jews of the generation after World War II rarely appears in films. There are sexually corrupt Jews aplenty in films made after World War II: for example, what Nathan Abrams calls "the subsurface, subliminal Jewishness" of Humbert Humbert's antagonist, Quilty (Peter Sellers), in Stanley Kubrick's 1962 film adaptation of *Lolita* ("Kubrick's Double," 26). Abrams points out that the segment in which Quilty poses as a high school psychologist draws on the stereotype of Jews as sex counselors as he tricks Humbert into believing he has legitimate insight into teenaged Lolita, whom he is actually exploiting sexually (29–30). He can certainly be interpreted as "a diabolical Jewish pervert," although Abrams argues this is a parody of anti-Semitism and specifically the Nazi take on Freud and his followers (31–33, 37). Quilty's nasty sexuality, however, is not presented as in any way a response to the Holocaust, although the parodic elements of the characterization may well be.

A more recent film, *An Education*, set in 1961, the same time period as *Lolita*'s theatrical release, presents us with a much less ambiguous but equally decontextualized predatory Jew, David Goldman (Peter Saarsgard), who seduces a sweet innocent Gentile teenager and almost ruins her life. This crass conman, as Irina Bragin points out, closely resembles "the parasitical Jew of *Der Ewige Juden* (*The Eternal Jew*)—one of the infamous 1930s Nazi propaganda films," a resemblance underscored by two references in the film's dialogue to the legendary Wandering Jew, a figure for the timeless perfidiousness of Jews. And timeless this slander is, as the film mentions the Holocaust only when the heroine's headmistress, in trying to persuade her not to go away with David, says, "We're all very sorry about what happened during the war" but that it is "absolutely no excuse" for the postwar behavior of Jews, nor is it any reason to treat them as the equals of Gentiles. Any impulse to strike out at Gentiles and any temptation to exploit them at every opportunity that a man like David might feel because he inhabits this intensely anti-Semitic environment is ignored by the characters in the film and by the film itself. Instead it simply treats Jewish sex criminality as a given.

I am not arguing that post–World War II, Jews were more likely to be sex criminals than Gentiles or that sexual criminality by Jews in this period should be excused, just that, as Foucault notes throughout *Discipline and Punish*, we are in an age where the backgrounds and extenuating circumstances of criminals are usually discussed. Foucault writes that one of the biggest shifts in the legal treatment of criminality was from asking only if a specific behavior violated the law to enquiring into "the causal process that produced" the crime and its origin with the circumstances of the offender (19). But apparently the cinema of Jewish sexual misbehavior does not follow this modern pattern by taking into account the trauma effected by World War II.

IV. Bad Jews in Reel Life

One rare exception is the British film *Villain* (dir., Michael Tuchner, 1971). Ian McShane plays Wolfe Lissner, a beautiful, bisexual petty criminal whom Vic Dakin (Richard Burton), a mobster modeled on notorious homosexual gangster Ronnie Kray, brutally forces into a sexual relationship with him. When the police try to get Wolfe to inform on Vic, he explains to them that as a Jew he is "a survivor." His pimping of reluctant young women and men, whom he first seduces, to powerful rich men, his selling of party drugs, and his sexual submission to Vic are all things he does to stay alive.

Jeffrey Epstein, who made headlines in the summer of 2019 for similar activities, although at a much higher socioeconomic level, could be compared to the fictional character; however, his life circumstances preclude the idea that he procured as a strategy for basic survival. In that the film *Villain* is apparently set in the time it was made, Wolfe would have been born at the end of the war, and his entire life shadowed by knowledge of the Holocaust. He might have played with one of the toy Paddington Bears modeled on the refugee Jewish children. He would have been well aware that the English turned away adult Jewish refugees and allowed them to die. His childhood, like my own, would have been filled with adults' accounts of the horrors that took place, in his case, just across the channel in Europe, and also of the lack of legal protections for or societal concern about Jews. He would have heard about Oswald Mosley, leader of the British Union of Fascists and of the Battle of Cable Street in 1936, in which Mosley and his followers received police protection for a march. The audience is assumed to understand all of this and to sympathize with Wolfe, whom we see being punched in the stomach by Vic prior to their sexual contact.

Because Burton plays Vic as a shockingly violent and psychotically unpredictable murderer, at the film's conclusion, when Wolfe finally refuses to go any further with Vic, causing him to miss his chance to escape arrest, we are pushed to feel empathy for Wolfe. He is right that Vic ruined both their lives and as Vic rages against the police, we see Wolfe being led away by an excessive number of officers. Wolfe stands among them, small and slight as he always appears in the film next to the burly criminals and cops, with his head hanging in despair. How strange, then, that this film stands almost entirely alone in its depiction of the psychological damage done to many sexually badly behaved Jews by the Holocaust.

V. Translating Trauma

A few comparisons to the art of the racialized and sexualized group most oppressed in the United States illustrate the oddness of this omission. In a groundbreaking essay on the putative masochism of women's blues

Fig. 4.1 *Villain*: Wolfe doing whatever it takes to survive.

songs, Angela Y. Davis argues that while songs like the versions of Porter
Grainger's "T'ain't Nobody's Business If I Do" recorded by blues luminaries
Bessie Smith and Billie Holliday seem to be celebrating women's submission to masculine abuse—"I'd rather my man would hit me than to jump
right up and quit me"—what they really celebrate is African American
women's postslavery ownership of their bodies with which they can do
whatever they please (30–31). Their audiences understood that "the early
blues women" created and shared personae representing "a tradition that
directly challenged prevailing notions of femininity" (A. Davis 37). Hazel
V. Carby argues, in "It Jus Be's Dat Way Sometime: The Sexual Politics
of Women's Blues," that because of the specific types of racism and misogyny to which Black women were subjected during slavery and the Jim
Crow decades that followed, "the blues singers had . . . no respect for sexual taboos or for breaking through the boundaries of respectability" and
this defiance of female propriety should not be considered an individual-
ist rebellion but rather a communal political stance (482). Indeed, African
American literature, theater, and film have a long tradition of showing how
sexual crimes and abuse fit into a history of specific types of oppression.
The most obvious example is Alice Walker's 1982 novel *The Color Purple*,
adapted to film by Stephen Spielberg in 1985. In these texts, we see Black
men whose sexist treatment of women is placed in the context of their own
subjection to racism, not in any way to excuse what they have done, but to
raise awareness of how their vile deeds are part of a much larger systemic
problem.

Black feminist scholars like bell hooks and Patricia Hill Collins talk in similarly contextualizing ways about misogyny in hip-hop culture. They never condone it; they call it out, but they do so by addressing its relation to a history of racist oppression and by insisting that ending the cycle is necessary to resisting racism and advancing the rights of their group. Their approach is deeply intersectional, as that of Jewish feminists should be. In a more recent example, Daniel Black's *The Coming*, a powerful tale of the experiences of a group of people in the Middle Passage and after, shows how the terrible abuse to which a previously decent and properly behaved young tribal member is subjected and, worse, the horrors he witnesses cause him to violently reject any further regulation of his behavior. None of these authors are implying that all Black people are evil or perverse because of how they have been treated in America, only that the ways they have been treated made some of them lose faith in the proprieties valued by their oppressors. This is something everyone who has not lived a sheltered, privileged life already knows, or so we might think. But again it does not seem to pertain to Jews.

In *Unclean Lips: Obscenity, Jews, and American Culture*, Josh Lambert traces a history of misrepresentation of Jews as inherently criminal sexually, beginning in ancient times and reaching into the present. Black Africans have, of course, been misrepresented in similar ways, yet few decent people, when observing departures from conventional sexual morality in members of this group, would fail to take into consideration the effects of colonialism, slavery, and other racist oppressions on the behavior of some group members. But when it comes to portraying Jewish rebels against sexual morality, many filmmakers seem to think the event that so deeply shadowed Jewish lives in the later part of the twentieth century need not even be alluded to.

The early years of the twenty-first century saw the release of two documentaries about the criminal prosecution of Jews accused of deviant sexual behavior: *Capturing the Friedmans* (dir., Andrew Jarecki, 2003), which follows the still controversial investigation of Arnold Friedman and his son Jesse for child molestation, and *Crazy Love* (dir., Dan Klores and Fisher Stevens, 2007), which traces the astounding relationship of Burt Pugach, a lawyer and his girlfriend and later wife, Linda Riss. Pugach served a fourteen-year prison term for hiring men to throw lye in Riss's face when she tried to break up with him, blinding and scarring her. She not only subsequently married him but also spoke in his defense in a later trial when he allegedly ordered a similar attack on a girlfriend who rejected him. The

Pugach marriage seems appalling, and the film plays it for shocks. The film on the Friedman case is shocking for a different reason. Since there was no physical evidence that the Friedmans ever molested anyone, many of the reports of abuse included claims that were physically impossible, and all the boys but one who originally accused them later recanted their testimony, all we can know for sure is that Arnold did collect child pornography. The films emphasize their subjects' Jewishness through many references to cultural and religious practices. Yet one area of contextualization remains absent.

That Burt and Linda met on Rosh Hashanah in 1957 is as interesting because of the year as it is because of the holiday. For many American Jews, the Holocaust was a daily topic of anxious conversation at this time. When a colleague of mine who teaches a class on the Holocaust asked me if I had ever had such a class, I replied that it went on for my whole childhood. Many Jews my age have agreed. Although some of us were not yet even old enough for kindergarten in 1957, we knew what the numbers tattooed on family members' and our parents' friends' arms meant. *Night and Fog* had been released the previous year and four years later Stanley Kramer would make the film *Judgment at Nuremberg*. Of course, there are crazy people in every racialized group (and plenty of white ones as well) and sex crimes occur for innumerable reasons. Still, it seems odd to go deeply into the psychologies of two Jews living in the wake of the Holocaust without even a mention of how the knowledge that 40 percent of the people in their group had recently been grotesquely murdered for insane reasons, often after being subjected to sexual torture, as the world watched doing little to help them, might have affected their sense of ethics and might even have had some influence on their crazy desire to cling to each other.

Capturing the Friedmans also takes an interest in the psychology of a Jewish family and yet similarly avoids any mention of the event that must have haunted the life of Arnold, the father, who was middle aged in the 1980s when the events in question took place. Based on what the film shows, it is difficult to conclude that either Arnold or his son Jesse forced sex on the boys in their computer class or on any other boys. Like the McMartin Preschool scandal,[7] the situation investigated here seems the result of grossly misused police psychology, including hypnosis, as Debbie Nathan, the journalist who helped exonerate the McMartins, reveals. But unlike the McMartins, who were ultimately cleared of all charges, at least one of the Friedmans, Arnold, was a self-admitted pedophile, who may have at least fondled a few boys in a way that he found sexually exciting although it did not involve touching genitalia. He apparently touched and sometimes stroked boys' upper backs, shoulders, and arms during the computer instruction. The film emphasizes that his lack of the complete innocence that America's current black-and-white sense of morality demands results in nearly inconceivable tragedy for everyone concerned.[8]

The family's obsessive documentation on home video of their life in suburban Long Island adds eerie material to the documentary's interview footage. Arnold spends almost all his time with his three sons, who adore him, and his admiring students (he teaches high school) and conducts a very popular computer class in his family's basement recreational room for boys aged from about ten to twelve. His nineteen-year-old son, Jesse, helps him teach the computer classes. Then one day an FBI kiddie porn sting results in his arrest for trading a magazine from Denmark. More porn of boys is found hidden in his home. The police start questioning the boys who took his computer classes. They relentlessly press them, saying over and over, "We KNOW what went on." At first the boys confess to looking at some silly stuff—an early CGI of a cartoon stripper, a "peter meter"—but finally they spin amazing and totally implausible tales of being repeatedly anally raped by Arnold and Jesse, who, if the accounts were correct, sodomized boys at least ten times during each weekly class. Despite their alleged brutalization by these fiends, in medical examinations none of the boys showed any evidence of physical molestation, and they were always happy and smiling when their parents came to pick them up after the lessons. One boy who claimed to have been raped and tortured about fifty times, begged his parents to sign him up for the second session of the class. Some of these boys now admit they said whatever the cops seemed to want in order to "get them off my back." We will never know what went on beyond the fact that the allegations were physically impossible, and yet the court accepted this nonsense as reality. It seems possible that some of the boys did have some improper but not physically injurious sexual interaction with Arnold and Jesse that they felt ambivalent about, as children generally do about all the sexual games they play, embarrassed, amused, and aware of being naughty. And, again, the unasked question is whether Arnold's bad behavior could be related to—although not excused by—Holocaust knowledge resulting in cynicism and disconnection from societal norms.

Well, a documentary cannot cover everything, so maybe these omissions should be overlooked, especially as the inclusion of Holocaust references in the films could be seen as implying that attempted genocide has made all Jews more susceptible than Gentiles to becoming crazy sex criminals.

VI. In the Embrace of Madness

So I will move along to a film that depicts us as just that, more susceptible than Gentiles to becoming crazy sex criminals and does so by ignoring the Holocaust and placing all the blame for whatever sex-related craziness Jews might exhibit on our race: the fictional film *Last Embrace* (dir., Jonathan Demme, 1979). The film could hardly be more filled with references to Judaism and Jewish life. It begins with a former CIA agent, now dying of cancer, receiving a goel hadam note—Hebrew for "avenger of blood." The previous twelve recipients of the note are dead under mysterious circumstances, so with the help of a Talmudic scholar, he begins to attempt to solve the mystery. It turns out that the avenger is Ellie, the seemingly nice Jewish girl with whom he is having an affair. She is out to kill all the descendants of some turn-of-the century Jewish criminals who raped her grandmother and forced her into prostitution, resulting in her subsequent death from venereal disease. After a confrontation with Harry at Niagara Falls, Ellie slips and tumbles to her death.

Initially the film seems to be implying that Harry is in danger because he has rejected his heritage. He is truly a "nominal Jew" in that he does not even recognize the writing on the note as Hebrew and makes no references to his own Jewishness. But the plot reveal of Ellie's motivation shows us that for Harry to know and embrace that heritage would mean embracing destroyers of innocent women. Many critics have noted the film's heavy allusions to Hitchcock's *Vertigo*, which include a large necklace with a red stone pendant playing a crucial role in unmasking Ellie's criminality, a bell tower where a murder takes place, and a final car trip down a long winding road to the place where the duplicitous love interest will accidentally fall to her death. But whereas in *Vertigo* we sympathize with the female love interest, who never intends to be an accessory to murder, here she is a psychotic killer whose motivation seems insane in that the men she slaughters had no knowledge of their ancestors' perfidious acts. Likewise, where *Vertigo* frames the sad tale of Carlotta Valdez, another nineteenth-century victim of patriarchal sexual exploitation, within a vision of the general corruption of 1800s California, and in particular the racism of the period, *Last Embrace* features no corrupt characters who are not Jews.

One must wonder, since the story (derived from *The Thirteenth Man*, by Murray Teigh Bloom) was to focus on a woman driven mad by horrific crimes committed against her grandmother, why not make that grandmother a victim of the anti-Semitic violence that resulted in so many Jews coming to America? Instead, the grandmother's story follows the early twentieth-century anti-Semitic propaganda (discussed in Jenna Weissman Joselit's study of Jewish gangsters, *Our Gang*) that inaccurately blamed Jews for the existence of "white slavery" (48). As Joselit shows, while anti-Semitic "social reformers suggested that Jewish 'merchants of vice' banded together in a kind of cartel, to control the white slave trade," in reality legal records suggest that Jewish procurers and pimps were a minority in the sex trade, which was dominated by Gentile immigrants (49–52).

Bloom's novel, like Joselit's historical study, makes clear that far from being all implicated in a sex-trafficking cabal, the majority of "the organized Jewish community kept on battling the [sex] trade in many ways," so much so that one character involved in that trade remarked, "They're worse than the anti-Semites" (Bloom 149). He feels this way because the sex traffickers are banned from the synagogues and denied burial in Jewish cemeteries. In contrast to the bad Jews who are not recognized by others as being Jews at all, having forfeited their right to belong to the community, is the "American Hebrew Leadership Council," with which Harry in the novel works to bring justice to the situation (218). There is a lot of emphasis in the novel on the idea that true Jews are virtuous, even to the point that Harry discovers from someone who knew his father that he was "born one of the anointed of the race"—that is, without a foreskin, making circumcision unnecessary (172). But just as in Nazi Germany, in the film adaptation, sexually corrupt Jews are blamed for every social problem.

The very phrase "avenger of blood" suggests a connection to the Holocaust, as one can see by consulting Deuteronomy 19:4–13 on "cities of refuge," which distinguishes between unintentional homicide and premeditated murder. The one who kills unintentionally "may flee to one of these cities and save his life. Otherwise, the avenger of blood might pursue him in a rage . . . and kill him even though he is not deserving of death, since he did it to his neighbor without malice aforethought." God's people were commanded to create cities of refuge "so that innocent blood will not be shed in your land." Only one who "out of hate . . . in wait, assaults and kills a neighbor" should be "handed over to the avenger of blood to die." Ellie, like the Nazis who are not once mentioned in the film, is no righteous avenger of blood. She lies in wait, assaults and kills men whose connection to the destruction of her grandmother is unknown by them. Her behavior is a sort of gendered version of the blood libel: Jewish men are evil destroyers of the innocent and so must die.

VII. Things Not Named

The celebrated film *Call Me by Your Name* is far more subtle in that its refusal to reference the Holocaust in any way can be seen as a simple choice of narrative focus. Why bring the Holocaust into every depiction of Jewish sexual behavior, one might ask, especially as this particular depiction lacks the emphasis on criminality so prominent in the other three films? Yet one response would be that the film's very popularity makes its falsifications (through omission) of Jewish history just as troubling.

It is easy to see why the film is so popular. As I mentioned in this chapter's opening, it is a fantasy designed to fill viewers with bliss. Although set in 1983, it takes us back to the sexual attitudes and behaviors typical of the 1960s–1970s sexual revolution. In that time period, sexual relationships between adults and teenagers that are now generally seen as psychologically damaging for adolescents were frequently celebrated in songs and films. Two extreme examples are Donovan's hit song "Mellow Yellow," which features the singer's joyous realization that a fourteen-year-old girl he is "mad about" is also "just mad about me," and Bertrand Blier's 1978 film *Get Out Your Handkerchiefs*, which deals with a passionate affair between an adult woman and a thirteen-year-old boy. *Call Me by Your Name* invites audience members who enjoyed sex with older partners when they were young, as well as those who merely longed for and fantasized about such relationships, to revisit those fantasies without guilt, simply reliving the excitement.

The film also belongs to the long Anglo tradition of portraying Italy as a place of sexual awakening. Think of George Eliot's *Middlemarch*, E. M. Forster's *Where Angels Fear to Tread*, and D. H. Lawrence's *The Lost Girl*, for examples. The two main characters of the film, Elio and Oliver, are physically beautiful, as is the Italian countryside, where their romance unfolds from a stereotypical rom-com "meet cute," during which both fight against their mutual attraction. Their depiction does little to challenge flattering Jewish stereotypes as both are intellectual, interested in high culture, art, classical music, and philosophy. So far, so good. Their attraction is immediately associated with shared Jewishness, as Oliver says, "I know what it's like to be the odd Jew out" and Elio, explaining why, unlike Oliver, he does not wear his own Star of David, says, "My mother says we are Jews of discretion." But these are slightly jarring moments, given what we see. Or rather what we do not see: any anti-Semitism. The Gentile Italians in the town are warm and welcoming to both young men and the local girls eager for sex with them. No one ever expresses any anti-Semitic views.

This was especially surprising to me as a viewer, for I had just finished teaching Elena Ferrante's novel *My Brilliant Friend* in a senior seminar on representations of friendship. The novel details the relationship of two girls who grow up in Naples in the 1950s and reaches into the present day. It is packed with references to how deeply World War II affected Italian everyday life and how persistent the prejudices of that time period remain even now. And, of course, one might look at history to see that, as Harry D. Wall says in his review of the Museum of Italian Judaism and the Shoah in Ferrara, "the history of Jewish life in Italy might seem like one long saga of suffering and trauma: slavery by the Romans; the Inquisition and persecution by the Church; forced segregation to cramped neighborhoods in the Middle Ages. The first of many ghettos was established in Venice in 1516. The 20th century witnessed the rise of fascism, anti-Semitic racial laws and the Holocaust, when nearly 7,700 Jews out of a total population of 44,500 were killed." Some have commented that this relatively small number of murders attests to the lack of anti-Semitism in Italy. It is true that "Mussolini showed no interest in deporting Italian Jews to their deaths" and even outside Italy, "Italian soldiers sometimes sheltered Jews" so that generally "Jews who had a choice would flee to zones of Italian occupation" (Wall 239–40). But in the end, a fourth of the country's Jews were slaughtered (Snyder 240). And to those who were marked for death, it probably did not matter that many Italians had been willing to let them live had it not been for the insistence of the Germans. As for anti-Semitism in Italy now, one can consult the Fundamental Rights Report of the European Union, "Discrimination and Hate Crime against Jews in EU Member States: Experiences and Perceptions of Anti-Semitism," which includes the testimony of almost six thousand Jews.[9]

Just because dislike of Jews, or any other racialized group, does not always result in a country's enthusiastic adoption of an official policy of murdering them, as it did in so many Axis countries, does not mean that the people of that country were not anti-Semitic. One might think of the attack on the Great Synagogue of Rome a year before the events taking place in *Call Me by Your Name*. While it was carried out by Palestinians, it could be considered part of the rising hostility by Italians toward non-Israeli Jews in this time period due to their being blamed for Israeli governmental policies on which, obviously, most Jews living outside Israel have no influence. Arguing from statistics, in a 2015 article, Anna Momigliano claims that the danger of Italian Jews being subjected to anti-Semitic violence has decreased since the 1980s. However, fairly consistently since World War II, as she notes, both the extreme political Left and the Right have encouraged Holocaust denial and promoted the idea that Jews conspire to deceive and deny the human rights of others. Cnaan Liphshiz reports on the results of this in his discussion of a poll that revealed that 15 percent of Italians now are Holocaust deniers, while almost 24 percent believe Jews are in control of both the economy and the media. And a personal observation from Deborah Lipstadt adds a chilling note. "During a recent trip to Italy," she sees that there, as in Germany, Austria, and the Netherlands, Jews are reluctant to wear kippot in public for fear of verbal or physical attacks and instead wear baseball caps ("Antisemitism," 10).

Not the tiniest glimpse of this World War II heritage appears in the film. Instead of reflecting the attitudes toward Jews in Italy in the early 1980s, let alone the alarming growth of anti-Semitism in Italy at the time the film was made, it adheres to the requirement that to be a text of bliss, as described by Barthes, the film must ignore political and historical realities in order to stimulate joyous feelings, the sort many of us have had during vacation trips to places in beautiful Italy where, for whatever reason, we were not subjected to prejudice against Jews. And it does so by denying that those prejudices ever existed, let alone persist today.

As Richard Brody argues in one of the film's few negative reviews, this is so unrealistic as to challenge our credulity. Among the characters that he considers woefully undeveloped and "sanitized" are "the middle-aged cook and maid Mafalda (Vanda Capriolo) and the elderly groundskeeper and handyman Anchise (Antonio Rimoldi), who work for Elio's family, the Perlmans. What do they think, and what do they say? They're working for a Jewish family . . . the only Jewish family in the region, even the only Jewish family ever to have set foot in the village—and they observe a brewing bond between Elio and Oliver. Do they care at all? . . . Is there any prejudice anywhere in the area where the story takes place?" As well as denying the existence of anti-Semitism in rural Italy, the film is also gay positive to the point of implausibility, with Elio's parents encouraging the affair in every possible way. This is 1983, in the early years of the AIDS pandemic when

American parents were so terrified that their teen-aged children might have sex and thus be infected with HIV that many began to support the disastrous abstinence-only sex education movement. In gay cultural centers in San Francisco and New York, people were beginning to see celibacy as a valid form of self-protection, and in the same year, even some former gay rights activists, like Larry Kramer, advocated a return to monogamy. However, no one mentions HIV or condoms, including Elio's highly educated and sophisticated parents. We are apparently also to believe that people in 1983 rural Italy find gay sex so unproblematic and wholesome that no girl would have any qualms about sex with a gay man and parents would urge a gay teen to act on his feelings with an older, more sexually experienced, and apparently free-spirited man. The father treats them, and us, to a slide show of statues from antiquity of beautiful young men, commenting on "their ageless ambiguity as if they're daring you to desire." And when Elio mocks an effeminate older gay couple, his father admonishes him to show respect. After the affair ends, he tells Elio that what he and Oliver had was special and "I envy you." Even Marzia, the girlfriend Elio uses for his own sexual initiation and then dumps for Oliver, is understanding and supportive.

The film also avoids any sexual coarseness except for some small touches, such as a urination scene and one of Elio sniffing Oliver's shirts. An hour and twenty minutes passes before we are shown a passionate kiss. Oliver retreats teasingly from Elio's clumsy advances, but finally they have sex, although the camera cuts away to a tree outside until they are in the tender stage after intercourse. Nathan Heller argues that this is not, as some critics claimed, an instance of "homoerotic shyness" because "that consummation suffuses much of the film," through such sounds and images as "the villa's shutters beating in the wind like a headboard" (67). Yet this kind of symbolic rather than direct representation of sexual activity suggests that the sight of actual gay intercourse would be offensive. We do see Elio digitally penetrating a peach and then, the film suggests, he masturbates with it. But the focus is on his shame afterward.

Here the film, unlike the supportive parents and Marzia, includes a slight suggestion that the affair may not be a cause for pride. This echoes Oliver's claim, when he first resists Elio's advances, that they have not yet "done anything to be ashamed of." His implication that sex between them would be shameful seems reasonable enough because at the time of the film's release, the #MeToo movement was gaining momentum, often through stories of intergenerational sex that seemed consensual to the younger participants at the time but in retrospect was understood as having been a violation that caused them imperfectly understood trauma. We are told that Elio is a seventeen-year-old high school student, while Oliver is a twenty-four-year-old doctoral student working with Elio's archaeology professor father. In other words, their affair fits the legal definition of statutory rape in most of the United States, of which both are citizens. And even more pertinently, it is very like many #MeToo reconsiderations of past events previously recalled as love affairs.

Oliver's behavior toward Elio conforms to the general view of the "grooming" of teens by sexually predatory adults. Oliver's eponymous request, "call me by your name and I'll call you by mine," an attempt to position them as equals, belies the huge difference in their situations in life and sexual experience, negating Oliver's greater power. We see him dominate Elio through withholding, as when he begins fellatio on him and as soon as Elio responds with desire, retreats and slams the door in his face. Jake Marmer argues that "Oliver's obliviousness to his affection is a form of seduction." I would agree but add that the obliviousness is clearly feigned. Oliver teases and even taunts Elio for not being able to initiate sexually, making it clear to the boy that he will have to prove his maturity through admitting his desire for Oliver and accepting Oliver's response whatever it may be. Again this is typical grooming behavior in which kids are made to feel that telling an adult they want him sexually will show they are grown-ups. Marmer adds that "the age difference between the two characters seems all the more dramatic in the film, where gawkish, slightly awkward Chalamet and studly Hammer appear to belong to different worlds of experience and prescience." Ofri Ilany remarks that Oliver "is meant to be 24 but looks as though he's in his thirties." The actor who plays Oliver, Armie Hammer, was thirty-one at the time of filming; Timothée Chalamet (Elio) was twenty-two. I agree with Ilany that the age difference seems greater than nine years, in part because of Hammer's muscular physique and Chalamet's slight one and also because Hammer is five inches taller than Chalamet. Elio looks more like fifteen to me than seventeen, creating somewhat disturbing images as Oliver looms over Elio, smirking superiorly as he dominates him emotionally and goads him to confess that he wants sex.

While I believe that many people in their late teens are ready for sex and that age of consent laws that criminalize sex between seventeen year olds and people in their early twenties are often unrealistic, what I see in this film is a sheltered and naïve boy being manipulated into an affair that

Fig. 4.2 *Call Me by Your Name*: Oliver and Elio, another way size matters.

he sees as expressive of true love by a man who sees it primarily as a diversion. Like Judith Levine, I think that people in their late teens are more likely to be hurt by love, when it leads to "romantic disappointment" than merely by sex that they want (137). But I do not think that is a reason that adults should feel fine about seducing and then abandoning them, as Oliver does here. The famous gay "sexpert" Dan Savage often opines that affairs between gay teens and young adults are acceptable as long as the adult follows the "campsite rule": leaving his partner in better (emotional) condition than he found him. In cinema this improved condition need not be immediately evident to the young person, so long as it is to the audience, in order for the presentation of the relationship to avoid reinforcing stereotypes of such affairs as inevitably detrimental to the young person.

For instance, the British version of the television series *Queer as Folk* begins its first season (1999) with a one-night stand between Nathan Maloney (Charlie Hunnam), who is, at fifteen, a year under the age of consent at that time in the United Kingdom, and Stuart Jones (Aiden Gillen), who is nearly twice his age. Nathan imagines himself to be in love with Stuart and, unsuccessfully, pursues him, hoping for a real relationship. But Stuart, although narcissistic and in many respects amoral, never gives Nathan any false hope that they can be lovers rather than sex partners for a night. Through Stuart's friends, Nathan learns about the diversity of the gay world and gains confidence and the comfort of belonging to a community. In contrast, Elio is isolated from Jews, other than his parents, and from other homosexuals, other than the one middle-aged couple who are their friends. So, to me, this is a story about an adult who takes advantage of a lonely boy. One of the few entirely critical reviews of the film comes from Andrea Merodeadora, who flatly condemns it as romanticizing sexual abuse of minors.

The conclusion can be considered bittersweet or simply tragic, depending on how we feel about intergenerational gay sex in which the younger partner is in love and the older one just experimenting with homosexuality. At the end, the film cuts to winter and the lighting of the Hanukkah candles and a call from Oliver, who says he is engaged and plans to marry in the spring. Perhaps by way of explanation of this return to heteronormativity, he says Elio is lucky his parents accept him as his own father "would have carted me away to a corrections facility." As the credits roll, Elio weeps. Ilany says, "No one is punished for this pure love." But is that really true? Elio seems devastated at the end, and we can assume he remains so because this is a memory piece without any commentary on a subsequent acceptance of what happened as a good thing. There is nothing in the framing or conclusion to suggest that Elio recovers from the pain this abandonment inflicted or gains a positive view of his own sexuality from learning that he was the summer romance of a person who would never deign to live openly as gay.

I am more inclined to agree with Ilany that while the film draws on the ancient Greek tradition, through the archaeologist father, to naturalize the sexual initiation of young boys by men, this ignores the intense rejection of "pederasty" by early Jews such as Philo of Alexandria. And I agree that by ignoring the ancient Jewish tradition of repudiating such unequal relationships, the film falsifies history. I am not so inclined to agree with the critics who praise the film for its equation of the experience of being racialized as a Jew with the experience of being sexualized as gay. Equating Jews and homosexuals in the most demonizing terms possible is an ancient and still continuing tradition among anti-Semites. Larry Kramer crudely parodies this tradition in the opening pages of his novel *Faggots*, writing, "There are now more faggots in the New York City area than Jews. There are now more faggots in the entire United States than all the yids and kikes put together" (16). I do not see a film that celebrates a same-sex affair between a Jewish adult and the minor he seduces and then renounces in the name of heteronormativity as successfully countering this sort of equation. Ilany sums up: "It's all too sunny and harmonious" and "at moments the soul yearns: a little darkness, please." Such realistic darkness might have been provided by a bit of depiction of Italian anti-Semitism and a look at why the parents have become Jews of discretion in Italy, which, lest we forget, eventually accepted and implemented the Nazi plan of genocide, however reluctantly.

From the anxieties surrounding the onset of the AIDS pandemic to the reenergizing of lingering anti-Semitism in Italy as the extreme political Left turned against Israel, the film leaves out everything that might supply a sense of danger and darkness. It is true that the film interestingly equates homosexuals and Jews, but it fails to address what such othered subjects have in common by failing to recognize that the sexual attitudes and behaviors of Jews, just like those of homosexuals, took, and continue to take, form in response to prejudice, hatred, and persecution.

VIII. Conclusion

The lack of attention to historical context in all of these films does not do the Jewish sex criminals portrayed an injustice because they themselves are unjust. The ones who are treated unjustly are the Jewish audience members, who, if we have the knowledge to understand what we are seeing, can recognize why the characters—and real people in the case of the documentaries—might behave so lawlessly. But we are left without any indication that the rebellion against the dominant culture's sexual laws could have been productive of empowering Jewish identities rather than destructive of them. As Hortense Spillers contends in her famous essay, "Mama's Baby, Papa's Maybe," changes in the concepts of gender and family structure held by people who have been subjected to a "dehumanizing, ungendering, and defacing project" such as slavery (72)—or, as I wish to add, the Holocaust—need not leave them incapable of acting as decent, caring people. Nor does being placed outside the bounds of normative, Christian white supremacist patriarchy mean that one necessarily becomes a vicious predatory outlaw. Instead, as she persuasively argues, it provides an opportunity to reimagine bonds between people and to exercise agency in constructing an identity (75, 81).

In the next chapter, I will take a look at one television series that does contextualize Jewish sexual illnesses with references to the Holocaust, but in such a way that one might wish it did not, and also at another television series that takes the opportunity to resignify, in a more encouraging manner, Jewish subjects made sexual outlaws by their intersectional racialization and sexualization.

Notes

1. David Duke, Louis Farrakhan, and other anti-Semitic writers have made much of the role of Jews in the pornography industry. They reference such scholarly work on the topic as Nathan Abrams's essay "Triple Exthnics" in order to support their view that Jews use pornography to promote the destruction of Gentile family values.

2. In addition to Weinstein's case, he mentions "James Toback, the former *New Republic* editor Leon Wieseltier and the journalist Mark Halperin. And Brett Ratner. And Jeffrey Tambor. And now Sen. Al Franken and *New York Times* reporter Glenn Thrush."

3. There is plenty of pushback against the argument that the Holocaust is now "ancient history" and irrelevant to today's politics, a notable instance being the exhibition "Auschwitz: Not Long Ago, Not Far Away" that opened on May 8, 2019, at New York City's Museum of Jewish Heritage.

4. See Wilkerson's chapter 9, "The Evil of Silence."

5. See Florian Peters, "Remaking Polish National History."

6. Many of us also saw a parallel to the situation of African Americans, who, under slavery, had been sexually abused in every possible way in the United States, generally without any legal restraints put on their tormentors.

7. The McMartin Preschool case shocked Americans in 1984, when it was the first of many cases of daycare centers where children were reportedly tortured and sexually abused, often in ritualistic ways. It initiated a moral panic described by scholars such as Mary de Young and Philip Jenkins as the result of investigators' encouragement of children to lie about their experiences. Some of the lies were fantastical and reminiscent of the witch trials of the 1500s and 1600s, including children being carried through the air by their tormentors, who could fly like birds, and subjected to extreme physical tortures that mysteriously left no marks on their bodies.

8. Obviously his possession of child pornography is a crime and also unethical and immoral. Getting sexual stimulation from touching children in socially acceptable ways—that is, by patting their backs or squeezing their shoulders—while being repulsive, seems to me to be in a gray area of ethics, so long as the children do not know that the adult is aroused by this behavior.

9. See also Giorgio Bassani's 1962 novel, *The Garden of the Finzi-Continis*, and Vittorio De Sica's 1970 film version.

5

TWO FUNERALS AND A WEDDING

Not So Nice Jewish Girls in Transparent and Broad City

I. (Sex) Culture Wars

Someone who learned about Jews only from TV programming in the first two decades of the twenty-first century would probably think of them as freer sexually than the American mainstream, based on the series *The Sarah Silverman Program*, *Girls*, *Inside Amy Schumer*, *Broad City*, *The Marvelous Mrs. Maisel*, and what was the most lauded of these shows, *Transparent*. It makes sense that the Jewish sensibility is associated, in these programs, with progressive sexual politics, since Christianity in America has long been defined by fundamentalism mainly in terms of its hostility to women's sexual freedom, abortion rights, homosexuality, and increasingly, due to the movement's greater visibility, transgender people's rights. Whereas, as Nathan Abrams observes, "Jews in America have been sexual revolutionaries. A large amount of the material on sexual liberation was written by Jews. Those at the forefront of the movement which forced America to adopt a more liberal view of sex were Jewish. Jews were also at the vanguard of the sexual revolution of the 1960s. Wilhelm Reich, Herbert Marcuse and Paul Goodman replaced Marx, Trotsky and Lenin as required revolutionary reading" ("Triple Exthnics," 28). Of course, there are Jewish religious conservatives, as well, and ones with very misogynistic and homophobic beliefs, but they get little press and almost no representation on television. The Jews we see on that media tend to be secular, urban, and generally liberal politically. As a Jewish feminist sex radical, I am pleased to see this turn toward celebrating Jews, and especially Jewish women, as leaders in the struggle against patriarchal heteronormativity. I am not so pleased, however, to see *Transparent* celebrated as the best of the bunch of shows that are both focused on Jews and also support the rights of sexual minorities.

Just as the radical feminist erotica magazine *On Our Backs* (1984–2006) was a response to the antiporn radical feminist publication *Off Our Backs* (1970–2008), the pornographic film *Nice Jewish Girls* (dir., Matthew Blade, 2009), whether intentionally or not, responds to the feminist collection *Nice Jewish Girls: A Lesbian Anthology* (1989). All four highlight areas of contestation in narratives that attempt to categorize a specific group in terms of a posited shared experience of sexuality. These visions of putatively representative Jewish girls' desires engage debates that have been ongoing since ancient times. As numerous theorists of Jewish racialization note, debates over the possibility of Jewish sexual difference have been revived since the 2008 economic crash due to the conflation by anti-Semites of images of Jews as sinister manipulators of world finances with images of Jews as corrupt and corrupting sexual subjects.[1] So it is perhaps not surprising that two twenty-first-century television series acclaimed for their sexual daring, *Transparent* and *Broad City*, narratively frame their characters' experiences in terms of their identification as Jews. There is a culture war in America over sex, and Jews are at its center. And no television shows did more to showcase that centrality in 2014 than *Transparent* and *Broad City*, which both debuted that year.

Transparent and *Broad City* invite comparison for many reasons. Beyond focusing on the relationship of Jews to sexuality in current times, both focus on Jewish women embroiled in the pursuit of sexual pleasure through finding identities with which they can be comfortable. Both series are comedies, although *Broad City* is farcical, often slapstick, comedy, while *Transparent* is comedy-drama, infused with a great deal of melodrama. This generic difference results in some significant differences in the attitudes about sexuality that the series' plots imply. While both series feature women protagonists who are determinedly nonconformist to mainstream gender and sexuality mores—what Kathleen Rowe calls "unruly women"—they do so with often apparently contrasting aims. As Rowe argues, "As romantic comedy's shadow genre, melodrama remains an uneasy reminder that the unruly woman's power is fragile, subject to social and generic forces that would shift the register of her outrageousness from comedy to pathos" (114). The structure of each series adds to the creation of this distinction. *Broad City* has, as dual protagonists, two young women, Ilana (Ilana Glazer) and

Abbi (Abbi Jacobson), whose lives in New York City are depicted through sketch comedy–like episodes. All the other characters who appear on the show are peripheral, and all the action is unrelated to anything other than Abbi and Ilana's attempts to enjoy life in various ways. Over and over, they satisfyingly, if often farcically, succeed in amusing themselves and their audience while affirming that sex can be great fun. *Transparent* has a more serious concern: the impacts of the Pfefferman family patriarch's decision to come out as transgender and begin life as a woman. The core of the show is the family members' struggle with their vexed gender identifications and frequently thwarted sexual desires. In *Transparent*, sex is depicted as almost always disappointing and usually as causing unpleasant life complications. This decision of Maura Pfefferman's (Jeffrey Tambor) causes not only her wife, Shelly (Judith Light), but also their adult daughters, Sarah (Amy Landecker) and Ali (Gaby Hoffman), and their son, Josh (Jay Duplass), to reassess what their genders and sexualities mean to them. And the meanings they find rarely lead to any joy.

II. Visions of Sadness / Visions of Joy

Despite being marketed as a comedy rather than a melodrama, *Transparent* seems glum in its overall view of life. It truly fits the designation of melodrama more than that of comedy. The title of episode 3 of the first season, "Being Alive Is Being Sad," could stand as the subtitle of the entire first two seasons. And Jewish life is particularly sad here. Contrasts with Gentile characters make this clear. For example, at the wedding, which opens the second season, of Maura's daughter Sarah to her college sweetheart, Tammy Cashman (Melora Hardman), Tammy's Gentile family are blithely happy while the Pfeffermans are mostly miserable, as always. And as I shall discuss in more detail later, the wedding comes to naught when Sarah decides not to sign the official papers, a decision that mystifies and upsets the Cashmans but that the Pfeffermans understand all too well—because anything sexual or romantic in their family always has tragic outcomes.

While *Transparent* could easily be understood as a melodramatic family saga, *Broad City* is structured as a buddy sit-com, so its light-hearted comedic tone fits its genre. As my opening remarks suggest, the series is also thematically aligned with a number of millennial television comedies that, as Maria San Filippo says of *Girls*, "examine and validate women's bodies, desires, pleasures and voices through sexually explicit imagery" (29).

Here sex is mainly depicted as a source of pleasure. Both Ilana and Abbi are constantly looking for sexual fun and are able to find entertaining sex partners. Ilana even has a male buddy—Lincoln, the charming Black pediatric dentist (Hannibal Buress)—who is consistently there to help her in times of trouble, as well as making himself available for sex they both enjoy. Even encounters that do disappoint the protagonists' expectations are treated as life-enriching adventures.

Many elements of mise en scène—especially costuming, music, and establishing shots—convey the series' sense of sex: either the exuberance of *Broad City*'s or the grimness of *Transparent*'s. *Broad City*, in keeping with its creators' roles as the main characters, consistently uses close-ups and POV shots, including crosscuts between a balanced two-shot of its protagonists, Ilana and Abbi, and whatever they are both looking at. Like most television series, it uses lots of shot–reverse shots to convey reactions, but unlike *Transparent*'s use of these shots to emphasize disconnections, as one person stares in shock or incomprehension at another, the shots in *Broad City* tend to emphasize Ilana and Abbi's sharing of a reaction. These shots are often accompanied by the energetic rhythms of party songs, to remind us that we are sharing their basically cheerful perspectives. In contrast, we rarely see the events of *Transparent* through the perspectives of the characters; instead, we look on from a distance, as if voyeuristically, although without the pleasures that watching pornography usually offers. Music choices in *Transparent* tend toward the melancholic. Long shots that give us a view of characters moving through rooms and not apparently connecting with anyone in them are a common feature of the series. These perspective shots are intrinsic to the mood of each series.

Through its presentation of sexual acts and behavior, *Transparent* suggests that for cultural reasons Jews are disproportionately victims of a sexually repressive society and as a result alone and lonely. This view is advanced by Ali in the episode "Cherry Blossoms," where she expounds on connections between the Holocaust and her family's sexual and gender dysfunctionality, which has rendered them not only "late bloomers," as one of her lovers calls them, but unhappy ones. There is no worry about Holocaust denial or erasure in this series; it is a continual reference throughout. In contrast, *Broad City* suggests that for reasons intrinsic to Jewish culture, Jews are able to have enjoyable sex lives that connect them happily to each other and to partners. As Hannah Schwadron discusses, in this series contemporary Jewish women's "joke-work leans on" the portrayal of identities that are, in terms of the majority culture, "not quite right, and not quite not, whether construed in racialized or sexualized terms" (77). Jews are raced and sexed continually and insistently in both series; here Jewishness is never under erasure. Consequently both series powerfully demonstrate how sexual narratives about Jews are informed by racial and gender intersectionality.

III. The Wedding Fail

The wedding episode, "Kina Hora," that opens season 2 of *Transparent* exemplifies the series' vision of Jewish intersectionality as blighting the character's lives. The title expression is a Yiddish one that forbids the evil eye, but we almost immediately get evil eyeballing as the wedding photographer in the first scene makes anti-Semitic remarks and insults Maura by calling her "Sir," although she is dressed, as always, in very feminine attire and wearing obvious makeup and a long-haired wig. For four full minutes, not only does the photographer try to take the picture, but the TV camera itself remains fixed on the fidgeting and arguing members of the Pfefferman family. Seeing them all dressed in white, crowded into the frame, and unable to smile for the photo pushes the audience to feel as uncomfortable as they seem to be. The darkly brooding Pfeffermans are contrasted visually, as the photographer sets up the next shot, to the blond Cashmans, whose cheerful demeanor fits the sunlight-flooded scene and the white clothing everyone is wearing.

Ali complains to her brother, Josh, that he should not have included his girlfriend, Rabbi Raquel (Kathryn Hahn), in the photo, but he explains she is now a family member because she is carrying his child, a secret that Raquel had wanted kept until they could be married. Ali immediately tells her sister, Sarah, and soon their mother, Shelly, embarrasses Raquel by disclosing her secret to all the guests. Raquel's happiness with Josh is destroyed because she now knows she cannot trust him. The camera spins away from their miserable faces to show the crowd. The lighting changes, and the wedding reception appears increasingly swamped by darkness.

This incident carries on the theme of the previous season and sets the tone for this one: sex is a problem because it creates humiliating and hurtful situations, a theme reiterated by the presence of Maura's hostile sister, who scolds Maura for having gone after pleasure in life while she had to care for their mother; the absence of Sarah's discarded ex-husband, Len (Rob Huebel), which their little children are saddened by and cannot understand; and

Fig. 5.1 *Transparent*: Postwedding windows full of woe.

finally by Sarah's rejection of the marriage when she decides she can do better in terms of sexual satisfaction.

The episode closes with peeks into the hotel rooms of the major characters after the wedding reception. As in Hitchcock's *Rear Window*, a drama that is famously framed narratively by the reluctance of the hero to propose to his girlfriend due to his view of marriage as entrapment, the windows open onto rooms that each contain mini-dramas commenting on the possibilities for sexual unhappiness. Each one appears as a square of light in a literally dark world, but the illumination their contents provides is hardly cheering. First we see Josh and Raquel trying unsuccessfully to get past her sense of betrayal; then in the next window, Sarah and Tammy, the latter of whom has just been devastated by the news that Sarah asked Raquel not to file the papers to make the marriage legal; then Shelly flattering Maura with a compliment that causes her to patronizingly kiss her former wife; then Ali, alone and lonely.

On a wedding night when one might expect to see a sex scene that is informed by hope and love, we see only the failure of sexuality to make anyone happy. If this is not sad enough, there is then a cut to 1930s Berlin where we see their doomed transgender great-aunt Gittel (Hari Nef) sitting alone and looking as wretchedly lonely as Ali. Jews and transgender people, obviously, cannot enjoy happy sex lives if this dismal wedding is anything to judge by. If James Stewart's character, Jeff, in Hitchcock's film had seen this out of his rear window, he probably would not have ended the film engaged to be married.

IV. Shiva Success

Perhaps because such occasions better fit the series' mood, *Transparent's* Shiva episode, the finale of season 1, is a little more upbeat than the wedding that follows it as the second season's first episode. The title of the Shiva episode, "Dreamboat Annie," references an earlier moment in the series. In episode 4, we saw a longtime family friend, Syd (Carrie Brownstein), attempt a sexual interlude with Josh. It ends badly. Syd accuses him of being so desperately lonely that he clings to any woman in his life. Before going out the door, she borrows Heart's album *Dreamboat Annie* from him. The lyrics of the eponymous song refer to someone who is "alone in the crowd" and "the lonely one" who observes "sad faces painted over with those magazine smiles." We hear the song again, playing in the background, as the body of Shelly's second husband, Ed (Lawrence Pressman), is prepared for the Shiva. The song is being sung by the new band Josh put together when the failure of his affair with the lead singer of the old one ended his involvement with it.

At first everything at the Shiva seems peaceful—so much so that we can almost ignore this disquieting sonic connection suggesting inescapable sexual failure and loneliness and also that Shelly wanted Ed to die so he would no longer require her care. But there are tensions, primarily due to the presence of Josh's long-ago babysitter Rita (Brett Paesel) with a teenaged boy who turns out to be the child she had as a result of the affair she had with Josh when he was fifteen. Soon the painted smiles fall away and the family members start attacking each other verbally over their resentments of the others' sexual behavior, past and present. Len lets Sarah know he will no longer tolerate her using him to sexually supplement her relationship with Tammy. And Sarah gets even with him by proposing marriage to Tammy, a move whose wrongness will be revealed in the next season's first episode. Ali gets revenge on Josh for having seduced Syd, who she knows is in love with her, by spoiling Raquel's joy over the tentative affair she and Josh have begun. And Ali angrily confronts Maura for allowing her to cancel her bat mitzvah when she was twelve, not really because Maura respected her loss of faith, but because of something Ali now knows. Maura (then still living as Mort) wanted, instead, to attend a retreat for cross-dressers.

Poor dead Ed gets almost no attention from anyone—he seems hardly even remembered—but the "magazine smiles" go back in place as the family joins Josh's son in insincere Christian prayer over a shared meal. Each one is as alone as only sex can make a person in this series. Ali believes that the persistent sadness of the family is the result of the traumas the previous generation suffered in Nazi Germany. The numerous crosscuts from the unhappy family to Ali's thoughts about the previous generation focus on Gittel, who died not only because she was a Jew but also because she was transgender. For this reason the antics of the other Pfeffermans always have a touch of dignity. They are not merely wealthy people with a near monstrous sense of entitlement but also victims of fascist transphobia that has blighted all their lives.

V. First World Problems

In contrast *Broad City* can seem insensitively frivolous. Numerous viewers have posted in online discussion threads about their anger at the comedic treatment of transgender people in the "Citizen Ship" episode of *Broad City*, in which the friends go on a pleasure boat trip to celebrate Ilana's gay Venezuelan roommate, Jaimé (Arturo Castro), gaining American citizenship. Ilana uses derogatory names for transwomen (although we might note that her riff about "Annas with bananas and Denises with penises" is a quote from *Paris Is Burning*) while joking about the sexual preferences of lawyers, who make up the majority of the boat's passengers. More transinsensitive comedy is provided when Abbi's roommate's boyfriend, Bevers (John Gemberling), backs out of making a promised public marriage proposal by instead announcing that Abbi is transitioning to being a transman. This causes some silly moments since Abbi has no such intention. Certainly *Transparent* cannot be accused of such insensitivity, although some viewers did object to the casting of a heterosexual man as Maura Pfefferman.

Transparent is rightly commended for its empathetic treatment of the problems and biases experienced by transgender people, although the series' transgender critics are also right to criticize its focus on an upper-middle-class white man and lack of attention to the situations of transgender people who cannot afford appropriate medical treatment and who do not have ample retirement income, like Maura, and therefore face more life-threatening problems than hers. Steven and Jaydi Funk, drawing on Judith Butler and Athena Athanasiou's theory of dispossession, argue that the series is neoliberal in that it "depicts Maura's gender transition as one that is isolated from the long history (and current state) of systemic prejudice and ideological violence perpetrated, especially by influential mental and medical health professionals, against gender expansive people in the United States and globally" (71). Like many of the transgender critics who labeled the show transphobic, they also note that the emphasis is almost always on the reactions of cisgender people to Maura rather than on Maura's feelings (76). However, they do concede the good intentions of the show's creator and executive producer, Jill Soloway, who has since come out as nonbinary. The show might also be commended for being what Debra Nussbaum Cohen calls "the Jewiest television show ever," since, as she quotes Soloway saying, "it's [now] more controversial to be Jewy than trans," a claim supported by a look at "some of the nauseatingly anti-Semitic comments left on YouTube under the series trailer."

Broad City is also Jewy, but in a distinctly different way. Especially in its second season, the characters frequently mention that they are Jews. They also have recognizably East Coast Jewish speech patterns from the series' beginning and, like the characters on *Transparent*, make jokes and references, including the use of Yiddish words, that mark them as Jewish. To be Jewish in *Transparent* seems to connote, as it does to anti-Semites, having the money to live a life in which most of the troubles one faces can easily be described as first world problems, such as how to achieve a sense of purpose when you have no need to work to support yourself (as is the case for Maura, Maura's ex-wife, Shelly, and their daughter Sarah as well as, to a considerable extent, their younger children, Josh and Ali).

Maura has spent sixty-eight years concealing her female identification from others in order to benefit from the privilege of her position as an assumed-to-be-male UCLA professor who actively fights the incursions of feminism into academe throughout his career. When she retires—with what seems to me an amazing income for a former political science professor—she comes out as a transwoman and struggles for acceptance and respect. Shelly seems to identify primarily as a housewife and mother and moves from one husband to another, shockingly deciding to euthanize her second one, Ed, when his Alzheimer's becomes too much of a burden on her. She, too, wants respect and also a financially supportive mate. Sarah, who appears to be in her forties,[2] is a bored housewife with a high-earning husband and two small children and is in the throes of a classic midlife crisis. She wants greater sexual excitement in her life and is unsure whether a male or a female lover would be best to provide it. Josh, unsuccessfully, attempts to manage girl bands and makes sporadic attempts to settle down into a conventional marriage. Ali suffers a series of identity crises as she struggles with her resentment of men and her uncertainty about what role in life would best suit her. Because there is nothing more at stake than their fulfillment, these difficulties seem minor and can easily be seen as comical.

Yet we are urged to take seriously these people, who have the wherewithal to extend the identity crises usually associated with adolescence into their thirties and far beyond by numerous references and crosscutting to their Jewish forebears in Nazi Germany. The tragedy of Gittel, who refuses to leave Germany when the Nazis take power, because it would entail using a passport that identifies her as male, works as a symbolic representation of the lives and deaths of transgender people today who refuse heteronormativity though they have few options for survival in their true gender. But to compare their situations to that of affluent Maura is a stretch. Still the show never allows viewers to forget that to be a Jew is to be in danger and to be a Jew who refuses heteronormativity means one is always on the brink of being killed.

VI. Joyous Jews

One could easily imagine the blank-faced confusion with which the lower-middle-class main characters in *Broad City* would hear such claims, because in that show being Jewish seems to mean being exceptionally free from the inhibitions that restrict the sexual freedom of American Christian conservatives. One way to understand the show is as a response to earlier sitcoms centered on young women trying to make their way in the big city, such as *The Mary Tyler Moore Show* and *Suddenly Susan*, which, as Linda Mizejewski points out, contrast an "all-American heroine," whose femininity is naturalized, to a female sidekick whose "Jewishness is often used as shorthand for bad taste and obnoxious manners, which in turn suggests a lack of femininity" (43–44.) Here Jewish women are not only equal partners in friendship; together they provide the series' definition of female behavior that springs from natural impulses. Yet the sexual freedom the young women demonstrate is never deracialized; instead, it draws on a long tradition, discussed by Mizejewski, of Jews as racialized outsiders who are therefore not invested in upholding American social norms (111–12). Although none of the Jewish characters seem to have much money—especially not Ilana and Abbi, whose low-level jobs annoy and frustrate them but cannot be given up because they barely scrape by in their small, shared apartments and are always searching, by necessity, for bargains—they do not see themselves as belonging to an underprivileged and under threat minority. As Jonathan Branfman shows, "*Broad City* often depicts Jewishness itself as an excess that makes Jewish women unruly" (5). Their Jewishness seems to lift them out of the pressure to conform to bourgeois propriety and into a transgenerational bohemia in which they pursue pleasure without any apparent restraint.

Transparent is not completely devoid of scenes in which sex brings happiness. "Grey, Green, Brown and Copper," the final episode of *Transparent*'s second season, at last shows us a sex scene with a happy outcome. Vicki (Anjelica Huston) rescues Maura from persecution by TERFs (trans-exclusionary radical feminists) at an event obviously modeled on the Michigan Womyn's Music Festival, which has drawn attention for barring transwomen. Vicki describes herself as NATO (not attached to outcomes), when Maura asks whether she minds sharing a hotel room. This sets the tone for a pressure-free erotic interlude. They spend the night spooning and in the morning they begin to kiss and then have sex with Vicki on top. Their sexual activity seems to consist entirely of rubbing against each other with their underpants on. The camera remains at a chaste distance from their crotches throughout the encounter, and a close-up of Maura's face fills the screen at the end. She orgasms and they cuddle. Both do seem happy with this outcome.

VII. Back to Black[3]

However, as always, there are plentiful sad notes. The episode title refers to Sarah's account of when the siblings stopped swimming together in the backyard pool. She turned twelve, got her period, and refused to swim; then the pool guy quit, meaning no one scooped out the pool, so it filled with multicolored leaves for two years. Now they are swimming together, and she goes from recounting this story to saying she wants to connect with Judaism, to become more religious and thus get some meaning into her life. This emphasizes the parable-like quality of the pool story. Although she points out that her period and the pool being clogged and ruined were not causally connected, it does seem so. Sexual development brings loss because sexual activities destroy possibilities of loving connection to others, as is emphasized by Josh's immediate reminder that reconnecting with temple will be difficult since Rabbi Raquel is out of their lives, thanks to her unhappy affair with him. They snuggle innocently, remarking on how this is the first time they are all "single" at the same time. The shot of the three siblings lying together smiling is one of the series' very few showing people happily bedded down together. That sex ruins intimacy is again strongly suggested.

Ali must have this in mind when she is given a choice by her father's former professorial antagonist, Leslie (Cherry Jones), either to be her lover or to work with her as a graduate student and she lets Maura know she chose the latter. Cut to Ali's great-grandmother Yetta (Michaela Watkins) and her daughter Rose (Shannon Welles) tracking down their husband/father and finding him with a new wife and child. Another cut takes us to Sarah's ex-husband, Len, mournfully telling Sarah that his new girlfriend dumped him. Except for Maura, the family members find peace in this episode only through putting sex aside. And even Maura seems more content with her reunion with her aging mother and previously cold sister than she was with the sex with Vicki. The episode ends with a flashback to young Rose (Emily Robinson) giving birth to Mort, whose father had predicted the child would be a girl. We know that Mort is a girl, Maura, but also that Mort will have to spend most of her life pretending to be male so as to fit the expectations mainstream society has of anyone who has a penis and is sexually attracted to women. If only Mort had not wanted sex with women, she might have been able to come out as the woman she is much sooner, as did the heterosexual transwomen Maura befriends after her own coming out. So this conclusion conveys once again the series' message that if it were not for the demands of sexuality that push us to adhere to one of two rigidly binary genders, we could live satisfying lives.

VIII. Sexuality and Its Discontents

In the politically polarized world of the early twenty-first century, two opposed visions of sex provide the foundations for most representations of sexuality. Either it is primarily a source of unhappiness or it is primarily a source of happiness. Those who hold the latter view see sex as one of the very few intensely pleasurable human experiences that are readily available to almost everyone free of charge and without any necessary ill effects. Those who see sex as generally unhappy believe it does have inescapable ill effects, including inevitable disappointment. These opposed visions have traditionally been gendered. Women are assumed to enjoy sex less than men for the most part, not only because they have to worry about birth control, but even more because their sexuality is often seen as incompatible with men's. Those who believe sex is a source of unhappiness generally subscribe to the idea that a woman can only really enjoy sex when she loves and trusts her partner or, more extremely, only when she is in a committed domestic relationship, while men see sex as a form of entertainment and try to avoid commitment. Consequently, in their view, heterosexual relations always involve struggle between people with opposed desires and goals.

Beyond this, many people who see sex as intrinsically unhappy believe that even in same-sex encounters, we cannot escape incompatibility and frustration, that sex is inherently unsatisfying as we always want what we cannot have. As academics well know, whole areas of psychoanalytic theory, from Freud through Lacan, argue that desire and lack are intrinsically linked, so sex can never be truly satisfying. But in popular media, the emphasis of the antisexual is usually on the disruption of social/family stability. And on television this emphasis has generally been very strong, with the less popular sexual orientations, such as bisexuality, nonmonogamy, and sadomasochism, being treated as markers of corruption or as indicative of damage from early trauma and as threats to happiness, especially the happiness of women.

Despite its admirable intention to depict the sexualities listed here and also transgender identities empathetically, *Transparent* holds to the patterns of associating sexuality with unhappiness and of emphasizing the dangers rather than the pleasures of sex, especially for women.[4] For instance, in the first two seasons, we are shown three sexual affairs Josh has. Two result in unwanted pregnancies. Inexplicably, the first one, which occurs because of the affair between a teenaged Josh and Rita, his babysitter, who is in her twenties, is not terminated. Most people might expect a sexually active young woman who is not religious and is living in Los Angeles in 1996 would choose abortion.[5] But instead she gives the baby up for adoption, and she and Josh both suffer when their child returns as an Evangelical teen. The second unwanted pregnancy is aborted, and Josh is devastated by this, as is his lover by his emotional response to her choice. Their love affair ends, because television and film abortions must always have tragic consequences. His third affair results in a pregnancy that his sex partner Raquel does want; however, the pregnancy's timing, before they are married or even engaged, is shameful to her and endangers her status as the community rabbi. This desired pregnancy ends in a miscarriage that spoils their relationship.

Josh's sexually inflicted wounds are not, however, presented as being caused by his inconvenient fertility. As Maureen Ryan enthuses in a rave review in the *Huffington Post*, *Transparent* emphasizes how "damaged" Josh was by the sex he willingly engaged in with Rita when he was fifteen. The series treats this as child molestation, although never dramatizing any aspect of the relationship that might be understood to have hurt him at the time it took place. Seemingly unable to endure the guilt, Rita suicides in season 3, right after Josh, who had previously insisted that their affair was consensual, tells her he forgives her for what she did to him. His new view of the affair is reiterated in season 4 when he finally achieves some peace by once again asserting, to her ghost, that he "was a victim." In this way, the show is in perfect accord with abstinence-only education ideology's insistence that any intergenerational sex between teens and young adults is horrific rape that will ruin the teen psychologically. The theme of life-destroying intergenerational sex returns in season 3, episode 8, "If I Were a Bell," when we learn that the reason Shelley has so many emotional problems is that she was molested by a teacher when she was a little girl. In her case, of course, any sort of consent was obviously not a factor because she was still a child. Still the message that all sexual encounters are destructive comes through in this implicit equation of rape of a child to sex with an eager teen boy.

IX. Inspirational Jewish Sexualities

As earlier remarked, *Transparent* connects its negative view of sex to Jewishness. Both through the many references to Jewish religious and cultural practices and through crosscutting to the experiences in Germany during the rise of fascism of family matriarch Rose and her sister Gittel, the series suggests that both being a member of a sexual minority and being minoritized as a Jew are at least somewhat parallel experiences in their resultant alienation and anguish.

Broad City also connects Jewishness and unconventional sexual experiences but in a decidedly sex-positive way, as we see in this series' Shiva episode. Ilana and Abbi demonstrate no dissatisfaction with their Jewish identities and, as one might expect of New Yorkers, do not seem to see themselves as minoritized subjects just because they are Jews. One might imagine that their complete lack of moralistic attitudes about sex is related to their particular type of secular Jewishness, which imposes no religious burdens. This is most evident in "Knockoffs," the episode that features the Shiva for Ilana's ninety-two-year-old grandma, Esther. No one at the event shows any apparent reverence for religious practice, and Ilana and her mother, Bobbi (Susie Essman), both behave in comically inappropriate ways that go unreproached by the other attendees. Esther is remembered with pride by her descendants for having sung at the Cotton Club and having had sex with Little Richard. Ilana says they do not mourn her grandmother because "that bitch did everything she wanted to." She is described as an inspiration to Abbi as well as to Ilana's whole family.

The episode begins with Abbi, Ilana, and Bobbi, bonding merrily over Abbi's date for afternoon sex with her neighbor Jeremy (Stephen Schneider) on whom she has had a crush for a long time. "Don't forget to wear a condom," calls Bobbi as Abbi leaves, and Ilana explains, when Abbi says in annoyance that she only made that mistake once, that this is just the way her mother "says goodbye to people." And why not? In their world there are few restrictions—if any—on the pursuit of pleasure. At one point Ilana tells Bobbi that she read on the internet that New York water has microscopic shrimp in it and so "we have shrimp inside us at all times. . . . Sounds delicious." Neither mentions that this unconscious shrimp consumption is a serious violation of kosher food laws. One cannot imagine Abbi or Ilana expressing rage, as Josh does in an episode of *Transparent*, by rebelliously eating ham and other foods forbidden by Jewish dietary law. Over and over, *Broad City*'s dialogue disassociates Jewishness from rules and restrictions and strengthens its association with seeking whatever gives one joy. Jon Stratton explains the high valuation that has been traditionally placed on Jewish assimilation in American films as being motivated in part by Jews' "nagging suspicion . . . that the real white people lead more fulfilling, exciting, *complete* lives than [they] can ever have" (158, original emphasis). *Broad City* rejects this view and, in insisting that class status is something reserved for Gentiles, reminds the audience that Abbi, Ilana, and her family have the freedom that comes from being considered hopelessly lawless, vulgar outsiders. This identification is in keeping with a fairly large movement, as Josh Lambert points out, "identifying oneself as a 'dirty Jew' in the 21st century has become a means for signaling one's opposition . . . to the banalities of a 'sanitized culture'" (184).

Throughout the episode, Bobbi is preoccupied by her obsession with acquiring counterfeit designer handbags (the titular knockoffs). At the Shiva, while their father, Arthur (Bob Balaban), tells Ilana and her brother,

Eliot (Eliot Glazer), that their mother is "all broken up," she is actually complaining bitterly about sales taxes on legitimately purchased handbags. As the family gathers in a weepy group hug, "Feel something," Ilana says to Bobbi, who is standing aside examining Abbi's handbag. Bobbi replies, "I'm feeling the inside of this bag." The lack of censure for these breaches of decorum suggests a milieu in which all pleasures are accepted as part of the fullness of life for the living. Abbi tells Jeremy that she has been surrounded by death lately and it makes her think about life; then she clicks beer bottles with him and says, "To Life!" The episodes' crosscuts between their sexual interlude and the Shiva reinforce this vision of a world in which sexual fun is the antidote to mourning, though such a position places one in the position of an outlaw.

The family's place outside the law is exemplified by Bobbi and Ilana's arrest after leaving the Shiva. Because Bobbi left her phone in one of the bags she obtained from some designer purse counterfeiters in Chinatown and is carrying in a rolling suitcase, she and Ilana empty the bags out on the sidewalk. Bobbi's loud and delighted exclamation, "bags, bags, bags!" as they lay them out, draws the attention of two beat cops, and they are arrested for attempting to sell counterfeit bags. They yell at the cops from the back of the squad car and berate them first for the arrest, which they consider unfair, and then for releasing them, which they believe happened only because they are considered white. As Branfman argues, "Jacobson and Glazer present their racial status in contradictory ways: they call themselves white while depicting Jewishness as an embodied, racialized difference" (11).

These merrily intersectional Jews are up for whatever opportunities for fun life presents. And the one the funeral episode focuses on, through crosscutting, is Abbi's pegging Jeremy. The series consistently presents Ilana as the more sexually adventurous of the two friends, but mainly because she is much more sexually self-confident than Abbi. When Abbi tells Jeremy, as he lies on top of her in bed that she wants to "switch. . . . Mix it up a little," he wrongly assumes she means penetrate him and eagerly hands her his strap-on, rolls over, and says, "Right in the butt!" She retreats to the bathroom and phones Ilana for advice. Ilana who is helping her mother pick out handbags for her Jewish friends back on Long Island in an under-the-street illegal store, is so ecstatic about this development that she begins to twerk and does a handstand. We soon hear that she has always wanted to use a strap-on and regularly wore one to bed in college in case the opportunity suddenly presented itself. Abbi is persuaded to give it a try and obviously

Fig. 5.2 *Broad City*: Intergenerational bonding over pegging.

finds the adventure very satisfying, as we next see her lying in Jeremy's bed radiant with afterglow. However, it is the reactions of Ilana's family to news of the event that convey the series' sexual attitudes most strongly.

As soon as Abbi joins the Shiva and Ilana gets the news of what transpired between Abbi and Jeremy, the celebration of sex lives unrestricted by propriety begins. As Eliot prays with the rest of the family gathered in front of the grandmother's portrait in the background, Ilana, in the foreground shouts, "This is the happiest day of my life!" Bobbi's examination of the interior of Abbi's handbag discloses the dildo she has bought to replace Jeremy's, which she accidently melted in the dishwasher after he left for work. The nuclear family gathers around as Ilana and her brother explain pegging to their father in a completely normalizing fashion. Abbi explains that this is not her ordinary way to have sex but that she did it "for Grandma Esther."

Everyone but Bobbi, who remains preoccupied with the purse, sheds sentimental tears over this tribute. Afterward, they are all eating and happy. The parents mention a swingers' party they attended, and Bobbi says heartily to Abbi, "Good for you for trying something new." Scenes like this clarify why women like Kendra Decolo, in an essay for *Bitch* magazine, praise the show for providing them with models for sex-positive feminist Jewish parenting. She writes that she "would like to give my daughter a sense of freedom and possibility while disrupting oppressive systems" and that the "joyful" kinky transgressiveness of the show's Jews conveys this sense.

X. Darkness Dildos

Transparent also shows us a woman, in this case Ali, wearing a strap-on, but the tone is quite different. After beginning a sexual affair with her best friend, Syd, Ali walks into the room wearing Syd's strap-on. Syd is sitting working on her computer, and Ali keeps poking her with the dildo, although Syd complains that this is making her uncomfortable. "Why have you been hiding this from me?" Ali asks. Syd replies, "It's a nighttime only thing . . . [that has] never seen the light of day before." Ali continues to embarrass and annoy Syd with it and then says she wants to do everything from now on "with a dick on." The episode's opening sequence, with Ali and her sister Sarah at a women's spa discussing their sexualities, tells us that Ali has entered a phase of anger against men and male privilege. Ali says she will now have sex only with women because that constitutes resistance to patriarchy. Sarah explains that she is attracted to women but has no interest in feminism and says she never thinks of patriarchy, just fantasizes about being sexually dominated by their long-ago high school disciplinarian Mr. Irons. Like Sarah, Ali clearly associates having a dick with being able to bully and dominate women. We do not see or hear of the strap-on being used for sex between Ali and Syd. As is typical of the series, its vision of the use of sex toys, like other aspects of sexual activity, is kept in the dark, just as Syd says the dildo should be.

Ali's bullying of Syd with the dildo is complemented by a scene in which Ali and transman Dale (Ian Harvey) try to have sex in a public restroom with a newly purchased dildo, but it falls to the dirty floor. Jack Halberstam has this to say on his blog:

> the final straw for me, late one night, deep into a binge watching cycle of *Transparent*, was when Dale, a transman, struggles to get his sex toy out of its child proof packaging in anticipation of hot sex with his fem date, Ali, and then drops his dildo on the floor. In that moment, I felt my faith in the series slipping away as fast as Ali's desire, and when she turns to leave, giving up for now on the potential of a heated and sexy exchange, turning her back on the fallen Sparkle Unicorn tool, I was ready to go with her.

Moreover, Halberstam notes that because this "scene is intercut with a failed sexual interaction between Josh and Raquel," detumescence becomes the theme of the episode. As Halberstam goes on to discuss, the show is pathos heavy in its representations of sex.[6] Sex is dirty and dangerous and problematic whether a flesh-and-blood penis or a dildo is involved. To pursue it is to travel away from pleasure.

In *Broad City*, Abbi and Bobbi do both encounter roadblocks in their pleasure journeys. When Abbi enters Jeremy's room wearing the replacement dildo, he rejects it and picks a fight because, he claims, the melted one was specially made for his rectum, while this one is a "cheap" substitute bought off the shelf. Their nascent relationship ends in anger. But later platonically in bed together, Ilana comforts Abbi saying, "You'll find someone else to peg. . . . There are infinite holes in the sea," and Abbi agrees because she is now "wild and free." Bobbi, too, finds consolation for her loss. After the confiscation of the knockoffs, Bobbi wails that she has not even been able to say "goodbye" to the handbags, and Ilana holds her (in a parody of the family's earlier mourning) until a male passerby berates them for "blocking the whole sidewalk." They curse him and redeclare their love for each other. The episode ends with Bobbi and Arthur in their kitchen, as she answers condolence emails, arguing about whether she can peg him. He reluctantly agrees since otherwise, she implies, she will no longer allow him anal access to her. "Oh, all right," he says, and offers to "stop by the mall" and pick up a strap-on. No one is depressed, let alone devastated; no one needs references to the Holocaust in order to justify their departures from heteronormativity; and there are no cuts to Nazi-era Berlin. Instead, we see lots of love and happiness in this world where sex is fun and sex scenes are funny.

XI. Forbidden Pleasures

One cause of the contrasting sadness of *Transparent* is pointed out by Spenser Kornhaber, in a review in the *Atlantic* subtitled, "When your own happiness hurts others, what do you do?" He notes that the show's negativity about sexual freedom is closely connected to its insistence that such freedom is gained through acts of "brutal" selfishness. "Again and again, the show plays with the fact that doing what feels good can make other people feel very bad." He describes the second season as being structured by "a plot motif that sees characters expend great energy getting into seemingly desirable situations, only to suddenly and somewhat inexplicably want out—prior promises and collateral damage be damned," including the nullified wedding that opens the season, Josh's abandonment of his plan to marry Raquel and have a child with her, and Ali's sexual experimentation with and refusal of a commitment to Syd. What it all adds up to is a vision of sexual freedom as alienating one from human community. This is certainly a major message of the narrative, but it is also communicated in more subtle ways.

Establishing shots help create the mood in both series. One of *Transparent*'s most daring episodes, in terms of the sex it shows us, "Flicky-Flicky Thump-Thump," exemplifies the way these shots are used throughout the series. Maura, dressed for a pool party in an ill-fitting swimsuit that does nothing to conceal the male bulge in her crotch, reluctantly masturbates Shelly who is in the bathtub. Since television almost never shows us people in their late sixties performing sex acts, this is revolutionary. But the potential for sex positivity is undercut by the look of distaste on Maura's averted face and then her rejection of Shelly's offer to return the favor. We can guess why Maura demurs; it would involve taking out her penis and so compromise her carefully constructed appearance as feminine. The scene works metaphorically to remind us that Maura's gender and sexuality are not reconcilable. Then the show cuts to a short series of exterior shots.

These shots work two ways. First, because of Los Angeles car culture, the exterior scenes are almost always empty of people, emphasizing the loneliness of the characters. The frame also often, as in the establishing shots in "Flicky-Flicky Thump-Thump," centers on the electrical wires— including phone lines—going into buildings. In the age of Wi-Fi, these wires no longer connect many people. They symbolize the disconnection of a world of isolated people who have little fully present contact with other people. Every episode of the series includes a sequence of shots of the exteriors of buildings, which the camera will then enter, and in each one we first see a stretch of emptiness, usually with a webbing of wires at the top of the screen. Sometimes the camera lingers on the wires, as if we might then go to something they bring into the story: a landline phone ringing or a plugged-in desktop computer delivering email or even a television being watched by a family member. But instead we see the usual bickering and misunderstandings, if people are gathered together, or the wistful looks of another lonely person who has failed to make the connection he or she yearns for. Jim Croce's song "Operator," which we hear in the series pilot, brings in the idea of failed attempts to connect and feelings mismatched to appearances that will dominate the series.

All of this speaks to Maura's tragedy: it is all too late for her. Unlike Caitlyn Jenner, but like most people in their sixties, Maura is not glamorous. She has the heavy, lumpy body and square, sagging facial features of an aging man. So when she retreats to a bar for transwomen and their admirers after the pool party, she is well aware that the men who approach her more medically modified, and younger, friends are not interested in her. And she is not oriented toward men anyway. So she dances alone with her image in the dance floor mirror, the usual slightly sour, depressed expression on her face.[7]

XII. A Breath of Fresh Air

The sort of isolation in loneliness characteristic of *Transparent*'s mise en scène seems impossible in *Broad City*, which takes us out on the crowded New York streets. Someone is always coming along and interacting with the characters. As the acrimonious interchange with the pedestrian in the "Knockoffs" episode suggests, there is no getting away from human contact in New York City, even when one does not want it.[8] Even the underground den where the counterfeit handbags are made and sold is crowded with people. Passersby interact with Abbi and Ilana constantly when they are outdoors, and when they are inside any building, they are almost never alone. In fact, the ubiquitous presence of Abbi's roommate's boyfriend Bevers is a running joke. And the establishing shots reinforce the sense that whatever problems the characters have, solitude is not one of them. We are given sweeping views of bustling crowds and buildings where neighbors are always looking at and speaking with each other.

In a review of the series' second season, Matthew Polland finds the opening of the first episode emblematic of *Broad City* as a whole in its evocation of a New York City packed, like the subway train they fight their way through, with all sorts of eccentrics and pests. But rather than depict their claustrophobically crowded world as a serious problem, the series focuses on "portraying the camaraderie that helps us shrug off such inconveniences. The series reasserts these desires when the friends step off the subway; any sense of irritation dissipates, and the pair quickly find themselves in a playful slapping match, their laughter echoing through the station. . . . It's that exuberant depiction of female kinship as being inextricably bound to the anarchy of daily living that gives the series its unexpected sweetness." As Susan J. Douglass enthuses, Abbi and Ilana "have become feminists heroes, in part because of the power and centrality of their friendship" (16). The third season finale, "Jews on a Plane," strongly reasserts this vision when Ilana and Abbi cause chaos in what is meant to be a matchmaking trip to Israel by insisting on sitting together instead of with the men with whom they have been paired,[9] because as important and joyful as they find sex, their friendship is even more important. And this is because it provides the support that makes sexual adventuring pleasurable.

Where *Broad City* imagines a world in which it is a source of consolation that there are always new people to experience sexually, and no matter how these experiences go, we can always at least laugh about them later with a good friend, in *Transparent*, that the characters "throw themselves" at lovers as a way to understand themselves, as Inkoo Kang observes, is what makes their lives so sad. Because once they do, they are likely to fall flat.

XIII. Tragic Jewesses

Sophie Mayer claims that with *Transparent*, "two decades after the florescence of the New Queer Cinema, TV brings us sex-positivity on demand." She argues that the date chosen for the series' main flashbacks, 1994, "points to the legacy of New Queer Cinema, its promise and its falling away. B. Ruby Rich named the phenomenon in articles for *Sight & Sound* and the *Village Voice* in 1992 and noted, even then, that a phenomenon that had begun as truly diverse and political was translated into the indie mainstream as largely white, middle class and cismale." In Mayer's view, *Transparent* counters that sort of narrow representation through such moments as the depiction of a Shabbat dinner presided over by Sarah and Tammy in which the patriarchal tradition is "dismantl[ed] movingly and precisely" because the patriarch "has been doubly replaced by queer female parents." Yet a closer look at the Pfeffermans reveals problems in representation (or the lack of it) of Othered queers similar to those identified by Rich. While it is true that the family members do mostly choose partners who have vaginas, as they laughingly claim in this scene, that choice is of cisgender women. The Pfeffermans also almost always choose partners within their own racial group, and Ali's departure from this, to try a three-way with two Black men, is a disaster,[10] yet another sex scene that begins with a tease and then quickly comes to nothing.

Furthermore, the family can hardly be considered representatively "middle class," as Mayer describes it, unless we believe that it is normal in California or anywhere else for middle-class families to own houses that Sotheby's real estate agents eagerly seek to list. And finally, this episode can be considered lesbian-positive (or positive about rich, white cisgendered lesbians) only if we ignore the later disastrous failure of Sarah and Tammy's relationship. Instead, one could easily read the episode the way Sarah's jilted

husband does, as indicative of the way Sarah's misguided attempt to alleviate her boredom through returning to Tammy, the lesbian lover she had
long ago in college, has disrupted and rendered more unhappy his life, hers,
Tammy's, and the lives of all their children.

Mayer goes on to praise the show for its endorsement of a woman-
centered perspective equated with life itself. She concludes by discussing
Melanie Klein's theory that, because men are forced to repudiate their early childhood identification with their mothers, they create a gynophobic
patriarchy." In her opinion, "*Transparent* resonates with this profound observation . . . making visible the possibility of social and cultural transformation. Not just from homophobia and transphobia to integration,
nor from male to female but—from Mort to Maura (a version of Mary, the
quintessential mother)—from death to life. *L'chaim!*" I wish I could feel this
way about the series, but its concept of female identification is too narrow
for me to see it as an affirmation of woman-centered values that result in
celebration of life. Repeatedly in its dramatization of Maura's struggles to
use the right cosmetics, to fix her hair in an approved manner, and to deck
herself out in the restrictive and uncomfortable clothing the mainstream
deems feminine, the series presents a particular view of being a woman that
centers on consumerism and the conformity to beauty standards that seeing oneself as a commodity demands. We are shown the stereotypical femininity not of the powerful mother but of the weak daughter who is always
seeking a daddy: a search literalized in Ali's excited acquiescence to Dale's
demands that she call him "Daddy" and submit to his sexual bullying as a
form of foreplay. Not only does Ali give up her usual comfortable-looking
androgynous attire for Dale, but she also costumes herself in a constricting
ultra-femme dress with a push-up bra in order to fit his fantasy and allows
him to shave her pubes so she can appear even more childlike and consequently subordinate. As Halberstam puts it, this scene is "one major buzz
kill" for anyone who thinks of equality between the partners as a basis of
eroticism. Sarah goes even further than Ali with her masturbatory fantasy
of being spanked by a father-figure. It is only when she realizes she cannot
get the abuse she craves from a man that she resorts to paying a lesbian
dominatrix to beat her.

Yes, the Pfeffermans prefer people with vaginas, but they also, if cisgender females, seem to prefer being punished for having vaginas and to crave
being forced into conventional femininity. This preference is emphasized
by montage in the episode "Bulnerable." The main event of this episode is

Raquel's miscarriage and Josh telling her he does not want to try again. She is shattered because she wants to be a mother more than anything else. It cuts directly from Josh going out one door to Sarah's Dr. Steve (Jason Mantzoukis) walking in another door for a night with her. Sarah unsuccessfully tries to get him to act abusive and treat her like a "slut." So we see that men come and go in the women characters' lives, always causing misery by failing to give them the traditional subordinate sex role they desire, whether it is mother or whore. However, it is sex that ultimately emerges as the problem, not men.

As guides to the terminology of nonbinary gender identifications, such as the online GLAAD Media Reference Guide, tell us, there is a difference between being transgender and being transsexual. Transgender is "an umbrella term" that encompasses both those who opt for hormone treatment and sexual reassignment surgery and those who do not but reject the gender they were assigned at birth. In contrast, transsexual is "an older term that originated in the medical and psychological communities. Still preferred by some people who have permanently changed—or seek to change—their bodies through medical interventions (including but not limited to hormones and/or surgeries)" (https://www.glaad.org/reference/transgender). And as experience of those who identify as transgender and those who identify as transsexual can tell us—and have often told me—another difference is the emphasis on sexuality in one term and on gender in the other. For its entire first season, *Transparent* avoids any possibly controversial emphasis on Maura's sex life, choosing, instead, to focus on Maura's gender identification and the sex lives of her children. And when we finally do get a sex scene involving Maura, she is still too inhibited to take off her underwear. The series title tells us that while Maura is trans, her role as a parent is the most important thing about her. And thus the series' replication of traditional gender binarity is indicated from its title on.

Whatever is radical and new about the show, and it has certainly been heralded by critics this way, there is little nontraditional about Maura's concept of womanhood. From her first explorations of her true, inner gender identity, she understands being a woman to mean wearing feminine clothing, cosmetics, jewelry, and a hairdo. Kang notes approvingly that Soloway says she made the sex scenes to show how women feel during sex rather than how they look. Yet we are reminded continually by the costuming that in the show's vision, one must conform to the most rigid gender stereotypes in order to experience oneself as a woman. Of the women characters, only

Leslie, the butch lesbian women's studies professor, dares to present herself to the world without obvious makeup and a carefully constructed hairdo. And she is bitter and angry due to the way she has been treated because she refused to conform to gender norms, as she indicates when she confronts Maura in support of the exclusion of transwomen from the women's music festival. So the message seems to be that while everyone should have the freedom to choose their gender identification, the only prudent choices are between traditional dominant masculinity and submissive, commodified femininity.

For many people today who live in conservative areas, this depiction of gender politics may seem realistic, and furthermore, *Transparent*'s dour view of the consequences of exercising sexual freedom may resonate with their own observations and experiences. They may even share the view of Sylvia Plath's poem "Lady Lazarus," that being a sexually active woman is equivalent in the torture it inflicts to being a Jew subjected to the horrors of the Holocaust. Certainly sex is not productive of happiness for large numbers of people. Moreover, because the series envisions gender in binary terms—male dominance/female submissiveness, male naturalness/female artifice—sex has to have unhappy outcomes or else the show would be blatantly antifeminist because it would endorse conformity to traditional gender roles. *Transparent* can certainly be understood as a critique of our sexist, and racist, society, which makes sexual pleasure difficult to attain and impossible to sustain for many people, especially for those who, like Jews, are subject to racialization.

Consequently, this comparison of *Transparent* to *Broad City* is not meant as a criticism of the former as a bad television series that should not be seen. Instead, it is simply meant to call into question whether *Transparent* is sex positive. I believe it is not. I wince when its sex scenes begin, knowing that heartbreak will follow, and for that reason, I have been grateful that the series has not included many. What I love about *Broad City* is that it keeps saying that life does not have to be that way. One can resist gender binary and reject racism and so treat oneself to a seemingly endless series of pleasurable sexual encounters.

XIV. No Conclusion, Just Go On Forever!

And further I agree with Amy Friedman, who in her blog for the *Guardian*, enthuses about the way *Broad City* reflects her own reality and also her feminist ideal. The series reflects my own life experience and is my Jewish ideal as well. Friedman writes: "Ilana and Abbi are our people. They are truly casual about sex, not simply feigning detachment in the name of empowerment. . . . They are feminists who . . . exhibit very real imperfections without the self-loathing. This strikes me as a huge step forward. Abbi and Ilana don't just reject the exacting standards most women feel they have to live up to, they still feel great about themselves. And their self-esteem is probably directly attributable to their unflinching support of each other and the pleasure they take in each other's company." I would add that it is also attributable to the pleasure they take in sex as a form of entertainment and a way to connect with others in their sex-positive community, including those so marginalized by their racial or ethnic identifications as to have rejected mainstream standards and strictures as ludicrous. For those who see sexual encounters as inherently fraught with danger and possible causes of destructive life disruption, *Transparent* deals with difficult reality in an encouraging way. But I must join Friedman in saying that *Broad City*'s sex scenes realistically reflect how sex can be experienced if we ask nothing of it except that it entertain us, and like Friedman I prayed that it would run "forever and ever. Amen." I was as sad as Abbi and Ilana are to see the series end with its fifth season, when Abbi decides to leave New York for an art residency in Colorado. But I was consoled by the sight of the graffiti they left on the Brooklyn Bridge: "Abbi + Ilana Forever."

Notes

1. See Josh Lambert's *Unclean Lips: Obscenity, Jews, and American Culture* for extensive discussion of this issue.

2. A somewhat confusing part of the series is that Landsman, who plays Sarah, was forty-five when the first season premiered, yet she seems meant to be understood as younger, despite the lines in her face, due to the flashbacks to her childhood when she seems only slightly older than her siblings. We know that Josh is thirty-two or thirty-three because we are told he fathered a child at age fifteen and that child, Colton (Alex MacNicoll), returns to find him when he is seventeen. In season 2, Ali says she is thirty. Sarah's behavior makes better sense if we take her to be the age she looks, rather than in her early thirties, since major identity crises around sexuality are usually the province of adolescents or people at midlife.

3. "Back to Black" is a hit song in the repertoire of tragic Jewish blues singer Amy Winehouse.

4. *Pleasure and Danger: Exploring Female Sexuality* remains the definitive study of the balance women seek between yearning for sexual pleasure and fearing sexual dangers.

5. However, to treat a single woman's decision to go through with an unwanted pregnancy as needing an explanation would go against the series' conformity to the

convention of television and films avoiding annoying religious conservatives by representing abortion either as unthinkable or as catastrophically causing infertility. The show finale in season 4 returns to the theme of extramarital sex resulting in unwanted pregnancies when Lila, the polyamorous partner of Len and Sarah, seems to be pregnant.

6. Halberstam is much less critical of the series in his book, *Trans**, praising it for refusing "to trade only in positive images of trans people, never mind Jews" (97).

7. In light of later revelations, it is tempting to imagine that some of the show's general sourness resulted from the unhappy atmosphere during filming. As Christi Carras reports, two transgender actresses on the show, Trace Lysette and Alexandra Billings, accused Tambor of persistent sexual harassment.

8. Because I have lived downtown in cities all my life, I like to joke that "people who need people are the luckiest people in the world," not for the reasons given by *Funny Girl*, the film this song features in, but because there is no way to get away from other people.

9. In season 3 of *Transparent*, the Pfeffermans also go to Israel, but as always, their trip is filled with unhappy events.

10. They begin to caress her, but when she shares her view that these two roommates and friends are using her body to connect with each other, they end the encounter and throw her out on the street. Disturbing racist aspects of this incident include that both men are seemingly mindless body builders, that Ali clearly sees and treats them as nothing but bodies, and, worst of all, that both conform to disagreeable and untruthful stereotypes of African Americans by being the most homophobic characters we encounter in the series, as is shown by their exaggerated panic at the suggestion that they might be attracted to each other.

6

MONSTROUS JEWISH SEXUALITIES AND MINORITARIAN CINEMA

I. Subtle Pleasures

I return to film analysis in this chapter to elucidate the ways more subtle than the celebration of sexual wildness central to *Broad City* that contemporary visual narratives have offered transgressive pleasures to Jews, and to all audiences, through the portrayal of Jews as racialized subjects. The greater length of films, usually double or more than an episode of a television series, makes possible sustained character development that can be more complex and subtle than that which a television episode can provide. Of course, the string of episodes that make up a television season could do far more character development than a single film, but that goes against the conventions of representation in the medium, which, until the advent of binge-watching "quality," or artistic, TV, strongly favored stand-alone episodes. As numerous critics have noted, television has generally relied more heavily than cinema on easily recognized stereotypes and maintained greater consistency in the behavior of its characters throughout a season so that these stereotypes are reinforced. When we think of the most famous characters in television history—the ones everyone recognizes immediately by name, from Lucille Ball to Mulder and Scully—this becomes obvious. In fact even in a series that calls into question many common ideas about the stability of human identities, like the science fiction series *Orphan Black*, in which one actress (Tatiana Maslany) plays several clones, each of her characters is easily distinguishable because each acts and reacts in a specific, unchanging manner that adheres to stereotypes (e.g., Because she is a scientist, one clone is always less emotional and more rational than the other clones). In contrast, films, like novels, often include substantial character development, and frequently make in-depth exploration of complex personalities the focus of the plot. Here the compactness of films also works in favor of complex characterizations. Just as one episode of a television series hardly allows time for serious character development, to draw out a character's development through several seasons of a series would try the patience of many viewers. Thus, *Broad City*'s Abbi and Ilana begin as unrestrained sexual adventurers and end five years later pretty much the same, although with more experience and more confidence.[1]

However, cinematic subtlety does not necessarily destroy the pure, visceral pleasure that Roland Barthes describes as the essence of the text of bliss. On the contrary, for me the films of the Coen brothers, like the revisionist historical fantasy of *Inglourious Basterds*, are texts of bliss. This may not be readily apparent because the films do not avoid stereotypes, but instead, as Barthes says the texts of bliss can do, push stereotypes to such an extreme that they explode (43). In the Coens' cinema, everything that makes a stereotype legible as grounded in social and historical realities is both figured forth and then exaggerated beyond the point of credible reality, calling into question the received ideas that made it recognizable in the first place. The Coens' films are also Deleuzian minoritarian cinema, which closely resembles the text of bliss in offering us unsettling new visions of what we believed was familiar. In this chapter, I go into detail about how these two descriptors, the text of bliss and minoritarian cinema, fit a few representative Coen films and, in doing so, make a case against the critical condemnation of their work as anti-Semitic.

II. Brothers in Trouble?

The depictions of Jews in the cinema of Joel and Ethan Coen have frequently confused audience members. Are the depictions anti-Semitic, as J. Hoberman, among many others, claims? Or are they, as many of their defenders claim, parodying anti-Semitism? The Coens' most controversial film in this regard is *Barton Fink* (1991). Richard Goldstein's 1991 *Village Voice* article about the cultural background that he feels led to the racially motivated murder of Yankel Rosenbaum, "The New Anti-Semitism: A Geshrei [Yiddish for shriek]," accuses the Coen brothers of being part of the problem. He interprets the unpleasant movie studio heads in *Barton Fink* as exemplifying the sort of "'anti-Semitism with an edge of irony' Jewish artists use to deal with the horror of anti-Semitism [by] deflect[ing] it onto an evil

Jewish other. But this strategy only fuels the fire" (36). On the other side of the critical spectrum, many see the film as depicting the close relationship between the everyday American anti-Semitism that plagues the title character (played by John Turturro), a young Jewish screenwriter who has just come to Hollywood, and the rise of fascism in the era in which it is set, 1941. Charlie Mundt, the Gentile false friend with whom he metaphorically and literally wrestles turns out to be a serial killer who causes official suspicion to fall on Fink. Mundt also hints he has murdered Fink's parents and uncle back home in New York. Although Mundt's murder of a Gentile woman with whom Barton has sex is a major part of the plot, the film has little to say about the sexualization of Jews or our racialization, for that matter, and so I only evoke it here to indicate the difficulty of analyzing the Coens' films' treatment of anti-Semitic stereotypes, such as the crass commercialism of the studio heads and the pretentiousness of Fink.

Difficult though such analysis is, I begin with the idea that the Coens are trying to do something else entirely than either condemn such stereotypes or reinforce them. Instead, I believe they are resignifying them but not in such a way as to create stable meanings. Instead, the resignifications are highly unstable, constantly shifting away from anything we try to make them mean. In Coen films, it becomes almost impossible to retain an idea of a positive or negative portrayal of Jews, let alone designate Jewish characters good or bad.

The concept of minoritarian cinema articulated in Gilles Deleuze's *Cinema 2: The Time-Image*, can help us understand the Coens' characters, who are so often seemingly protean, monstrous figures. In this, his second book on film, Deleuze draws on his and Félix Guattari's *Kafka: Toward a Minor Literature* to describe a "minor cinema." While this cinema, as he describes it, is realized in the so-called third world, the qualities he ascribes to it could just as easily be seen in the films made by members of minoritized groups in any of the countries called the first world. As Constantine Verevis says: "Deleuze describes this minor cinema as one that sets out, not to represent the conditions of an oppressed minority, but rather to invent new values and facilitate the creation of a people who have hitherto been missing. Like Kafka's minor literature . . . minoritarian cinema ceases to be representational and moves instead towards its limits."[2] And at those limits, we can find the Jews created by the Coen brothers and the bliss that contemplation of them can bring. Such a reading goes against those of critics like Hoberman, who has been particularly critical of the Coen brothers' films for depicting Jews as, in his words, "grotesque."[3] Yet we cannot understand why the Coens' Jewish characters look and act the ways they do without thinking of the films in terms of cinema history. Just like their contemporary, Quentin Tarantino, the Coens deliberately place their films in an intertext of traditions and conventions of cinematic representation. Their Jews look and behave the ways they do in relation not only to the way Jews look in other films, but also in dialogue with the meanings attached to those appearances and behaviors.

It would be a serious mistake to see these characters as figures meant to represent real Jews such as we might encounter—or might be—in everyday life. Instead, we might think of these Jews as being experimental figures, like the characters in Kafka's work. The Coens, and all filmmakers who create films from the subject/subjugated position of Jews in a Gentile-dominated society, are like Kafka as artists in that they are trapped within what Deleuze and Guattari describe as "the ambiguity of the Jews" who are without a fixed and thus legible national character to define them (12). The Coens, therefore, reimagine Jews outside the necessity of fighting anti-Semitic stereotypes with equally false admirable archetypes. Instead, they make of their Jewish characters the sort of monsters that push the stereotypes beyond their limits to a point where we might imagine Jewishness anew. As this book has argued up to this point, Jewish sexualities, including Jews' physical appearances, are central to the racialization of Jews. But before venturing into the world of the revisionary deconstructions—or, as Deleuze and Guattari would have it, deterritorializations—of Jewishness the Coens create, I first look at some American stereotypes and then make a little side trip to India to summon a corrective to the stereotypes that the Coens must grapple with in order to begin their experimentation.

III. American Beauty and American Ugly

If, as Sam Mendes's 1999 film *American Beauty* suggests, there is a specific type that defines this term, there is also a corresponding American ugly. The well-known American beauty standard applies to women only. Male beauty is always suspect of homosexuality (but more on homosexuality anon). The stereotypical American beauty, like "the shiksa goddess" pursued by many real and fictional Jewish men, is blond (Deliovsky 49–50). Her hair is the premier mark of her Anglo-Saxon or Germanic/Nordic heritage, as it is always very smooth, kinky hair being the signifier of African or Jewish blood (Deliovsky 56). Since the 1960s, frizzy hair, as featured in numerous underground comic depictions and later in films, identifies women as "dirty" hippies or other sorts of counterculture political dissidents whose rebellion includes the refusal to use commercial beauty products. It is often associated with feminists, as the refusal to wear the appropriate hair products is taken to mean that a woman rejects the norm of making herself attractive to men. The naturally straight hair of most Asians and Latinas, is not, however, a mark of superior beauty. Americans may "wish they all could be California girls," but not that kind of Californians! Rather, blondness acts as the imprimatur of purity, also suggesting that body hair, now including pubic hair, will be minimal and nearly invisible. In addition, the American beauty should have the lower body of a young, athletic boy, slim hipped with tiny, high buttocks, her only curves provided by high, very firm breasts that are not so large as to be seen as comical. She should also have a narrow, high-cheekboned face. While, of course, in real life there are all sorts of Jews with widely different appearances, including many who meet these beauty standards, they—and certainly not the Jewish women typically depicted on film—are not the norm or the stereotype.

Women identified as Jews in cinema tend to have hair that is almost always both curly and frizzy (as untreated curly hair tends to be), sometimes to an arresting extent, as exemplified by the famous hair of Amy Irving or as revealed by the immigrant wife, played by Carol Kane, in *Hester Street*, to her husband's shock when he finally persuades her to abandon her Orthodox hair covering. Just as defiantly intransigent as this unruly hair, which is usually dark, their large features give them "excessively expressive faces,"[4] and the matching bodies are almost always either frighteningly bony or excessively zaftig (Schwadron 7, 31). Embarrassingly big breasts and full hips and behinds wobble as they walk, alerting us to their impurity, their disgustingly fleshy presence. And they are disgusting because in America, the land of shaved armpits and pubic hair and extra-strength deodorants, unaltered female physicality is always grotesque.

If the women are repulsive, the men are worse.[5] For decades, Woody Allen defined Jewish masculinity for moviegoers as neuroticism physically exemplified by a weak, inadequate body. The Jewish male on film is almost always unathletic, either small and skinny or fat and flabby. His kinky hair is often an unattractive halo around male-pattern baldness. And both sexes are afflicted with what may be America's most despised nose: a long, hooked one. As Hannah Schwadron discusses, "The Jewish nose [stands for] all that is inferior . . . about the Jewish body," and specifically, due to its phallic associations, in women this nose represents "defunct femininity" (113).

What this all adds up to is that, unlike European Jews, who have traditionally been described in literature and often depicted in cinema as dangerously seductive (Abrams, *New Jew in Film*, 43–67), American Jews most often appear in films as uglies that simply cannot inspire sexual desire, although they may be given a sort of pitying love. *Annie Hall* (1977) is a classic in this regard through its emphasis on the point that a Jew can only win a Gentile's love through his or her force of personality and persistence sexually, a theme repeated in many films. In *The Way We Were* (1973), for example, despite her tremendous charisma and the way the cinematography favors her, Streisand (as Katie) is consistently presented as inferior in appearance to Robert Redford's Hubble and as so lucky to have initially tricked him into bed with her that we cannot be surprised that she is unable to hold onto him and is replaced with a blond Gentile. As Eric A. Goldman comments, the story so heavily insists on her physical inferiority because of her stereotypical Jewish looks that "the seduction by the Jewess of the WASP seems plausible only because it happens without his knowledge [he is drunk]" (139).[6] It is the way we were, once upon a time in America, although in the film of that name, the central Jewish gangsters both desire a Jewish girl from the neighborhood. In Coen land, the past, as well as the present, are imagined differently.

IV. Bollywood Surprise!

But first off to India, because if the Coens' treatment of the physical appearance of Jewish women is surprising within the context of American cinema, it would have fit seamlessly into Indian films up until the recent past. In contrast to the Jewish female cinematic stereotype, Indian women are often described as the most beautiful in the world. What a bombshell to cinema studies, then, is Danny Ben-Moshe's 2017 documentary, *Shalom Bollywood: The Untold Story of Indian Cinema*. As Marcy J. Levinson summarizes the film: "From the early history of how Jewish women ('Anglo Indians') numbered only in the thousands but came from what the narrator calls a more 'progressive community,' the documentary introduces viewers to various Bollywood actresses, including the silent-era queen of the 1920s, Sulochana, 'the one with the beautiful eyes'—aka Ruby Myers. 'Shalom Bollywood' also introduces Miss Rose (Rose Ezra), Pramila (Esther Abraham), Ramola (Rachel Cohen), Arati Devi (Rachael Sofaer) and (Florence Ezekiel) Nadira." As ample clips of their close-ups demonstrate, these beautiful, dark-eyed, and delicately hooked-nosed stars, often seen with haloes of kinky black hair, had an undeniable "exotic" look the camera, as well as the audiences, loved. As Yudit Kornberg Greenberg discusses, they were liminal figures to Indian audiences, "neither white nor brown" (30). "The lightness of their skin combined with their [mixed] European and Indian dress marked their belonging as well as their Otherness, which was celebrated rather than denigrated or erased, as Jewish women's differences from the mainstream beauty standard so often were in Hollywood (31). In fact, many would argue the celebrated beauty of these Jewish stars originated the appeal associated now with Indian women, especially because, in 1947, Esther Abraham (Pramila) was the first Miss India.

The rise of Jewish stars in Bollywood made sense not simply because a Jewish Indian director, David Penkar, developed the singing and dancing style now seen as synonymous with Bollywood, or because he was only one of many Jewish cinematic innovators in India, but because anti-Semitism was rare in India. Even in the 1970s, when Muslim and Hindu women began to appear in films, Nadira continued to be cast as a sexy vamp that men just could not resist. A postage stamp was created to commemorate the loveliness of Ruby Meyers. During the same time period that Jewish women dominated the screen in Indian films (from the silent era up through the 1960s), in American cinema, despite the large and influential presence of Jewish directors and producers, Jewish women were deemed unacceptable as love interests in any way other than disguised, not merely renamed, as Gentiles, as was, for example, Rita Hayworth, originally the dark-skinned and haired daughter of a Sephardic father.[7] Other Jewish stars who are not widely known to be Jewish and who were cast repeatedly as blond Gentiles in their movies include Mae West, Laurel Bacall, Ellen Barkin, Dyan Cannon, and today Scarlett Johansson. So, while in India Jewish women were at the forefront of cinematic glamour, in America the beauty of Jewish women could only be acknowledged if their Jewishness was effectively erased from view. This relates to the cinema of the Coens in that the situation of the Bollywood stars shows the fallacy of there being only two choices for the depiction of Jews in Hollywood films: either as repulsively ugly people or disguised as Gentiles.

V. Between Goys

I begin this section by riffing off the title of Eve Kosofsky Sedgwick's groundbreaking gender studies book, *Between Men*, because her theory so perfectly fits the romance at the center of the Coens' first historical film,

Miller's Crossing (1990). I choose this film as the center of my investigation into the Coens' minoritarian approach to Jewish appearances and their effect on Gentiles because it is their most extended treatment of this topic. Set in "an Eastern city in the United States, toward the end of the 1920s," as an intertitle tells us, this is revisionist history of a nearly allegorical nature due to its stylized cast and sets, which give us an America that seems populated almost entirely by large groups of gangsters and their immediate hangers-on. The town has long been controlled by the Irish gangsters led by Leo (Albert Finney). But as the story opens he must fight for continued dominance against Johnny Caspar (Jon Polito), an Italian gangster, and his men. In what initially seems an inconsequential side plot, he is also being deceived by the Jewish woman he adores, Verna Bernbaum (Marcia Gay Harden), who is carrying on a secret affair with his right-hand henchman, Tom (Gabriel Byrne). A further complication is provided by her brother, Bernie (John Turturro), who has not only seduced Mink (Steve Buscemi), the effeminate boyfriend of Eddie Dane (J. E. Freeman), Caspar's right-hand man, but is selling Mink's inside knowledge about the fixed fights Caspar arranges. For most of the film, it seems that Tom has gone over to the Italian side because he disagrees with Leo's refusal to approve Caspar's request to kill Bernie, which causes a gang war.

But at least two things work against this interpretation. The first is intertextual. Viewers who know action films will be aware of the plot device that structures *A Fist Full of Dollars* (1964) and its inspiration, Akira Kurosawa's *Yojimbo* (1961), along with dozens of other less famous films, in which a man pretends to be angry at his boss so that he can infiltrate the ranks of his boss's enemy and destroy him. The second reason we may doubt that Tom has really betrayed his old boss is more subtle. The film includes three important gay characters and to a large extent normalizes male homosexuality through everyone's knowledge of their love triangle. And although the characters constantly make racist remarks, none make homophobic ones. Consequently, it seems possible that Tom may feel more than platonic friendship for Leo.

Byrne's acting suggests Tom's romantic feeling toward Leo. Byrne's trademark soulful eyes track Finney wherever he goes, and as Tom, he often seems to be almost swooning with devotion. Tom shows more affection for Leo than he ever does for Verna, as she remarks jealously on repeated occasions. She offers to stop seeing Leo and run away with Tom, but even after Leo has thrown Tom out of his criminal organization because of his affair with Verna, Tom refuses to leave Leo. He explains to her that although he and Leo are "through," it doesn't mean he doesn't still "care" about Leo. In fact, everything he does is for Leo's benefit, as she bitterly recognizes at last.

The scene in which Tom confesses his relationship with her and Leo beats him all the way down a flight of stairs and out the door is an S/M set piece classic, choreographed to the tune of an extra-diegetic rendition of "Goodnight, Sweetheart." Tom makes no move to defend himself and casts enigmatic but intense looks at Leo as he reels from the punches. As William Nolan notes, Tom's confession seems motivated by his competitive decision to break Leo's trust in Verna (55), but the audience is pushed to ask, as Verna does, why Leo's view of her matters to Tom since she is so willing to throw Leo over in order to have Tom. An earlier scene in which Leo singlehandedly defeats a gang of Italian thugs who attack him as he prepares for bed not only explains why Tom admires him but, because it is scored with the diegetic sound of "Danny Boy" playing on the gramophone, also tells us that the truest, most real love in these men's world must occur between them, not with the women who, as in Sedgwick's theory, serve only to strengthen and formalize their alliances—as ultimately happens here, at least until Leo agrees to marry Verna and so loses Tom.

The final scene is romantic to the extreme, and Verna is peripheral to the romanticism. At the beginning of the scene, she jumps into Leo's car and leaves the funeral of her brother, Bernie, when Tom shows up at the graveside, presumably because she knows he killed Bernie. Neither man seems at all bothered by her departure. Instead, they begin addressing the problems in their relationship. Leo tries to persuade Tom to stay with him as his adviser and tells him that he is no longer angry that Tom had sex with Verna, whose marriage proposal he has accepted. But Tom angrily rejects his forgiveness and tells him that he must leave. Leo sadly walks away and Tom stands watching him as he walks down a dirt road. The camera swoops in on a close-up of Tom's face, his eyes glistening with what seem to be unshed tears.

The revolutionary ideas about the romantic attachments beneath the surface of homosocial bonds between men, written about by Eve Sedgwick, and their outing (as it were) in sexually explicit homoerotic fan fictions, reported on by Constance Penley, are now old news to most of us working on popular media. Linda Mizejewski notes that "Tom and Leo seem to be rivals for Verna, but it would be just as easy to read Tom and Verna as rivals for Leo" ("1990," 40). The sort of closeness demonstrated in several scenes between Leo and

Tom—or "Tommy" as Leo always calls him—seem suggestive in the wake of films like *Brokeback Mountain*. For instance, when Tom warns Leo that he is in danger from Caspar, Leo replies, "I reckon I could trade body blows with any man in this town" and then adds tenderly, "except you, Tommy" and then a beat later, "and Verna." Tom looks mightily vexed by this added remark. Later, in exasperation over Tom's storming out after their disagreement, Leo says, "Goddamn kid's just like a twist." In 1920s slang *twist* means a "broad."

However, when the film was made, its reception was no doubt partly influenced by the silence that covered romantic feelings between otherwise conventionally masculine men. So Nolan's reservations about whether we are meant to see Tom as gay are justified, although, as Nolan quotes in his essay's title, Tom is described by Eddie Dane as "straight as a corkscrew." Nolan emphasizes the film's drawing of parallels between Tom and "the Dane," as Eddie is always called by the other characters. Unlike Nolan, however, I do not read the relationship between Leo and Tom as classically homosocial in its dependence on them and their community not recognizing that homosexual bonds between men are possible. There seems to me no evidence in the film that anyone fails to see Mink and the Dane as both sexually and romantically involved or Bernie as homosexual. Instead, like Christopher Orr, I see the film's conclusion as romantically tragic in a way that is only possible if we read Tom's feelings for Leo as sexual/romantic love. As Orr observes, "The ending of *Miller's Crossing* makes [a clear] reference to the immaculate final scene of *The Third Man*: a funeral, a protagonist abandoned by his car, who watches as the last person he cares for in the world walks away down a dirt road hemmed by trees. (Yes, the love interest and best friend roles are inverted here, but you get the point.)"

VI. A Glass Key

As many critics recognize, *Miller's Crossing* is based on Dashiell Hammett's *The Glass Key*, including several similar scenes, characters, and plot details as well as images of and references to hats, which play a crucial role in Hammett's novel.[8] Lines of dialogue, such as "it's the kiss off" (166), are repeated in the film, but the insertion of gay characters and a classic noir femme fatale into the film's narrative make it distinctly different, as does the importance of Jews in the film. Hammett's novel centers on a battle between politicians whose power has been legitimized and mobsters, as the American aristocrats and warlords. As Tom will say in *Miller's Crossing*, "Love is the wild card." Top mobster Paul loves a senator's daughter but won't allow the senator's son to dally with his own daughter. These two class crossers are the cause of the problems as the senator kills his son to keep him from making trouble with Paul over Paul's daughter and Paul shields him because he loves the senator's daughter. There is no reference to race or ethnicity in the novel—and absolutely none to homosexuality.

In the Coens' film, what might be called the Jewish theme and the gay theme overlap in enhancing the sense that Verna, the fatal Jewish woman, is the key to everything. In contrast to Hammett's story, which features five significant female characters—Paul's mother; his daughter, Opal; Bernie's girlfriend, Lee; Eloise, the newspaper editor's wife; and Janet, the senator's daughter—the Coens' has only one, Verna, the grifter Jew who is indirectly responsible for a series of gangland massacres (which do not occur in *The Glass Key*) because of Leo's decision to protect her brother as part of his courtship of her.

If we leave aside the role of Hammett's protagonist, Ned Beaumont, in helping to empower his mobster friend Paul, Ned is an honorable man. The novel repeats twice that Ned has only known Paul for a year, and Ned does not seem to be part of Paul's criminal mob. He deceives people in order to bring to justice the killer of the senator's son, and when he discovers that the senator himself is the murderer, he forces him to submit to arrest even though this ruins Paul's chance of seizing power through the impending election. Unlike Tom, who kills Bernie in cold blood, Ned never kills anyone or commits any crimes. Janet, with whom he leaves at the end, is also an honorable person who deceives Paul only because she wants justice for her murdered brother. Ned compares her to the biblical Judith (144–45), but Janet never has sex with Paul and is upset when he kisses her. In Janet's dream that gives the novel its name, she and Ned are trying to get into a room filled with food but the glass key to the door breaks. They force the door and are overwhelmed by the snakes guarding the place. This symbolic representation of their place in a world of violence and evil reinforces their difference from the others.

Janet, with her pale blondness, aristocratic heritage, and elegant appearance, exemplifies the qualities 1931 America, as well as our society today, associate with female value. She has a childlike belief that goodness and badness are absolute opposites. She reacts to a man unexpectedly and uninvitedly kissing her with outrage and nearly incapacitating horror. She turns to Ned as the protector she needs, trailing after him following her father's arrest. Perhaps the Coens were inspired by Ned's calling her Judith—in a reference to the biblical character who seduces her tribe's enemy to vanquish him—to reimagine this character, who is so set on protecting her brother, as a Jew. But that change necessitates many others if the story is to remain set in the late 1920s.

Because Verna is a Jew, she must be a survivor, not a protected princess, because anti-Semitism is the norm in her world. As Nathan Abrams says, "Verna's toughness ensures her survival in the male domain of the underworld" (*New Jew in Film*, 128) but also in the ordinary world where she is despised as a "Sheeny," "Hebrew," and "Yid," slurs used to refer to her brother throughout the film (101). Only Leo, blinded by his passion for her, sentimentalizes her, and even he eventually accepts that a woman like her could not be sexually chaste. As a member of an oppressed and despised minority who will soon begin to be systematically slaughtered in Europe, and who have been informally persecuted and murdered there and in the United States for generations, she has no faith in any justice system and is completely cynical. She is also self-hating, attracted to Tom because, as she tells him, she thinks he is a bad person like her. Her devotion to her brother has nothing in it of honor and decency, like Janet's determination to avenge the death of her brother, Taylor. Instead, it seems desperate. Though he apparently cares little for her, dismissing her as a "whore," he is all she has in a world of exploiters. Abrams's description of Verna as simultaneously "a coldly manipulative hyper-sexual Jewess" and "caring and family-minded" (*New Jew in Film*, 205) ignores the difficulties of her situation in which, despite her toughness, she clearly needs to secure a permanent male protector if she wants to avoid being prostituted to one man after another.

Verna gives up on Tom only when he refuses to leave town with her (as Ned does with Janet) and instead stays to make sure Leo's position is secure. She realizes that Tom has always put Leo first. The final blow is, no doubt, to learn that Bernie is dead, and although Tom has made it appear that Caspar killed Bernie, she probably guesses that Tom killed her brother himself. Then she chooses Leo. As we have seen, Leo risked his position and even his own life and sacrificed dozens of his soldiers rather than make her unhappy by giving Caspar permission to kill Bernie. Clearly, he puts her needs before his own or anyone else's. Given that she is completely vulnerable in a world of vicious violence, she makes a reasonable choice.

Tom's choices are harder to understand. Paul Coughlin remarks of Tom, "The central enigma of Miller's Crossing is Tom's agenda." As he says to Leo at the conclusion, "Do you always know why you do things?" Does he love Verna, as he once says? Or is that apparent admission just another of his many tricks? Why does he kill Bernie when he does and not earlier in the woods when doing so would have benefited him? Did he feel sorry for Bernie initially and then feel enraged by Bernie's blackmail attempt or was he simply saving Bernie to use later? But unlike Morgan Meis and J. M. Tyree, who argue that "the twisted motivations that make up *Miller's Crossing*" are not "decodable" (70–71), I see them as illuminated by close attention to the hints we get about Tom's nonnormative and essentially masochistic sexuality.

In *The Glass Key*, Ned's tormentors tauntingly accuse him of enjoying their beatings because he not only refuses to give the information demanded of him but maintains a smart aleck demeanor, but unlike Tom, who, as Sheila Benson notes, shows almost no sign of injury after enduring severe beatings, Ned suffers terribly and is hospitalized. The unrealistic lack of injury that allows Tom to deliver witty ripostes to his attackers and demonstrate a sort of self-satisfied defiance makes him seem like a participant in consensual and theatrical S/M scenes in a way Ned does not. Jeff, the gorilla-like thug who works for and, like Eddie the Dane, is eventually killed by his boss, calls Ned a "massacrist" (185), but we see little evidence of that. Ned is aggressive with anyone who tries to hurt him. Tom, in contrast, never fights back when Verna punches him in the face or when he is much more severely beaten by Caspar's men, Leo, and the enforcers of the loan shark Lazarre. Nolan is right to read the staging of these beatings as sexually suggestive (57), but what they suggest to me is that Tom is masochistic, taking perverse pleasure in being punished for his inability to conform to heteronormativity. This interpretation is supported by Tom's gambling. Unlike Ned, who is a professional gambler and consistently wins throughout Hammett's story, Tom perfectly fits the stereotype of a compulsive gambler who plays until he loses everything. In the same spirit, he plays his role in the plot he has devised to protect Leo until he loses Leo, Verna, and his place in the city.

We do not know, any more than he does, why he does what he does, but we have hints. The insertion of three sexually active and passionate gay men into the story allows for an interpretation that holds together, leaving no detail out—except why he has a sexual relationship with Verna at all. If Tom is in love with Leo, his devotion to him is not beyond reason, as it appears to Verna, but simply exists in that wild card zone where passion dictates all. If we follow the Dane's suggestion that he is bisexual, which is

Fig. 6.1 *Miller's Crossing*: Irresistible Verna.

the meaning Nolan ascribes to the Dane's saying Tom is "straight with your frail and queer with Johnny Caspar" (51), then the dalliance with Verna also makes sense. Tom and Leo are not having sex with each other, and there is no indication that Leo has any feelings beyond sentimental, platonic love for Tom. So, Tom would need the outlet of an active sexual relationship. Still, it puts tremendous weight on the idea of Verna's sexual irresistibility that he chooses her, since obviously there are other women in the city, even the hatcheck girl who pops into the story and slaps Tom for standing her up after his night with Verna.

If all Tom wants from a woman is that she be a willing sexual partner, why must he choose the one who will cause trouble between him and his real love, Leo? And why does Leo, after finding out that Verna is deceiving him, decide to marry her anyway? After a while it seems odd that Bernie refuses her offer to help him become straight by having sex with him since her sexual power is so great. Then again Bernie is busy getting Mink to risk his life, and finally lose it, through his own sexual allure.

VII. Those Darn Sexy Jews!

In this film the Jews might as well be stars in 1960s Bollywood. Or starring in an anti-Semitic fantasy of our subversive power. They ruin everything for the Gentiles and without ever conforming to American beauty standards. That last part is important because in American cinema Jews who inspire desire are almost always the ones who can pass for Gentiles, and when they cannot, they end up with unattractive (by American mainstream standards) Jews who look like them.[9]

Particularly interesting here is the role played by Bernie. A bit of a whore himself, he uses his rather sleazy charm to survive financially in the world in which he finds himself, easily taking away the kept boy's affections from his big Scandinavian protector. (The Coens mark Eddie as Scandinavian by having all the other characters call him *the* Dane, not Eddie Dane.) Bernie contrasts the Dane, whose cadaverous appearance is the antithesis of glamour and makes him seem the embodiment of death. The film makes the point that far from achieving power due to great wealth (obtained through trickery) most ordinary Jews have whatever power and influence we do through our ability to appeal to the ruling group, and that appeal is fairly frequently sexual. Small, weak, and whiny, Bernie is uncannily like an early Woody Allen character who can wheedle his way out of almost anything. He only fails the second time he attempts to talk Tom out of shooting him. It is vital to note that it is not his looks that cause this failure but his lack of the sort of militaristic masculinity that defines honor for Tom. He lacks the pride that makes a man willing to die rather than cry and beg. In other words, he chooses survival at any cost, as oppressed people under the threat of extinction must do if their group is to survive. And the price of that survival is always some sort of seduction of the powerful.

Like many Coen films, this one pushes us to see the world differently than it is conventionally imagined in American film. And if we cannot do that, then at least to recognize that another vision is possible. The Coens' Jewish brother and sister may look ugly by American beauty standards. Harden, who went on to play Jewish women in several other films, although Gentile, is dark, has very curly black hair and a long, slightly hooked nose and is curvier than Hollywood generally prefers in a serious drama's love interest. But both Verna and Bernie are highly desirable sexual objects to the other characters in the film—in fact, they are irresistible. And they do not use that sexual power to take advantage of the innocent, as sexy Jews tend to do in European films. They use it to try to survive in a world where they have no other power at all. And Verna, at least, does so successfully. We may be reminded of John Goodman's character in *The Big Lebowski* (1998), who converted to Orthodox Judaism for his ex-wife, as we see Leo wearing a yarmulke as he stands beside Verna at Bernie's funeral.

Bernie's nickname, "The Schmatte"—Yiddish for "the rag"—references the notorious Jewish rag-and-bone men, immigrants at the very bottom of urban economies. For that reason, it became a slur indicating Jewishness in America. The word also suggests the Nazi euphemism for Jewish victims, "pieces" in English. The idea of a huge battle over the killing of a Jew invokes World War II, an idea reinforced by our awareness of the events taking place in Germany at the time in which the film is set.[10] The film illustrates the shifting perspectives possible as art is viewed at different times in history and by different audiences. Like much cinema with cult followings, it functions like a lenticular print, which reveals different images depending on the angle from which it is viewed. And as is repeated by both Tom and Bernie, "There is always an angle." In our current age of awareness of sexual diversity, we can easily see Tom as being in love with Leo, whereas to the film's initial viewers, he probably typically seemed heterosexual. (As Mizejewski demonstrates, "later film scholars" commonly see the relationship between Tom and Leo as "homoerotic" [40].) Likewise Jewish audience members who see the film as commenting on the world of violence leading up to World War II may interpret Bernie and Verna as I do—as sympathetic characters—whereas those looking at them as representations of Jews pointlessly added to a Hammett tale may find them offensive. But whatever angle we approach the film from, what is always clear is the way Verna and Bernie cannot be resisted sexually.

Among many things that Ruth Wisse praises in the Coens' 2009 film, *A Serious Man*, is its use of a famous Yiddish song called "A Miller's Tears" about the exile of an old Jew who must leave his home because the mill where he has always worked is now closing and the people who tolerated him because of his job are now against him. He hears the townspeople talk of chasing him away since he no longer has a function serving them. Full of pathos and despair, the song invokes the precariousness of Jewish existence. I wonder if the Coens were inspired by this song for the title of their earlier film.

This song might help us see the differences and similarities between Bernie and Tom. Like the Miller, Tom must leave town, but unlike Bernie, who risks and ultimately loses his life because he cannot face taking to the road without money or friends, Tom belongs to the Irish immigrant group who, by the late 1920s, have been accepted in much of America as white and have consequently been able to provide some protection for each other as members of established power groups in politics, law enforcement, and organized crime, while Jews maintained a foothold only in the latter. As Bernie says, he cannot just go away the way Tom told him to when he spared his life in the woods as he has no resources, no money, and no friends to help him survive elsewhere. His choices are to become a vulnerable wanderer or stay and fight to survive in a hostile city. He makes the latter choice and loses everything, as did so many European Jews who chose to stay and fight in Europe in the 1930s. Bernie is a stereotype, as the film's detractors claim, but what sort? Is he a manipulator, a victim, or a hero? And what of his sister, Verna? Possibly they are all three things and more through their sexualization and racialization, simultaneously bad Jews and good Jews. And thus the overloaded stereotype explodes.

VIII. Somebody (Jewish) to Love

A Serious Man (2009) takes us into an era more than two decades later, May 1967, in which Jews are largely accepted as Americans, if not quite white ones, and like the Irish earlier, they have their own enclave, in this case in the suburbs, where they belong and have the numbers that provide some safety. Unlike Bernie, but like Tom, they can choose to be ethical and still survive, although as we soon see, the costs of ethical choices are just as heavy as those for unethical ones. The film begins with a prologue, in English-subtitled Yiddish, depicting a strange incident in a nineteenth-century Eastern European shtetl when a man brings home to dinner a person he claims is their famously holy rabbi but whom his wife believes is a dybbuk (according to Jewish folklore, a malevolent spirit that possesses a human body). We see her stab him in the chest. The film then cuts to 1967 suburban Minnesota and follows an unhappy period in the life of Larry Gopnik (Michael Stuhlbarg), a physics professor who must contend with his wife, Judith (Sari Lennick), leaving him for another man, the disgustingly smug Sy Ableman (Fred Melamed); his son, Danny (Aaron Wolff), abandoning Jewish traditions to get high on marijuana and listen to Jefferson Airplane; and his brother, Arthur (Richard Kind), sleeping on their couch and apparently suffering some sort of breakdown.

And then things get worse. Larry is forced by Judith to move to a hotel because she has cleaned out the couple's bank account. Larry finds that Sy has interfered in his tenure case with false allegations. A failing student, Clive Park (Kang David), tries to bribe Larry into giving him a passing grade, and his father threatens to accuse Larry of misconduct and sue if

Larry refuses the money. Larry learns that Arthur is under indictment for solicitation and sodomy. Then Sy is killed in a traffic accident.

Larry seeks help to understand all this from three rabbis but only finds deeper confusion. The first one simply foists on him some pop psychology about positive thinking, the next tells a bizarre story about a dentist who saw Hebrew letters spelling out the word *Hoshiayni* ("Help me, save me") engraved on a Gentile patient's teeth. When Larry asks, "What happened to the goy?" the rabbi answers in surprise, "Who cares?" The last of the three rabbis, the most learned and reputed for his wisdom, just (mis)quotes to him the lyrics of the song "Somebody to Love." Larry helps his brother escape to Canada, accepts Park's bribe so that he can pay Arthur's lawyer, and then immediately learns that although he has been granted tenure, his doctor believes he has lung cancer. Additionally, we see that a tornado is about to hit the high school Danny attends.

And if you have to ask why I thought this was so funny, you would not understand either why my mother laughed bitterly at the phrase "the luck of the Irish" and my father always told her, "Yeah, but at least it's better than being one of 'the chosen people.'" Although what got me at the end was the credit sequence in which we learn that the shtetl wife was right: that holy old rabbi was, indeed, a dybbuk. That is when I began rolling on the floor in glee at the idea that sometimes the holiest of holy ones just seems like another dybbuk sent to torment us. As Alan A. Stone says, the film is "simultaneously sad and funny, the defining emotional dialectic of the Jewish sensibility" (49).

Most critics of the film discuss the foundational role played by the biblical story of Job. Ian Nathan, for example, says that while it is filled with autobiographical detail, it is essentially "a rewriting of the Book of Job" (83). And John Anderson entitles his review "Job in Minnesota." But Wisse seems most astute in her claim that although Larry's "unmerited punishment is meant to evoke that man in the Land of Uz who was 'perfect and upright, and . . . feared God and turned away from evil,'" in Wisse's view, Larry is "less like Job than like the schlemiel of Jewish folk humor, Larry simply lacks the imagination to engage in the kind of thieving, adultery, and bearing false witness that goes on around him. He wants to believe in a perfect and upright world, and only when misfortune begins singling him out in earnest does he try to learn why bad things happen to good people." He also wants to believe that religion holds the answers, but how can it when spiritual leaders are a bunch of dybbuks?

Anne Brener, a rabbi who is most definitely not a dybbuk, praises the film's depiction of "a precise moment in time and place," post-Holocaust and just prior to the Six-Day War. She says the film expresses the angst felt by her (and my) generation who "learned from teachers who had likely not yet come to terms (literally) with what was rumbling in their shocked and tormented psyches. They foisted upon us a rote Judaism, whose essence we could not understand. . . . They couldn't help it. They were stunned and grieving. They were wrestling with their faith. For many of them, the words of the Jefferson Airplane song, which frame the film, might ring true, 'When the truth is found to be lies, and all the joy within you dies.'" And as she notes, the final rabbi substitutes the word *hope* for *joy* in his misquoting of the song. Harlan Jacobsen is harsher, praising the film for depicting "the rabbinate as just one more manifestation of American charlatanism" (47). Failed by spiritual leaders, and poised between being despised as victims and being despised as victimizers in a world without meaning or connection, we are left, as the film suggests, hardly able to think of God Himself as anything but another dybbuk.

Ian Nathan claims that "Larry's is not just the Jewish condition: it is the human condition" (85), but I disagree. The film is very much about the differences between Jews and Gentiles. And the weirdest aspects of the film suggest laudable things about Jews. The story of the goy's teeth could be read as indicative of the Jewish attitude that marks us as different from Gentiles even when the Jews in question are very religious and conservative. Non-Jews just do not matter, so the ultra-religious do not care about enforcing religious morality laws on non-Jews. The Haredi (ultra-religious Jews) have very strict rules about sex, including gendered dress codes and the prohibition of nonfamilial physical contact between men and women, but they treat them as choices. One can choose to practice Judaism, to obey all the rules, to live a moral life as dictated by rabbinical interpretation of Talmud. But one can also choose not to identify as a Jew on these or any other terms. Gentiles may still regard one as a Jew, but the ultra-Orthodox will not. And if you choose not to be a Jew, who cares what you do? As I discuss earlier, this is no doubt what annoys Christian conservatives about Jews. We do not care about other people's sex lives; like Christianity's own Jew, Jesus, we do not judge the woman taken in adultery. We do not demand that the entire world be constrained by civil law to do or not do specific things with their sexualities. We refuse to impose our religious rules on nonbelievers.

And the film, although anything but ultra-religious, takes this same attitude. Larry's teenaged daughter, Sarah (Jessica McManus), is constantly washing her long, silky hair and fussing about getting a nose job, although the camera loves her beauty and shows it to us amply. Stone calls her "the embodiment of vanity," but no harm comes to her for this vanity (49). Nor does any harm come either to Larry's dope-smoking, hedonistic, and adulterous neighbor, Vivienne, played by Amy Landecker, looking much more attractive than she does in *Transparent*, or even to Larry for fantasizing and literally dreaming about sex with her. As the Jefferson Airplane misquote suggests, when all the hope within you dies, what consolation is left but the joy of physical beauty and the sexual pleasure it promises? The way the film refuses to tell a morality tale that fits with the current fundamentalist Christian obsession with managing the sexuality of others as one's highest religious duty and instead treats the bad things that happen to good people as random and mysterious; the way it insists on the incomprehensibility of the ways of God, while still leaving room for there to *be* a God; and the way it values sexuality as a comfort are all quintessentially Jewish but also, as Rabbi Brener argues, belong to the Jewishness of a particular moment in time. We live in the moment in which Jews had to reinvent ourselves to recover connections to the world and the divine or else had to face a world in which all hope was irretrievably dead. And as the film's stereotypes suggest, through being stretched to the breaking point, we will need to continue to reinvent ourselves to transcend this historical moment and live on.

IX. Between Jews

Inside Llewyn Davis (2013) is aptly named because it takes us much deeper into the issue of Jewish identities and suggests that the Jew we do not see is more important than the one we do as it is that one who has all the beauty and power and sexiness, that one who avoids being caught in a confining stereotype and instead enters endless revisionary resignifications. Like *A Serious Man*, which begins in Yiddish, *Inside Llewyn Davis* refuses to define Hebrew and Yiddish terms in the main part of the film or to explain throughout such important plot elements as what the appearance of a dybbuk means or what is expected at a bar mitzvah, *Inside Llewyn Davis* was obviously made for a Jewish audience or at least an audience to whom Jewish identity issues matter.

Inside Llewyn Davis addresses self-identified Jewish audiences while also allowing for audience responses from those, Jewish and not, who believe that Jews are now seen as racially unmarked white people. As Jonathan Romney writes in his review in *Film Comment*, the film can be read as a compact history of the development of the folk music scene of the early 1960s. But in my reading of the film, concepts of Jewish identity, offered up for Jewish audience members' identification, urge responses that will differ from those of audience members who do not identify as racialized Jews. Where such audiences may see stereotypes, we have the option of recognizing their Deleuzian resignification. Crucial to this reading is the film's structure, in which the dramatization of Llewyn Davis's story is set between two scenes in which we can hear the beginnings of Bob Dylan's career, which was to revolutionize folk music performance. Such Jewish bookending is also a feature of the paired scenes in which Davis interacts with Jewish intellectual supporters of the folk music culture. This interpretation will lead to an examination of how such double address, pervasive in the films of the Coen brothers, functions in relation to a Jewish double consciousness similar to that which W. E. B. Du Bois and Frantz Fanon attribute to Black people but different in a few crucial ways.

The Coens' use of double address works as a subtle intervention into the usual racist cinematic portrayals of Jews. They use diegetic sounds that foster interpretation that goes against the grain of the images and the perspective privileged in the narrative through POV shots. In so doing, the film "facilitate[s] the creation of a people who have hitherto been missing," reinscribing the racialized Jews that cinematic histories of folk music often erase, but it does not stop there. Its real subject, the one we cannot actually see but who is omnipresent thanks to the framing, is Dylan, a master of self-reinvention,

When it comes to Jewish responses to film, *Inside Llewyn Davis* stands out as particularly polarizing, nearly as much so as *Barton Fink*. Hoberman ignited a firestorm of angry response when he wrote of the protagonist, "Llewyn is of indeterminate ethnicity but definitely gentile—if only because he is far too appealing to be a Jew in Coenville" ("Coen Bros. Torture Another Schlemiel"). In that the Coens, by their own admission, based Llewyn on Dave Van Ronk, who described himself as "mostly Irish, despite the Dutch name" and was raised as an Irish Catholic, Hoberman's claim about Llewyn's Gentile identity seems defensible. However, many self-identified Jews replied indignantly defending both the film, which

Hoberman harshly criticizes, as he does almost all of the Coens' work, and the idea that Llewyn is not meant to be seen as Jewish. Armond White dislikes the film but proclaims, "Llewyn is a modern Wandering Jew who, like Dylan, dare not speak his ethnicity (his name is a Welsh creation like Dylan's chosen's moniker)." As he sees it, the film's biggest flaw is that it "question[s] Jewish alienation [merely] superficially." In the online magazine *Reform Judaism*, Rabbi Andy Bachman not only praises the film as essential to an understanding of New York Jewish heritage, he jokes that Llewyn's singing "The Shoals of Herring" shows he is a Jew, because Jews love herring.

In *The Black Atlantic*, Paul Gilroy generously invites Jews to think about our own double consciousness in ways similar to that urged on Black people in diaspora by Dubois and Fanon (205–12). That is, we are invited to think of ourselves as having a colonized consciousness that splits our perceptions between a minoritarian consciousness determined by our situation as racialized subjects, and which makes us feel inferior and estranged, and a majoritist vision that we misrecognize as objective and universal but that is, in fact, derived from the dominant culture. But as Gilroy points out, the situation of Jews differs from that of Blacks for two major reasons (207). First, in most official political circumstances, we are in effect white. And second, even before being granted this privileged status, we could often pass for white by changing our names and rejecting any part of our heritage that our families of origin had maintained.

After World War II, many people came to see the racialization of Jews as a bad thing and Jewishness was often described as referring only to religious belief. However, as this seemed inadequate to many secular Jews and Jews who followed religions other than Judaism, others began to designate Jewishness as an ethnicity. We are now stuck with the bizarre situation I explored in this book's introduction. While some people profess or practice extreme forms of anti-Semitism inveighing against and sometimes physically attacking or killing people with Jewish surnames but without religious or ethnic community associations, and who (like me) do not even like herring, others insist impatiently that Jews need to stop pretending to be anything other than white people so that we can join them in confronting our white privilege. And let us not forget the contingents of anti-Semites who ignore the very existence of Middle Eastern Jews and argue that all European Jews are descended from converts and, consequently, there are no descendants of the biblical Jews alive today.

Into this madness move the Coen brothers as they place Llewyn Davis into their re-creation of the 1960s folk scene just at the moment of its shift from an intellectual focus on an authenticity defined in terms of faithfulness to archaic roots to a widely popular form, whose claims to authenticity derived from individual expression, a movement which Bob Dylan is often credited with disseminating. The film opens and closes bookended by Dylan's singing (off screen) at the Gaslight Theater while Llewyn is being beaten up in the alley by a man who is angry because Llewyn heckled his wife's performance on the autoharp. In the second version of the scene, Dylan's voice is much more audible, to the point that his set seems especially portentous. Francesco Sticchi argues that "the final appearance of Dylan, as [the] only authentic innovation in the musical panorama, reiterates and reinstates the state of immobility and fallacy of the main character" (141). But Dylan does not actually appear to us except for a moment, although he does to the patrons of the Gaslight Theater. We hear his song "Farewell" as a diegetic background to Llewyn's departure and the film's conclusion. Just as Llewyn considers his attacker's wife's singing and playing silly and outdated, so will the next generation regard Llewyn as one who never even made enough of a mark to be a has-been.

But in a context that is all about authenticity, what does it mean that Dylan is depicted as the opposite of Llewyn? One of the most interesting things to some Jews about Todd Haynes's postmodernist Dylan biopic, *I'm Not There* (2007), in which six different actors play different Dylan personas, is that the one persona missing is Bob Zimmerman, or Dylan the Jew. Llewyn, the folk purist whose Welsh heritage we are really given no reason to doubt, is blown out of the scene by the mighty winds of a Jewish fake Welshman in what could be read as a stunningly self-hating reiteration of the stereotype of Jews as crafty chameleons, one of the anti-Semitic stereotypes of Jews mentioned in every study of Jewish representation in cinema. But this reading, which would accord well with Hoberman's complaints about the Coens, is problematized by the film's other bookends: Llewyn's interactions with his would-be patrons, Mitch (Ethan Phillips) and Lillian Gorfein (Robin Bartlett), who are unambiguously marked as Jews, although reviewers are far from seeing them unambiguously.

While Hoberman predictably alludes to the couple as Jewish "grotesques," Adam Nayman describes the Gorfeins as "an older married pair of academics depicted, teasingly but affectionately, as endlessly generous and indulgent Upper West Siders who offer Llewyn food, shelter, and support in spite of his being a sorry mess." One could easily interpret them as foils to Llewyn. Llewyn's second attempt to mooch off them and spend a night on their couch ends when he bursts into a rage because, after making a place for him at their table and praising him to their other guests, Lillian invites him to sing a postprandial duet with her. Although he never explains why this request makes him so angry, it seems to be caused by his frustrated desire to be seen as a professional and to differentiate himself from mere fans of folk music. His rejection of the commercialization of folk music through efforts like Dylan's to use it to express—and market—the artist's own emotions is matched in angry intensity by his refusal to casually enjoy the music or tolerate anyone else doing so. That folk music can be consumed as casual home entertainment sends him into a furious frenzy. Yet he is also infuriated that his own approach to folk music as a historical preservation project is not financially rewarded and brings him no success.

In contrast the Gorfeins represent a sensible relationship to music. They know what they like, they support the artists who make the music as much as they reasonably can—offering their couch on a first come, first served basis—but they also realize that they need to have jobs outside the music industry so that they can be free to enjoy the music on their own terms. Next to them Llewyn seems absurdly childish.

And this helps clarify the relationship between his fall and Dylan's rise. While Dylan did initially present himself on the New York folk scene with a Gentile name, he was soon generally known to be a Jew. But beyond that outing of his racialized identity, which may not have been his own choice, was what he *did* choose: Dylan chose to depart from the two conventions governing the folk music scene in the early 1960s, protesting specific topical issues from a Leftist perspective and re-creating traditional songs and performances. Instead, Dylan chose, as Haynes's film celebrates, to inhabit a persona, to construct an identity from whom the songs seemed to emanate as if from the heart. Llewyn's performances are embarrassing because the more he strains to make them seem authentic the more mannered and false they sound. He does not sound like a turn-of-the-nineteenth-century fisherman or have the affect of one when he sings "The Shoals of Herring," nor does his rendition of "Hang Me, Oh Hang Me" evoke the world-weary outlaw of the lyrics. In comparison, when one hears Dylan sing, for example, "Don't Think Twice It's All Right" or "I Want You" or, my favorite, "It Ain't Me Babe" recorded around the same time as the film's setting, it is nearly impossible to believe he is not coming directly out of a personal experience and giving voice to exactly what he feels. The inclusion of "Blowin' in the Wind" in Regina King's film *One Night in Miami*, as an inspiration for Sam Cooke's "A Change Is Gonna Come," represents this personal experience more than the characters in King's film know. They see the song as being about their own experience of minoritization, but the opening question, "How many roads must a man walk down / Before you call him a man," could just as easily be interpreted as arising from Dylan's early life as a "Jew boy" in majority white and Protestant Minnesota. His songs are minoritarian musicianship par excellence in their refusal, as Deleuze puts it, "to represent the conditions of an oppressed minority" in general terms. Instead, the songs represent "the Jew" as a very specific Jew whose very specificity pushes us to see Jewish sexuality differently, not as being about rebelliously desiring to possess a Gentile woman in order to establish his manhood or defeatedly settling for another Jew but about desiring sexual satisfaction that does not come at the expense of freedom to self-define. And even though Dylan's physical appearance never matched American standards of male attractiveness, for his fans it was nearly impossible not to feel his sexual charisma. In contrast, Llewyn's sexuality and its expression are repugnant.

The darkly comedic subplot of Llewyn's attempts to mollify his friend Jim's wife, Jean, whom he impregnated, provides a gloss on Llewyn's character. He arranges for an abortion, at her demand, and, in doing so, finds out that three years earlier when he paid the same doctor to provide one for a girlfriend, she decided instead to leave New York and have the child, without informing him of her decision or his fatherhood. And this seems to be a wise choice on her part, since he shows absolutely no emotion at this revelation. While the singer standing in for Dylan off-screen reminds us of Dylan's amazing outpourings of feeling that made his work deeply moving to generations of fans, Llewyn seems as dry and cold as it is humanly possible to be. He faithfully preserves folk music as if he were the dead page on which the music is written. And whereas the Gorfeins choose again and again to accept the music makers into their lives so that they can feel the music inside them, can make it theirs through joining in, Llewyn is animated only by disdain, as when he heckles the earnest singer whose husband beats him in the end.

What really beats him in the end, though, is his steadfast attachment to his identity as a true heir of folk music. To a large extent, as the Coens make clear, a Jew simply cannot take on the role of an insider folksy American preserving his or her own heritage. (This is one of the things that makes the Coens' return to their Minnesota roots in *A Serious Man* so hilarious. Larry's battle with his Gentile neighbor over the legal boundary between their properties is a parody of the Six-Day War, an absurdity because, like the war, it entails a hopeless effort to be seen as in the right by people who do not consider Jews legitimate possessors of the land.) We come to the songs that came from Western cowboys and outlaws, Appalachians, dust bowl refugees, and East Coast fishermen from the outside. We do not learn them at our daddies' knees as we sit on the cabin floor. Never really accepted as true Americans, which is one reason we have never had a Jewish president, we construct provisional identities for ourselves that, like Dylan's, express a reality to which we relate despite a culture that tells us we are only imposters, and like the Gorfeins, we open ourselves to a world that is often hostile to us and take from it what hope and joy we can.

Through their positioning of Llewyn Davis between Jews, the Coens suggest to an audience of Jews "with no direction home"—a lyric from "Like a Rolling Stone" and the title of Martin Scorsese's 2005 documentary on Dylan's career—that we can make a home of America by embracing our outsider status and using it, as Gilroy exhorts us to do, to form coalitions with the others who are excluded. For Dylan, as for the Gorfeins, the music of the common people is there for the claiming, to be used to demonstrate that we do not want to ally ourselves with those unmarked ones, the privileged, the norm, the mainstream but rather with the poor, the workers, the outlaws, the failures, and, perhaps most of all, the racialized Others. Instead of claiming a right to the land and establishing ownership, Dylan casts himself over and over, as he does in "Farewell," as a wandering Jew, not by a cursed destiny but by his choice to throw in his lot with the dispossessed. Llewyn is an outcast who wants to get in but is too proud of his own bleak authenticity to bend enough to fit anywhere.

X. Conclusion

The film asks Jews, who lack an unrestricted range of choices, and from whom identity construction and reconstruction are demanded, who are culturally denied anything resembling a stable selfhood like the one of which Llewyn is so proud, what we want to belong to and what we need to make of ourselves so as to do so. The Coens make Llewyn available to Jews in the audience as a figure with whom we may identify, whom we may choose to interpret as Jewish, but they place him between Jews who are clearly identified as such to remind us of who we have been in the American past and how we might work with that heritage. All the Jews in the Coen brothers' films push the stereotypes of Jewish racialization to the limit, not to denigrate Jews, but to detach us from the myths of assimilation into whiteness and so to make possible future productive identifications, ones that do not exist in majority discourse but that are everywhere in minoritarian art.

Notes

1. Similarly, *Transparent*'s Pfeffermans begin the series dissatisfied with conventional heterosexuality and the gender roles it demands and struggling to find satisfying alternatives and end the series five years later the same way. The last complete season, the fourth, wraps up with revelations in which family members tell each other what the audience has known all along, that their behaviors and personalities were formed by specific early traumatic sexual experiences. The musical finale that constitutes season 5 is framed as what the matriarch, Shelley, calls "a Joy-ocaust" in which they try to overcome the sense of themselves as doomed losers and to accept themselves as they are and have always been.

2. Deleuze declares that "this acknowledgement of people that are missing is not a renunciation of political cinema, but on the contrary the new basis on which it is founded, in the third world and for minorities" (217).

3. Hoberman describes the characters in *A Serious Man* and *Inside Llewyn Davis* this way in a November 21, 2013, review of the latter film in *Tablet*, also remarking that Bernie in *Miller's Crossing* is "appalling."

4. As numerous nose-measuring studies have shown, Jews do not have larger or more hooked noses than people in any other group. This is a myth generated in medieval Europe as explained in Sara Lipton's *Dark Mirror: The Medieval Origins of Anti-Jewish Iconography*.

5. See David L. Reznik's *New Jews: Race and American Jewish Identity in 21st-Century Film* for extensive discussion of cinematic portrayal of Jews as physically unattractive.

6. In *The Owl and the Pussycat*, where Streisand plays a prostitute who aspires to be an actress and is paired with a would-be writer played by George Segal, she is represented as far more seductive. In the play on which the film was based, the relationship is interracial, Streisand's role having originally been written for a Black actress. Neither she nor Segal are strongly racialized in the film, but the audience would likely be aware of the Jewishness of both the actors and their characters. And the ultimate success of their love affair, therefore, seems possible because they are both Jews.

7. It is interesting, given the history of Jewish actresses in Bollywood films, that Christopher Sharrett says that if, in *Gilda*, Hayworth is presented as "the reigning 'sex goddess' of her era," she has the attributes of the Hindu goddess Kali (2).

8. Numerous critics note that, as the Coens themselves have said, Hammett's *Red Harvest* is also an influence on the film. Like *Miller's Crossing* and *The Glass Key*, it deals with a corrupt small town, in this case Personville (aka Poisonville), a corrupt mining town. And the novel includes a troublemaking woman, Dinah Brand, who is "thoroughly mercenary" and "cold-blooded" (27). She is also a double crosser, who has "a gift for stirring

up murderous notions in [her] boyfriends" (159). Corrupt boxing is also a theme in this novel, but there the obvious resemblances of *Red Harvest* to *Miller's Crossing* end.

9. We might contrast Bernie to Wolfe in *Villain*, discussed in chapter 4. Although Wolfe's gangster boyfriend, Vic, seems devoid of tender feelings, he is arrested and loses everything because he cannot bring himself to escape without his beloved "boy" by his side, and as Vic begs a reluctant Wolfe to come with him, a police dragnet closes in.

10. Nathan Abrams provides a useful overview of critical opinions on "archetypal Holocaust imagery" in the forest scene where Tom decides not to shoot Bernie (*New Jew in Film*, 102). However, I disagree with his reading of Bernie as a stereotypical Jewish villain whom audiences cannot pity. Responses to the film, such as William Nolan's queer-positive one, call this assumption into question.

7

OUR ERASURE IS BEING TELEVISED

I. Anti-Semitism as the Fabric of Our Lives

In this, the final chapter of this book, I focus once more on American television because it is the visual entertainment form that is seen by and influences the largest number of people. As popular as the Coens' films have been, the Coens cannot hope to reach an audience anywhere near as big as that of American television. The gap between the casual visual entertainment seeker and the cinephile is brought home to me each year as I teach film classes to students in both groups. The former group is representative of the average American. People in this group do not generally recognize the names of directors and, instead, think of films in terms of their celebrity stars or their genres. They rarely, if ever, see art films or foreign language films. They may stream a film at home or go out to see a blockbuster movie as often as once a week, although once a month is more likely. But they see television shows every day or evening of their lives.

Mike S. Ryan's 2015 essay on the differences between television conventions and those of cinema, although dated in some ways as TV continues to change, is instructive, as it can help us understand how the two different audiences have been conditioned by the two different media to receive information from narratives. First of all, television typically fosters a more passive approach to interpreting a story than film does: "TV is primarily told from a third-person, objective point of view. A whole story told from the limited perspective of one character, or even more radically, from a narrator's perspective—whose point of view may actually be unreliable or not shared by any one actual character—would be way too complicated to be carried through multiple TV episodes. Likewise, the story as a subjective or interior exploration of character, mitigated by the director's own subjectivity, is primarily the realm of cinema" (Ryan). He emphasizes that

TV usually lacks the ambiguity of art film and tells us in fairly direct ways how to understand what we are seeing: "The idea that the film demands the viewer participate in the creation of meaning is utterly not an option on television" (Ryan). There are some changes in character behavior, but in order to hold viewer interest, it consists almost entirely of surprising reveals and reversals. Ryan explains this rather contemptuously, claiming that "meek" characters must always "after a few episodes, become aggressive and assertive. A female character's husband has to at some point come out as gay. An aggressive mob boss will in later episodes show his vulnerable fearful side."

Stuart Heritage is one of many who contest Ryan's extreme claims about characters on TV, saying that television series' character development is superior to that in films because "the intimacy of television, combined with the amount of time that actors spend in specific roles, means that viewers can become far more invested in television characters than film characters." Yet investment in a character does not mean the characterization calls for audience interpretation or even adds real complexity. Heritage gives as a supporting example Walter White (Bryan Cranston), the antihero of *Breaking Bad* (premiered 2008). He says that we can see White "transforming over two years of his life in a way that could never be achieved in film." But I do not see this. Instead, I see a very slow, and suspenseful, journey through five seasons to the final reveal of something any attentive viewer knew all along.

From the beginning we are given numerous clues that Walter is not, as he claims, self-sacrificingly cooking methamphetamine in order to provide for his family after his inevitable demise from cancer but, as he finally admits, doing it for the excitement and personal power it provides him, which reassures him that although he is dying of terminal cancer, he is still alive. Indeed, in a guide provided for the online journal *Filmmaking Stuff* in 2020, Scott Kirkpatrick sums up the issue of character development on television with this advice to script writers: "If a TV series is successful, it should be able to continue endlessly (episode after episode, season after season). To get there, characters must remain static which allows their dramatic or comedic structure to provide a theoretically endless number of 'episodes' to write. If your storytelling style lends itself to a character's transformation, [films] might be the way to go. However, if developing a framework of great characters that allow continuous story scenarios to pass through, then write a TV series." For these reasons, as I argued in the previous chapter, characters on TV are more likely than those in films to be static in easily recognizable ways—that is, they tend toward stereotypes, which is not inherently a bad thing but can be problematic when the stereotypes rely on negative views of a specific race (or gender or sexual orientation).

II. Racialization and Stereotyping

Rather than going into depth here to compare contrasting depictions of Jews in two series, as I did in chapter 5's consideration of twenty-first-century television series whose primary focus is an intersectional approach to American Jewish identifications, I will provide here an overview of stereotypically disagreeable Jewish characters in contemporary series. Unlike the play with stereotyping in the Coen brothers' films that I have discussed, this stereotyping does not stretch anti-Semitic ideas to the breaking point, does not resignify standard representations of Jews, and does not make possible new ways of seeing stock Jewish characters like the sleazy crook, the victimized whiner, or the rootless wanderer. This stereotyping causes weariness, not bliss. As Barthes remarks, one can make a claim that simple repetition of a stereotype "creates bliss," but as he adds, "I am not the one who would make such a claim" (41). Although he never says why such claims are annoying to him, one can easily guess. Like any other gay man, he could not be reasonably expected to take pleasure in seeing the seemingly endless repetitions of stereotypes of homosexuals that mainstream culture presents to amuse the heterosexual majority. Similarly, as a Jew, I do not find bliss in seeing images of stereotypical pathetic or detestable Jews. I also agree with Fran Markowitz in finding it vexing that "the Jews, a diverse and dispersed people, are often predefined as a timeless category of humanity" (263). Consequently, in this chapter my aim is not only to continue, as I have done throughout this study, to show that Jews are racialized and often, as a result, represented in much popular entertainment media as bad people who harm others. Here, in addition, I show how this racialization in television series has included the erasure of the realities of our history and the complexities of our identities as human beings.

My starting point here is one that may come as a surprise, since the series has been greeted with so much approval for its portrayal of a Jewish woman as a true heroine whose spunky attitude and perseverance we should admire. This is the popular television series *The Marvelous Mrs. Maisel*, which has so far successfully drawn audiences interested in the period directly before the rise of the counterculture, the sexual revolution, the gay liberation movement, and feminism's second wave changed sexuality in the United States dramatically. This chapter opening allows an exploration of how Jews are imagined approvingly by some feminists as innovators of what was, at the end of the 1950s, a new sexual openness and with the problems in popularizing this view, especially when the approval is given as the result of an ahistorical approach.

The television series, like Brodkin's *How the Jews Became White Folks*, treats Jewishness as a form of ethnic whiteness, and it depicts Jews in 1950s America as already assimilated into mainstream culture. Consequently it shows a general disregard for historical authenticity and a specific lack of representation of the Jewish struggle for acceptance in America. As Rohkl Kafrissen notes, "*Mrs. Maisel* takes place in a supersaturated fantasy 1958 New York, one where anti-Semitism, racism, homophobia, and even sexism are barely a whisper." This feel-good false history makes an interesting contrast to the more realistic treatments of the past in many of the films I have discussed because it illustrates what is at stake if we fantasize away the world that those who came before us were compelled to grapple with. In that sense it can also be seen as offering the same sort of blissful disregard of history that pervades *Call Me by Your Name*. Again, this is the sort of approach to pleasing audiences the repetition of which does not bring me bliss, although many others, including some Jews, feel otherwise. So once again I play the Jewish feminist killjoy.

III. Jewish Dream Girl or Nightmare JAP?

With the premiere of *The Marvelous Mrs. Maisel* in 2018, *Transparent* gained some serious competition as "the Jewiest show on television" (Debra Nussbaum Cohen). The main characters of *The Marvelous Mrs. Maisel* are all Jews, and every episode includes references to Jewish holidays and typical cultural practices of the times, including a compendium of Yiddish vocabulary, as Emily Burack details in an amusing review. The show does get a few things oddly wrong, as many commentators on the web point out, such as the heroine, Midge (Rachel Brosnahan), buying the roast for the rabbi's much-anticipated Rosh Hashanah visit at a nonkosher butcher shop that sells pork chops. But on the whole, the show strives to educate Gentiles about Judaism and to depict a late 1950s world in which Jews in New York City treated Judaism as an underlying structure of their lives.

Unfortunately, the show also includes numerous ugly stereotypes, such as Midge's father-in-law's fixation on making and saving money to the exclusion of everything else. Midge's mother, Rose Weissman (Marin Hinkle), aggressively runs the family, while her husband, Abe (Tony Shalhoub), a mathematics professor at Columbia University, weakly assents to her bossiness so that he can study in peace.

Perhaps because of this role modeling of a bitchy Jewish mother and her schlemiel mate, Midge is unlike the depressingly insecure and masochistic Jewish women we meet in *Transparent*. She is self-satisfied to the point that when her husband, Joel (Michael Zegen), announces that he is leaving her and has been carrying on an affair with Penny (Holly Curan), his secretary, her response is indignation based on her angrily reiterated view that she is not only much more intelligent than Penny but also has a more beautiful body and has always provided him with an exciting sex life due to her wild techniques. Her complete lack of any self-doubt is one of the most amazing things about the series. She knows she is superior to everyone with whom she comes in contact and seems to have no inhibitions about saying so. One might therefore see the series as providing an image of a strong and effective Jewish woman others should emulate. However, one can only take away this message if one ignores the many unpleasant aspects of Midge's portrayal.

The Amazon teaser for the show features the song "The Greatest Star" from *Funny Girl*, presumably to connect Midge to Fanny Brice, as played by Barbra Streisand. But unlike Brice or Streisand, she is not from a family that had to struggle financially but is instead a stereotypical Jewish American Princess (JAP) from the upper West Side. We see her dependence on her wealthy parents and her husband, who is also pampered and protected by his rich parents, to provide her with all the luxuries of life. Of course these characterizations play into the stereotyping of Jews as all belonging to a privileged wealthy elite. They are ahistorical since in the late 1950s not only were there many descendants of the impoverished Eastern European Jews still struggling to come out of poverty and enter the middle class but also an influx of refugees from the Holocaust were scrambling to reach that status in New York.[1]

But the series' focus is always on Midge as a feminist role model for twenty-first-century women. In keeping with current beauty standards, she is very thin and obsessed with her appearance, constantly exercising to maintain her perfect figure, the dimensions of which she measures every day. (And this is one of many false notes in the depiction of the fifties, because she does not aim for the soft, smooth appearance admired in women in those times but rather for the well-defined muscles admired today, as we see with her sculpted arms.) This battle to avoid conforming to the stereotypical film image of the Jewess as unathletic, overweight, and unfashionable is always connected to her contempt both for other Jews and for all other women. One of the few flashback scenes we see of her college life is of her, with the other young women, suffering the burning pain of dyeing blond not only the hair on her head but also her pubic hair. The scene is reminiscent of one in Paul Verhoeven's *Black Book* when the heroine, Rachel, does this to hide her Jewish identity from the Nazi she will seduce. Although in far less threatening circumstances, Midge similarly begins as a woman who seems to want to pass for Gentile, which would be easy to do as the actress playing the part, Rachel Brosnahan, is not Jewish.

In her comical wedding speech she confesses to treating college as a husband hunt and the names she gives of her dream husbands are all popular Gentile ones, and just in case we do not pick up on that, she emphasizes that she wanted her husband to be blond. She is pertly defiant of the propriety required of upper-class Jewish women who wished to be admitted to the Gentile social world of her times, as her mother's shocked reaction to her behavior tells us. But she also has no respect for Jewish religious beliefs, especially dietary laws. Her glee at horrifying her wedding guests with the revelation that the eggrolls they have just eaten contained shrimp gives us a preview of the naughtiness she will later exhibit as she bares her breasts, swears, and talks about sex in her standup comedy routines.

But rather than seeming truly groundbreaking, as the series seems to want us to think—and which only someone completely ignorant of the history of Jewish women comedians would think—she comes across as one of the bratty JAPs who exercise their privilege in numerous films and television series.[2] Traditionally Jewish American Princess was a term used to describe the spoiled and demanding daughters and wives of affluent Jewish men who deferred to their greedy consumerism and endured their selfishness and emotional coldness. As Nathan Abrams points out, in films made from the 1990s on, we see a "more modern JAP [who] is not as pernicious as her earlier incarnations" (*New Jew in Film*, 53). Still this does not seem to indicate things have changed much in representations of Jewish women, since Gretchen Weiners in *Mean Girls* (2004), Rachel Green in *Friends*

(1994–2004), and Shoshanna Shapiro (Zosia Mamet) in *Girls* (2012–2017) all fit the old stereotype, although Shoshanna, as Emily Shire argues, only does in the early seasons of the series. Shire provides a history of the JAP character noting, "The JAP image became so pervasive that in 1971, Julie Baumgold's article 'The Persistence of the Jewish Princess' appeared on the cover of *New York Magazine*. Baumgold defined Jewish princesses by their sense of entitlement, their self-absorption and their overconfidence in their subpar beauty." Examples Shire provides of entertainments that used the "crass, one-dimensional JAP for laughs" include Lila Kolodny (Jeannie Berlin) in *The Heartbreak Kid*, Elaine Lefkowitz (Dinah Manoff) in the TV series *Soap*, and Rhonda Weiss (Gilda Radner) on *Saturday Night Live*. She identifies Fran Drescher's Fran Fine on the 1990s show *The Nanny* as "the television character most commonly associated with the JAP stereotype," remarking that "Fran's nasal whine, love of shopping and general lack of decorum drove the plots and jokes of the series." Shlomi Deloia and Hannah Adelman Komy Ofir contest this view of Fran Fine, claiming "Drescher resurrected the 1920s image of the loud, flashy, and flirtatious Jewish ghetto girl to comically subvert the stereotype of the self-centered, manipulative, spoiled, and frigid Jewish American Princess" (133). I remain skeptical, first because, as I have discussed, the vulgar, sexual Jewish girl character features in numerous films and television series made long after the 1920s and because this stereotype is not incompatible with the stereotype of the JAP, as *The Marvelous Mrs. Maisel* shows through Midge's combination of self-centered, spoiled, manipulative behavior and flashy sexual vulgarity.

Reality television is the worst offender in terms of presenting us with JAPs to detest, in Shire's view, since "every Jewish woman on a 'Real Housewives' series seems like a living punch line for the corniest jokes. Materialistic, pampered and lazy, they embody the most obnoxious and obvious JAP traits." This claim is borne up by the heavily criticized *Princesses: Long Island* (2013). In contrast, as *Girls* progresses, Shoshanna "displays a vulnerability and earnestness that was notably lacking in previous JAP characterizations" (Shire). And like Nathan Abrams, Shire sees hope for the future as "Shoshanna is not the only JAP on TV that goes beyond a flat, stock character." She praises Rachel Berry (Lea Michele) on the TV series *Glee*, because while Rachel "is known for her self-involvedness, impatience and sense of entitlement," she "uses these qualities to move closer to her goal of becoming a Broadway star. She makes good on her kvetching through commitment to her professional dreams." One might say the same of Midge Maisel; however, unlike Rachel Berry, she does not mature and learn to treat others with respect and kindness.

In fact Midge reminds me of no one more than the petulant pixie persona Sarah Silverman often assumes, but in Silverman's case to mock the stereotype of the immature, self-centered JAP rather than embody it.[3] Critics are divided on this issue, with Marjorie Ingall arguing that by becoming a comedian who foregrounds her Jewishness and her femininity, Midge subverts the stereotypes that were being promulgated by Jewish male comics and novelists of the period in which the series is set. These male writers and comedians depicted Jewish women as unattractive scolds who cared about nothing but money. Marissa Brostoff, in contrast, argues that the show avoids analyzing the position of Jews in this crucial era of assimilation and "fall[s] back instead on tired tropes: dueling *machatunim* (in-laws), overbearing Jewish mothers." Emily Nussbaum is particularly hard on the show, calling it "cloying" and discussing the grossly unrealistic way it depicts its heroine as so absurdly adored by everyone she encounters that one must ask, since "her act rarely matches her charmed life—why would Midge, so wooed and worshipped, rave about how women are experts on rejection?" (89). This question is important because in this series, as in many fictions of all sorts, from novels to films, and notably in political commentary, Jews are represented as having an overblown sense of entitlement, being privileged but exhibiting an unearned sense of victimization.

The history of Jewish women as feminist leaders is also erased by the show's treatment of the other women characters. You would never know from this show that an era of feminist activism led by Jews like Betty Freidan and Gloria Steinem was in the making in the late 1950s. As Nussbaum notes, "Despite its feminist theme, 'Mrs. Maisel' has more one-line bimbos than 'Entourage'" (89). And it is an understatement to say that Midge has no sympathy for them. Midge's relations with other women are primarily competitive and bitchy. One of the first things we learn about her is that she was happy in college because her roommate was fat and greedy and so, as she triumphantly crows, no competition to her. When she perceives other women as potential competition she reacts with intense hostility. We see her, before she has any inkling that Joel's secretary Penny is having an affair with him, shooting her a contemptuous look as she struggles with an electric pencil sharpener. Midge later remarks scornfully that Penny must be an imbecile. In her second wedding speech, in "The Punishment Room," the third episode of season 3, she takes the opportunity to insult and humiliate another bride, supposedly her friend, by pointing out that the wedding was forced because of an unwanted pregnancy.

Her hostility to other women reaches a head with the episode much lamented by feminist viewers like Feifei Wang, in which she turns her stand-up act into a tirade of criticism and mockery of the more popular woman comedian, Sophie Lennon. Although there is a lot of speculation about whom this character is modeled on, the most obvious answer would seem to be Sophie Tucker due to the name and the "blue style." Midge decides to publicly humiliate Sophie by exposing her for dishonestly representing herself as fat and poor when she is really skinny and rich. But as June Sochen tells us, Sophie Tucker was as genuine as a comedian could be in this time period ("From Sophie Tucker," 75), so this constitutes an attack on her integrity. Sochen also recounts how Tucker, who "disliked" being required to perform in blackface would remove her gloves at the end of her acts to show the audience the truth of her pale skin ("Fanny Brice and Sophie Tucker," 47). Joyce Antler praises Tucker as "an early champion of women's liberation" (*The Journey Home* 149).

Nussbaum makes the interesting argument that Sophie Lennon is modeled on Joan Rivers, who was also an inspiration for Midge's character, according to the show's creator, Amy Sherman-Palladino. Nussbaum claims that "Rivers's more unsettling qualities—her vengefulness, her perception of women as competitors, her eating disorder—all get displaced onto Midge's foe, fat-joke Sophie, who lives in an opulent French-themed apartment, like the one Rivers lived in, collects furs, and, like the real Joan, wanted to be a serious actress. It's as if Rivers has been split into good Joan and bad Joan, because it's too hard to make such a caustic trailblazer seem cute, to acknowledge how much her success derived from being shaped by misogyny, not from transcending it" (89). But which Joan is it that Midge represents when she congratulates herself on her perfect body and expresses rage that her husband did not value her conformity to beauty standards as the culture of her times said he should? Sochen observes that "by exposing forbidden topics to public scrutiny in outrageous and tasteless ways, Rivers acts as commentator on social mores. She repels her audiences by saying disgusting and unladylike things" (76). In contrast Midge delights her nightclub audiences with her pixyish posturing and petulant complaints. She only outrages when she goes after her rival Sophie.

The attack on Sophie Lennon is not an isolated incident in the show. The principal way of establishing Midge's marvelousness, as Wang argues, is through contrast with other women. Honey Bruce (played by Caitlin Mehner), gorgeous and witty in real life, here appears as a plain, stupid and exasperating drag on her husband, Lenny (Luke Kirby), who, like everyone else is delighted by Midge and makes it his business to foster her success. Midge's agent Susie (Alex Borstein) is modeled on Sue Mengers, but instead of being a brilliant lesbian with an enviable sex life, like the real and legendary Mengers, she is a sometimes pathetic example of gender confusion, dressed as a boy but seemingly asexual and unsure of how to present herself to a world that consistently mistakes her for male, as indicated by her childish choice of a nickname and her self-pitying complaint that she will always be alone. Ultimately then, while Jews are anything but erased in the series, to a large extent our complexities and our history are. As Paul Brownfield says: "However 'Jewish' Sherman-Palladino wants the show to be, 'Maisel' fails to grapple with the realities of the moment in Jewish American history it portrays. Which is ultimately what leaves me queasy about its tone—the shtick, the stereotypes, the comforting self-parody. The stereotypes aren't that comforting anymore."

IV. More Bad Jews

UnREAL (premiered 2015) is another television series that features a physically attractive Jewish woman protagonist, Rachel Goldberg (Shiri Appleby), who achieves success in the entertainment industry. However, this protagonist, unlike Midge Maisel, is not portrayed as a heroine but as an antiheroine. Nonetheless, she has many of the same attributes as Midge. The series gives us an account of the horrible life of Rachel, who has just barely escaped her wealthy and psychotically cruel psychoanalyst mother (who drugged her for various mental disorders she misdiagnosed throughout Rachel's childhood and adolescence) only to fall under the spell of evil Quinn King (Constance Zimmer), who is the executive producer of a reality TV show *Everlasting* (a parody of *The Bachelor* and *Who Wants to Marry a Multi-Millionaire?*). In the first season, the show-within-a-show, which is absolutely grotesque, features ten stereotypical bimbos trying for seven weeks to get a wealthy man to propose. They are each managed by "producers" whose job it is to create "good TV" by tricking them into losing their tempers, crying, having physical fights, and throwing tantrums. Rachel is excellent at doing this, and her ability to ruin lives extends to that of the cameraman, Josh Kelley (Jeremy Caner), whom she seduces, then dumps for one of the shows' bachelors, and finally returns to when the rich man dumps her. Every time the series builds sympathy for her, it subsequently dramatizes her destruction of another person.

How bizarre that this hateful and seemingly criminally insane woman is modeled on the woman who created the show, Sarah Gertrude Shapiro! The show strongly supports the old idea that Jews have an inherently twisted sexuality that poses a danger to others, since Rachel could hardly be more stereotypically perverse and still be a heterosexual who has vanilla sex. It seems that nothing sexually excites her that does not involve deception and nefarious plans. Robyn Bahr describes Rachel as mentally ill, remarking that "the only work she knows how to do is steer people to become their worst selves." Lisa Yelsey says, "She schemes her way into sabotaging female contestants, destroys her own relationships, and convinces or forces people to humiliate themselves on television." Her sadistic behavior extends even to the point of precipitating the suicide of one of the contestants. But Rachel avoids trouble for herself and Quinn by planting a fake suicide note absolving the show of any blame.

JTA, blogging in *New York Jewish Week*, defends the character, claiming, "Rachel is complex in the way that all humans are complex—though she masterfully encapsulates the neuroses commonly found in highly driven people in certain industries. She's manipulative yet self-sabotaging, vulnerable yet strong and, perhaps most of all, extremely good at her job." She also notes that "'UnREAL' smacks of authenticity—that's because one of its co-creators, Sarah Gertrude Shapiro, spent three years as a producer of 'The Bachelor.'"

In JTA's opinion, it is laudable that "Jewish references are sprinkled throughout the series, such as the time Rachel memorably said, 'sheket b'vakasha,' Hebrew for 'be quiet'—or, more aptly, 'shut up.' And, this being about 'the industry' there are loads of Jewish characters, too." This is the sort of review that raises the issue of Jewish minoritization for me. If the series were on Israeli television, I would not have qualms about its portrayal of the protagonist as a perverse, selfish, money grubber, because she would simply be a human being, and some humans are bad people, but outside of Israel—and India, which is the one major country in the world without a history of anti-Semitic racialization of Jews—the way Rachel's behavior fits pernicious stereotypes is disturbing. In a summing up of the show in its fourth and final season, Arielle Bernstein challenges the view of Rachel as complex: "Rachel's casual and consistent cruelty doesn't end up making her into a more interesting character. Instead, her character becomes repetitive, as every increasingly horrible action seems to actually make her character flatter, rather than more nuanced." Anyone familiar with the one-dimensional criminal Jews who appear on the sidelines of action and crime stories on television or in cinema should recognize this type: the Jewish bitch whose villainy appears as a racialized cultural heritage.

Rachel contrasts with the more developed criminal characters in some of the historical dramas I have discussed, such as *Once Upon a Time in America*, *Casino*, *Villain*, and *Miller's Crossing*, and even with the killers of Nazis in *Inglourious Basterds*. All these characters are presented to us within a context that allows us to interpret criminal behavior as a response to oppression by the dominant culture. Of course this is most evident in *Inglourious Basterds*, since most rational people can easily see why Jews would take great pleasure in slaughtering Nazis, including Hitler and his minions, during World War II. However, as I have attempted to show, the other three films make the point that when Jews behaved in corrupt and criminal ways in the past, their crimes were largely motivated by their situation within an anti-Semitic society where they had to fight, seduce, or otherwise undermine Gentiles to survive. No such excuses exist for Rachel's behavior, as her psychological damage is directly attributed to her mother's abuse of her as a child and that mother is also depicted as a powerful, and toxic, sadistic Jew. But at least in this television series the stereotypes are out in the open, not sliding into view as if in glimpses through a half-opened door.

V. Lost in Space

In many other series that is not the case. *The Expanse* (premiered 2015) has been praised for its diverse cast, and I agree with Tasha Robinson about the importance that the story, adapted from a book series with a similar multiracial and multinational group of characters, "takes place in our universe, around 200 years from now, in a future . . . where racism and sexism have become obsolete. Without fanfare, the creators behind the show have created one of the most egalitarian futures on television." Yet Ruta Kupfer's claim that "again and again, T.V. shows acclaimed for their nuance and character development rely on a two-dimensional depiction of Jews" is applicable to this otherwise excellent series.

David M. Perry goes further than Robinson in praising the show, comparing *The Expanse* to another speculative fiction series, *The Man in the*

High Castle, which he rightly criticizes for creating a world in which the Axis won World War II without giving serious attention to "the Nazi anti-Semitism, or Japanese or American racism undergirding World War II–era societies." He then goes on to praise *The Expanse* for focusing on "resistance to authoritarian and fascist regimes." Yet given that the ability of humans, in the show, to inhabit the solar system asteroid belt is only possible because of the scientific invention of a character named Solomon Epstein, it is odd that neither Robinson nor Perry ever mentions the Jews of *The Expanse*. Perhaps that is because their inclusion in the discussion might call into question Robinson's and Perry's claims that the show avoids in any way supporting a patriarchal heteronormative white supremacist worldview.

The show does, as Perry argues, strongly support the idea that women are and should be treated as fully equal to men and does, as Robinson details, show us many women and people of color acting responsibly and effectively in positions of power. And it does make a powerful case for resistance to fascistic oppression. But it also, in the third season, gives us a gay Jewish villain named Cohen, whose selfish behavior causes lots of trouble. That this cowardly and unpleasant man is clearly a Jew but not identified as one by anything but his name undermines, for me, the antifascist intentions of the rest of the show. In that the authors of the book series on which the television show is based also have recognizably Jewish names (Daniel Abraham and Ty Franck) this use of a stereotypical "bad Jew" is as annoying as the way the Jewish creators of shows like *Transparent*, *Mrs. Maisel*, and *UnREAL* and directors like Woody Allen reinforce damaging stereotypes. And that the sneaky coward Cohen is also gay puts the poison cherry on top of the rotten cupcake.

But wait, one might say, what about the way the women in the popular prison drama, *Orange Is the New Black*, another show rightly acclaimed for its resistance to stereotyping minoritized people, celebrated Jewishness in the sixth and seventh (and final) seasons? Doesn't this series mitigate the impression that shows well-known for breaking racial and gender stereotypes fail to do so when it comes to Jews? Arielle Kaplan, among others, praises season 3's depiction of the African American convert to Judaism, Cindy Hayes (Adrienne C. Moore), whose "tak[ing] Judaism very seriously" leads to her ethical reformation. This, however, may well be the ultimate ambiguous use of a Jewish character in that the series' treatment of Jews valorizes religious belief at the expense of racialized Jews. Sigal Samuel earlier asked in an essay in the *Daily Beast* "Does 'Orange Is the New Black' have a Jewish problem?" And her answer is a resounding yes: "Because the writers behind 'Orange' are so amazingly good at creating complex, stereotype-busting characters, it comes as a shock when we meet Larry, his mother, and his father—the show's Jewish characters, all of whom feel cut from cardboard." Samuel focuses on one scene in which Piper (Taylor Schilling) is released from solitary confinement due to the intervention of Piper's boyfriend, Larry Bloom (Jason Biggs). As Samuel notes, no one mentions that this well-connected man is a Jew because "the implication here is veiled but obvious. Piper, the liberal, wealthy offender, is connected to Larry, a liberal, wealthy Jew. And *he* has connections on Capitol Hill; in fact, the prison personnel allow themselves to speculate (albeit hyperbolically) that he's got a direct line to Obama himself. . . . What emerges from this scene, then, is a continuation of the stereotype of the modern American Jew, who is understood as a powerful and intimidating bully." And what emerges in the series' concluding seasons is that while Judaism is a beautiful and inspiring religion, and Black American converts make good, virtuous Jews, people who are born Jewish are the same corrupt creeps they have so often been portrayed as in popular entertainments.

Another frustratingly stereotypical depiction of a Jew created by a Jew for television audiences who otherwise demand realistically nuanced portrayals of racialized subjects is Maury Levy (Michael Kostroff) on *The Wire* (2002–8). Kept on retainer by the drug trafficking Barksdale Organization, he is depicted as "the most repulsive piece of garbage in the city of Baltimore" (Plotz). As Keith Kahn-Harris observes, in a much-cited essay, other characters in the series who do reprehensible things are given complexity and made somewhat sympathetic as a result, while Levy is a shallow reflection of the avarice and dishonesty traditionally attributed to Jews by anti-Semites. In season 2, the difference between Levy and the other characters involved in the drug trade is emphasized by a courtroom scene in which Levy tries to discredit witness Omar Little (Michael K. Williams) by calling him a "parasite" for profiting off the drug dealers as a stick-up man. Omar, who became one of the show's most popular characters,[4] counters this charge by observing that Levy is also a parasite on the drug trade. But as we ultimately learn, Levy is not only profiting from the drug trade as an attorney for the cartel but also secretly directing its actions. And unlike Omar, whose criminal career is a response to his extreme poverty and marginalization as a gay Black man, who operates according to his own ethical code, and who is punished in the end, Levy's villainy is motivated only by excessive greed, and he prospers to the end. The difference in their fates reinforces the ludicrously ahistorical anti-Semitic view that Jews are soulless minions of the devil who all reap material rewards on earth for our evil actions and will not be held to account until the afterlife, when we will finally be carried away to hell.

David Simon, the show's producer and writer, has defended this depiction, depressingly arguing that, in his experience, the majority of lawyers for criminals in the drug trade are Jews: He claims that "when I was covering the drug trade for 13 years for the Sun, most of the major drug lawyers were Jewish. . . . Anyone who is anyone in law enforcement in Baltimore knows the three or four guys Maury Levy is patterned on" (Schleier). In another interview, he asserts that "the four biggest drug lawyers during my years of covering Baltimore were all Jewish, one of them quite observant" (Beiser).[5] However, this attempt at verisimilitude does not explain why Levy's Jewishness is constantly emphasized on the show through his use of Yiddish, his religious practices, and even his references to his wife's brisket. Seth Madej takes particular exception to the final episode in which "Simon had the opportunity to give Levy some nuance to make the stereotyping in the earlier episodes forgivable. Instead Simon not only passed on that opportunity but also chose to write a scene that *emphasizes* those stereotypes and all but guarantees that the audience will be left associating them to the show's only Jewish character" (emphasis Madej's).

Adding insult to injury, *The Wire* also emphasizes Levy's adherence to Judaism. It is hard to understand what Simon intended to accomplish with this depiction. Jews who care about racism in the justice system, not to mention those of us who identify as people of color, are already doing what we can to fight the injustices done to African Americans. It is highly unlikely that a portrayal of Jews in a television show as vicious criminals secretly running the illegal drug trade to the detriment of Black lives and community will have any beneficial impact on corrupt Jewish drug lawyers, causing them to change their ways. So the only effect this is likely to have is to confirm the view of anti-Semites that not just secular but even devoutly religious Jews are evil beyond redemption.

VI. Just Sad Victims

A much less unpleasant use of a Jewish character occurs in the television adaptation of Stephen King's horror/suspense novel *Mr. Mercedes* (premiered 2017). I must confess that I love Stephen King's work and consider him the Charles Dickens of our times, but without Dickens's racism, sexism, and anti-Semitism. I particularly delighted in King's honest portrayal of the vicious anti-Semitism in Dallas and its environs at the time of the Kennedy assassination in his novel 11/22/63, although the television adaptation downplays this. My family had moved to Irving, Texas, during the time of the assassination, and we were subjected to continual name-calling and harassment because we were racialized as Jews, just as King shows happening to other Jews in the Dallas/Fort Worth area. Consequently, I do not blame him for what I saw as an annoying and unnecessary addition to the television version of *Mr. Mercedes*.

The series, like many television and film versions of King's books, departs from the original in numerous ways. Some changes seem designed to avoid offending anyone in minoritized groups or inspiring violence, both moves I support. In the book the psychopathic villain Brady (Harry Treadway) impersonates a cerebral palsy victim, twitching and drooling repulsively in his wheelchair full of explosives and so gets past security for a stadium performance of a popular boy band. King feared inspiring copycats; thus, the venue is changed to an art gallery opening with far fewer people, and Brady masquerades as an intellectual in a wheelchair, providing a more attractive view of the handicapped. In the book Brady's coworker and friend Freddi Linklater is a disagreeable butch lesbian with contempt for other women. In the television series, her name is Lou, and she is a cute and funny baby butch who loves her Black girlfriend and is played by charismatic actress Breeda Wool. Also in the book, the Black boy genius Jerome loves to annoy the hero, Bill, by talking like an exaggeratedly ignorant rapper or a stereotypical field slave in a classic antebellum melodrama. In the television series he is played with dignity by Jharrel Jerome and always comports himself in the manner one might expect from a proper Harvard-bound young man. And finally in the book Holly, who will emerge as the heroine, is a sort of idiot savant with Asperger's syndrome who is barely functional until Bill (Brendan Gleeson) rescues her from her abusive mother. But in the television series Holly (Justine Lupe) just seems a bit nervous and to be suffering from low self-esteem. All of these changes make the series less nasty than the book.[6]

However, the biggest change injects a bit of annoyance for Jews via the addition of a next-door neighbor yenta (Yiddish for busybody), Ida Silver (Holland Taylor), who is not in the book and who tries unsuccessfully to seduce Bill and is broken-hearted when he chooses the Gentile Janey

(Mary-Louise Parker) instead. I would hesitate to call this an anti-Semitic addition, especially as Ida is not depicted as a bad woman, merely an intrusive one whose intrusiveness sometimes benefits Bill and often brings him comfort. She is not identified as a Jew except by her name and her stereotypically Jewish speech patterns. But her depiction does reinforce the trope in American visual entertainment of the Jew who is unattractive but desperately, comically, and hopelessly attracted to a Gentile.

Abrams, in his essay "Jews in Contemporary Cinema and Television," responding to the article by Kupfer that I discuss previously, asks whether Jews really are negatively stereotyped in twenty-first-century television shows or are notable primarily for "their almost total absence" and whether the Jews we do see are "two-dimensional or nuanced," and then he declares, "The answer is both" (216). His primary example of a series filled with complex representations of Jews is *Sons of Anarchy* (2006–14), in which we see Gemma Teller-Morrow (Katey Sagal), "the matriarchal head" of the titular motorcycle club, whose toughness he compares to that of Shoshanna Dreyfus in *Inglourious Basterds* (221). The Jews in this series fight neo-Nazis and, due to their toughness, are accepted into and even run outlaw motorcycle clubs, breaking typical representational stereotypes. However, much of the toughness manifests as endurance of victimization, as when Gemma conceals the fact that she was gang raped in order to avoid starting the gang war her rape was meant to provoke.

Similarly Jewish victimization advances plots in other series, such as the men's prison drama *Oz* (1997–2003), in which members of the Aryan Brotherhood kill Jewish inmate Alexander Vogel (Brian Smyj) to demonstrate their power to others. The Jewish victim plays a more active role in the horror-drama series *The Strain* (2014–17), which centers on a battle between good and evil in which the latter issues from former Nazis who have turned into vampires. The hero is advised and aided by Professor Abraham Setrakian (David Bradley) a pawnbroker[7] who knows the vampires from his time in the concentration camp they ran during World War II. He is bitter, understandably angry, and ruthless.

VII. The Worst Jews Ever

Such ambiguous inclusions of stereotypical Jewish characters pale in relation to the Jews of *Breaking Bad*, who misbehave terribly without any defensible justification. This portrayal of stereotypical Jewish characters somewhat blighted, for me, the otherwise bracingly sharp pleasure of this show, which has been, so far, my favorite television series. The pleasures of *Breaking Bad* are sharp because they derive from some unrestrained and, to many viewers, disturbing truth telling about contemporary life in America. The protagonist, Walter White, is a high school chemistry teacher so underpaid, due to the anti-intellectualism of the United States, that like many of us who teach, even at the university level, he must moonlight in order to pay the bills for his modest lower-middle-class home and small family. And like some chemistry teachers who work in underfunded schools with unsafe laboratory conditions, he has developed lung cancer, despite never having been a smoker. But the most American thing about his story is his lack of good enough health insurance to be able to fight the disease. He strikes back by becoming a methamphetamine cook and laboriously building a drug empire. The satisfaction offered to angry viewers by this tale of revenge against a system that penalizes people so heavily for choosing important, useful work that corporate America and the taxpayers do not value is mitigated by casting and narrative details that seem racist.

The turf battles between Latin American drug cartels that disrupt life in White's Albuquerque and the struggles of the DEA to police the border prefigure Trump's obsession with the supposed threat of Mexico. Hostile critical responses have the easy target of the names of White and his protégé, Jesse Pinkman (Aaron Paul). In a drama that pits white men against Latinos and Blacks, these names certainly stand out. The most influential and frequently cited essays on racism in the series are two by Malcolm Harris in *New Inquiry*, one a follow up. His thesis is that the series is filled with misinformation about the drug trade that is designed to promote the idea of white people's superiority.[8] Chris Prioleau provides additional critique with detailed analysis of the show's depiction of Latinos and African Americans as expendable violence victims or psychopathic murderers: "And while brown blood flows, as free and unlamented as tap water, any time a white character is killed it signals a moral turning point in the show, a sign that things may have gone too far" (Prioleau). Paul Elliott Johnson adds to the critique of the show's putative racism analysis of ways it can be read as a sexist drama that offers angry, disaffected white men the vicarious pleasure of seeing violence erupt when their "perceived right to happiness is unsatisfied" (22).

For some viewers and critics, the show was redeemed from any possibility of advancing a racist agenda by the conclusion, in which Walter battles, and defeats, a gang of hideously awful Aryan Brotherhood members who have captured and enslaved Jesse. Among the ways the show does present the deaths of people of color as deeply lamented occurs when Todd Alquist (Jesse Plemons), the nephew of the brotherhood leader, Jack Welker (Michael Bowen), kills Jesse's girlfriend, Andrea Cantillo, and threatens to kill her little son if Jesse continues to refuse to cook meth for the brotherhood. Jesse appears profoundly traumatized by this event and subsequently loses his ability to fight back. Through such characters as decent Andrea and her sweet little son, the show counters what could be seen as an anti-Latinx bias. Ultimately, there is no critical consensus on the series' representation of African American or Latinx characters. But what remains interesting in the various critical and fan responses to the show is the dearth of commentary on its anti-Semitic aspects, especially among those accusing the show of racism.

One anonymous commentator on Quora stands out. In answer to the question, "Which mainstream films are known to be anti-Semitic or Islamophobic, or at least have strong overtones that way?" they note that "there are several Jewish characters in this show, and they're all trying to hurt or manipulate Walter White, they're all greedy, and they all fit classic antisemitic stereotypes" (September 26, 2018, www.quora.com/Which-mainstream-films-are-known-to-be-anti-Semitic-or-Islamophobic-or-at-least-have-strong-overtones-that-way/answers/101349087). A bullet list of problematic Jewish characters follows. The first is debatable, Saul Goodman (Bob Odenkirk), a truly criminal lawyer (a word play like that of his assumed name, which is a contraction of "it's all good, man"), is not really Jewish but pretends to be in order to meet the expectations of crooks who think Jews make the best unscrupulous and deceitful lawyers. The next on the list, Jane Margolis (Krysten Ritter), is not identified as a Jew except by her surname. And as the anonymous commentator remarks: "According to Nazi propaganda, Jewish women exert their own uncanny influence over society by seducing Christian men and using sex to steal money. That's exactly what she does in the show. She seduces Jesse, a naive Christ like character, and then manipulated him so he would betray Walter White and take the money Jesse made cooking Meth and escape to New Zealand. So we have here another greedy Jewish character who manipulates people for personal gain." I would add to this that unlike the similarly manipulative Jewish brother and sister in *Miller's Crossing*, Jane has no need to trick or corrupt people in order to survive. She has a loving air traffic controller father who wants to care for and protect her, but she is just a very bad person who takes sinister pleasure in persuading Jesse to begin injecting drugs.

Another bad Jew is Ted Beneke (Christopher Cousins), who also is not discussed in the show as Jewish but is identified as such by his surname, as Jane is, and also, as the anonymous commentator observes, has a mezuzah attached to the front doorframe of his home. (Viewers must zoom in on the image of the door to see it clearly.) And as the commentator explains, "Like Margolis, Beneke seduces someone for his personal gain," in his case "Skyler (Walter's wife [played by Anna Gunn]), and then he forces her into giving him 600,000 dollars by blackmailing her. Another greedy, cowardly, scheming, seductive Jewish character." However, the worst Jewish characters are clearly Walter's longtime frenemies, Eliot and Gretchen Schwartz (Adam Godley and Jessica Hetch). We might note that *schwartz* is German/Yiddish for "black," so their contrast to Walter *White* could not be more strongly marked.

Walter is a genius chemist who should not have been reduced to a position teaching high school, which is another source of the rage that causes him to "break bad." He attributes his downfall to the Schwartzes, and we are given no reason to doubt his story that he worked with them developing patents but that they subsequently took advantage of his financial problems by accepting a low-figure buyout in order to cut him out of the billion-dollar company he helped them found.[9] They are marked in many ways as Jewish, including a reference, in the last season, to their celebration of the Jewish holidays with their friends the Cohens. Kupfer sums up the scene in which Walt forces the Schwartzes to accept $9 million of his drug money and use it to set up a trust fund for his son this way: "The representation of the scared, money-grubbing swindlers who prefer to fraternize with their own kind, standing next to a pile of money they aren't allowed to touch, is a stereotype. In the series, set in a world of crime, there are people far worse than the Schwartzes: Todd, the soulless psychopath; Tuco, the violent, cold-blooded gangster; and even, some would say, Walt himself. But there aren't any characters more loathsome or corrupt than the Schwartzes."

In their conclusion, the anonymous commentator on Quora angrily points out that "Walter White's street name was Heisenberg. Heisenberg was a real life scientist who worked for the Nazis. Heisenberg was the German scientist in charge of the Nazi atomic weapons program." True enough, and one might also note that Heisenberg defended himself against the SS accusation that he was a "White Jew" (the Nazi term for an Aryan

Fig. 7.1 *Breaking Bad*: The Schwartzes burdened with Walter's drug money.

who behaved like a stereotypical Jew). Which brings me back to the possible exoneration of the show from charges of racism/anti-Semitism through its conclusion. Walter White is never presented as heroic, nor, as Kupfer argues, is his world populated by decent people. Pretty much everyone we meet in the series is either amoral or decidedly and proudly immoral. Everyone is greedy and manipulative, not just those with Jewish surnames. And if Jesse is "Christ like" as the anonymous commentator claims, he has an odd way of showing it, since he is an addict and meth cook who is not above murdering to protect himself from the consequences of his crimes and also breaks the cardinal rule of both organized and street crime by becoming a snitch to the DEA. So I would prefer to think that, like his chosen hero Heisenberg, Walter comes in the end to understand that there can be no safe accommodation of Nazis because if you ignore their crimes, then they come for you. It may be only coincidence, but Walter White was the name of the Black/multiracial man who first infiltrated the Ku Klux Klan before the one featured in Spike Lee's 2018 film *Blackkklansman*, to which I turn in the book's conclusion.

VIII. Better Watch Out

But first, a look at a very different sort of racial masquerade in the 2019 limited television series *Watchmen*. Based, rather loosely, on Alan Moore and Dave Gibbons's 1987 DC Comics series *Watchmen*, the story was extended by show creator and writer, Damon Lindelof, into a drama set in our current era, although in an alternative America with a different history. The plot engages the issue of the rise of the alt-right in real America. (The show includes many allusions to the United States' current division along racial lines.) The complicated plot concerns the efforts of a group of Tulsa, Oklahoma, police officers costumed and masked to fight the Seventh Kavalry. This white supremacist organization was formed to end a program of reparations for victims of racial violence by eliminating the politicians and police who support the program.

The protagonist, Angela Abar (Regina King), is an African American policewoman who disguises herself as the superhero Sister Night. She discovers that her grandfather Will Reeves (Louis Gossett Jr.), whom she has just met, is a former victim of the real historical event the 1921 Tulsa Race Massacre, seen by many as the worst single instance of white violence against Blacks since the end of the Civil War. As a result of watching mobs of armed men and men in planes killing the inhabitants of a successful Black business district and losing his parents to this attack, he decides to join the Tulsa police force as soon as he grows up. But when he is half lynched as a punishment for arresting a white supremacist for torching a Jewish delicatessen, Will transforms himself into the vigilante Hooded Justice who must conceal his race in order to be accepted as a force for good. His granddaughter, Angela, marries the series only true superhero, Jon Osterman, also known as Doctor Manhattan, a German Jewish watchmaker's son who was transformed through a nuclear accident into a sort of god, "one of the most powerful characters in comic history" (Li). The situation of Angela's husband is something of a reversal of her grandfather's story in that he presents himself as Black in order to avoid being recognized and so forced to use his powers to contribute to the world's evil.

Due to his need to pass as an ordinary human and so escape having his powers stolen by the bad guys, Jon takes on the identity of a dead man. His superpowers allow him to re-create his body to match that of the man whose identity he assumes. He asks Angela to choose one whom she would be comfortable having as a husband, and she chooses Cal Jelani (Yahya Abdul-Makeem), whose African American likeness Jon happily appropriates. Abdul-Makeem said of the role, "In a world where white supremacy is the antagonist of our story, it makes sense that a god is inhabited by a black man . . . [that] God can be black" (Li). Since white supremacy is embodied by the Tulsa chief of police, many of the officers, and a Republican senator from Oklahoma who is scheming to become president, Doctor Manhattan, in his Black incarnation, gives an answer to the series' implicit question—"Who will watch the watchmen?," a translation from *The Satires of Juvenal* usually understood to mean, who will hold the powerful accountable? The answer could be imagined to be Black Americans, especially after the 2020 presidential election, when their votes are generally considered to have determined the outcome.

IX. Conclusion

However, as the show intermittently reminds us, Doctor Manhattan is not really a Black man; he is a Jew in a science fiction full-body version of blackface. As I discuss in this book's introduction, and as Michael Rogin argues, Jews did not use blackface simply appropriatively but also as a way of dealing with their racialization in America. Nicole Kassell, *Watchmen*'s executive producer and director, says as much in an interview with Travis Clark when she talks about her "very personal" connection to the material. She is from Charlottesville, Virginia, where the 2017 Unite the Right Rally took place. She told Clark, "Since the 2016 election, I've felt upset and shocked, and as an artist I didn't know what I could do with that energy. When I read the ["Watchmen"] script, I said 'this is it.' This is tackling everything I want to talk about." And one additional reason she gives for wanting to address the rise of American white supremacy is that she is "half Jewish" (Clark), as is Lindelof.[10] In some ways the series achieves the dream of some politically progressive Jews, to finally be racialized in a way everyone can agree is truly a racialization—that is, to be seen as Black and to have the love and acceptance of Black people, here represented by Angela and Will. While it seems that this can only happen in an alternative universe, because of all the vexed history that stands in our way in this one, in the book's conclusion I return to the historical Walter White to begin a final consideration of how we, the Jews, might at least fight back against the erasure of the realities of our racialization and so bridge the divide between ourselves and other people of color.

Notes

1. Because of the milieu in which I was raised, I did not realize that by the mid-1960s most Jews were no longer low-income factory workers. I was shocked to discover, when I started college, that rich Jews were fairly common, since I had never met one.

2. See Nathan Abrams's *The New Jew in Film*, 43–58, for a very detailed history of cinematic representations of the Jewish American Princess.

3. Linda Mizjewksi describes Silverman's live performance and television persona as "putting Sarah through the antics of a cartoon character" and calls the character a "hybrid boy/girl, or beauty/beast," as is reflected in Silverman's farcical claims to be half monkey, half Jew, yet pretty, cute, and sexy, claims that are always in service of incisive parodies of sexism and of racism, very much including anti-Semitism (103, 109–11). Her petite, pert feminine beauty becomes a tool in her "offensive" comedy designed to deconstruct identities naturalized for all women and for Jewish women in particular (92–94). The most striking feature of *The Sarah Silverman Program*, for me, is the way this parody often centers on wild exaggeration of the type of fictional character given the name Manic Pixie Dream Girl in a review of *Elizabethtown* (2005) by Nathan Rabin (who has now expressed regret for the implicit sexism of this review in an essay in *Salon*). This term, which is now frequently used to describe a trope of visual entertainments, was meant by Rabin to critique ridiculously child-like, alternately petulant and overly cheerful women who exist in narratives only to help immature men learn to enjoy life. Sarah's distinctiveness derives from her refusal to present herself as romantically interested in men at all. She exhibits the polymorphous sexuality of a small child. She discusses wanting to marry her dog! And all her manic energy goes into her self-promotion. She sulks and burbles giddily about herself and no one else.

4. Robert Bianco explains Omar's appeal in his *USA Today* article, "Ten Reasons We Still Love TV."

5. Another Jewish showrunner, Jenji Kohan, creator of *Weeds*, responded with similar indignation to criticism of her series' portrayal of "an array of Jewish characters" racialized as stereotypically "effeminate, parasitic, or chameleonic" and also "sexually perverse" (Deloia and Ofir 130, 135, 139). With determinedly "honest" depictions of Jews like this in the drug trade, it is little wonder that anti-Semites feel certain that Jews run every criminal operation blighting life in America.

6. Such changes are typical of television adaptations of King's stories. The revolting rape and torture of a little boy in *The Outsider*, for a recent example, is downplayed considerably in the TV version.

7. This may be a response to *The Pawnbroker* (dir., Sidney Lumet, 1964) in which Rod Steiger plays Sol Nazerman, a former professor turned morally compromised pawnbroker by his experiences in a German concentration camp. Unlike Setrakian, he does not fight evil but instead begins to embody it through his cold refusal to care about anyone anymore.

8. See also Lindsay Beyerstein's rebuttal of Harris's claims in the *Nation*.

9. This backstory could be compared to the main story of David Fincher's Mark Zuckerberg bio-pic, *The Social Network* (2010). This tale dramatizes, and to some extent fictionalizes, the legal battles between Zuckerberg (played in the film by Jesse Eisenberg) and the Winklevoss twins, who claimed Zuckerberg stole the idea for Facebook from them. Zuckerberg has been a controversial figure from the beginning of Facebook's rise to fame, due to its reputation for data mining and political manipulation. And, of course, Zuckerberg is a Jew and one who, in this depiction, fits the stereotype of a sexually unsuccessful man who prioritizes making money over achieving emotional closeness with others or advancing a progressive social agenda. However, his antagonists, the Winklevosses, as played by Armie Hammer and Sean Parker, are much worse. In what the film depicts as their arrogant sense of entitlement and absurd insistence that the vague idea of theirs that Zuckerberg developed

is their intellectual property, they are villainous. And because they represent the wealthy as enemies and exploiters of those who lack their inherited class privilege, the audience, like Zuckerberg, yearns to see them brought low.

10. Being personally of the opinion that, to paraphrase *Westside Story,* "When you're a Jew, you're a Jew all the way," I find the term "half Jew" as inaccurate as "half Black." This simply is not the way racists, who are the ones who create and maintain racializations, think now, although the Nazis did seem to like this term.

CONCLUSION

The Erasure of Jewish Identities and Their Reinvention

I RECALL BEING HURT AND ANGERED WHEN, IN 1984, I first read in Barbara Smith's chapter of *Yours in Struggle: Three Feminists on Anti-Semitism and Racism* by her claim that "almost all Jews in the United States are white people of European backgrounds, and therefore benefit from white-skin privilege, which is often combined with class privilege" (80). This did not fit the way I had understood my Jewish identity when I was growing up surrounded by family members and their friends who were not privileged intellectuals but union-supporting factory workers and who, when they went down South, were subjected to Jim Crow exclusions because of their dark skin and kinky hair. It did not fit with the way the children at the elementary school I attended when we moved to Texas would taunt me by saying, "I saw your father in the yard and he's a Negro!" And it certainly did not fit with the poverty I had to fight so hard to overcome. But over time, as a result of entering academe and rising up into the middle class, I have understood that Smith was right; most Jews in the United States pass for white most of the time, and as a result, many of us have gained consider-able class and economic privilege we would not have had if we had insisted on being seen as people of color. In other words, sad to say, the painful distance we often experience from Americans racialized as Black is our own fault. Unlike other groups considered "ethnics," American Jews have a choice about whether to identify as white. As Isabel Wilkerson shows, for most European immigrants, "becoming white meant defining themselves as furthest from its opposite—black" (50). People of Irish heritage, like my maternal grandmother, had no real choice because their entire group was classified by law in the United States as white whether they liked that or not, and today no reasonable people in America considers those of Irish ancestry nonwhite. However, as I have shown, for Jews the situation is quite different, what with all the neo-Nazis daily declaring us nonwhite on the web and in demonstrations. When our racialized identity is erased in real life, as opposed to visual entertainments, it is because we ourselves effected the erasure. No one can refuse to be racialized if others insist that they are other than white, but Jewish Americans have been offered the option of being considered white in specific places and times by those who are always seen as white. And many of us have taken this option although it entailed erasing our history and the identities it confers.

One of the most complex and fascinating explorations of the dynamics of a representative Jewish attempt to rectify this situation of self-erasure and so to reconnect with Black people is contained in what I will call the race relations subtext of the film *Joker* (dir., Todd Phillips, 2019). The main plot of *Joker* traces the transformation of Arthur Fleck (Joaquin Phoenix), an unsuccessful comedian who lives in poverty and is frequently the victim of bullying and abuse, into the psychopathic villain of the Batman comics and films, Joker. Fleck suffers from brain damage from abuse inflicted by his stepfather when he was a child. The brain damage causes him to laugh uncontrollably when he feels stress, and the laughter first attracts the attention of people around him and then, as it persists, infuriates them so that some subsequently harm him. He snaps one night on the subway and shoots three stockbrokers who turned on him when he tried to stop them sexually harassing a frightened woman passenger. After this incident, his rage against the world builds until he decides to use the makeup he has from his job as a party clown to re-create himself as a vigilante. Soon he begins to target those who have hurt him in the past. Finally, he becomes a sort of general avenger of class privilege–based cruelty. In this role he finds himself the leader of a nihilistic movement whose rallying cry is "kill the rich."

First of all, Phoenix, although not raised Jewish, is technically a Jew through the maternal line. More importantly, though, the character he plays is undeniably Jewish. The race relations subtext begins with Arthur being attacked by a group of Black and Latinx boys who take away the sandwich board he wears to advertise the party clown company and, when he tries to get it back, beat him in an alley. For a Jewish viewer this is an important moment of double address. As J. Hoberman points out in a rave review of the film, Fleck is a Jewish name. Not only is the fictional setting of the film, Batman's Gotham City, "New York, circa 1981," but also Fleck and his mother live "in a slum tenement on a grim street that's recognizably the Bronx. (Given his family name, he and his mother might be the last remnants of a once-Jewish neighborhood)" (Hoberman, "Joker"). Hoberman finishes his review by claiming that "no other movie so cogently addresses the crisis of the present moment, both in Hollywood and the world," and, in this case, unlike that of the Coens, I fully agree with Hoberman. I would add that for the Jewish viewer, the crises addressed by the film include the one we are now experiencing as racialized subjects.

In a January 2020 essay, Carly Pildis, speaking powerfully as "the only white presenting person in my Jewish household," discusses the tensions of relations between African and Jewish Americans in the Trump era. As she notes, "These last few months have tested our ability to hear each other. It doesn't help that the tabloids are pushing stories about how black-Jewish relations are imploding and that black Americans are behind the recent rise in anti-Semitism, even though only 33% of those arrested in New York for anti-Semitic hate crimes were black. There is no data that suggests black people, as organizations or individuals, are driving the rise in anti-Semitic violence in America." In other words, it is once again divide and conquer time. A good example of what she is talking about is that white supremacists in Ohio marched with signs blaming Jews for the coronavirus and featuring an image of a human-faced rat wearing a Star of David and labeled "The Real Plague" (Hancock). This conspiracy theory is now a staple on the internet, and it always involves the accusation that Jews are cynically manipulating African Americans in order to advance our plot to disempower and destroy white people. We will not get African Americans, who have been the hardest hit in this country by the pandemic, to take our side simply by demanding it. The solution to the social problems of both groups, Jews and Black people, that Pildis passionately proposes is that Jews show solidarity with Blacks and fight for social justice for all. Despite his claim to be apolitical, this is exactly what Fleck does as he transforms into Joker.

His first move after the beating in the alley is to reach out in friendship to his Black neighbor, single mother Sophie Dumond (Zazie Beetz). Far from lumping together all Black people as his enemies, he forms a romantic attachment to her. We are led to think, through the first part of the film, that she reciprocates his feelings and provides emotional support for him. We might even begin to imagine that his parodic assumption of the white face of his clown disguise, which becomes, as he transforms, a recognizable anarchy mask, signals the solidarity that they have as raced and marginalized subjects who can only mock and reject whiteness. But then comes the film's big reveal. The relationship with Sophie exists only in his delusional imagination. In real life she is afraid of him, and rightly so, because even if he were not at this point a serial killer, he is still white-identified and life experience, if not familiarity with statistics, could tell Sophie that white men are more likely to attack Black people than the other way around.

Joker's subplot exposes the Jewish ego-boosting, feel-good fantasy of Black acceptance of a white hero that we get in *Watchmen* as just that: a feel–good, ego-boosting fantasy. Once again we see masks and identity concealment. Once again a devoted and affirming Black woman stands behind the embattled Jewish would-be hero, but this time, that support is revealed as pure illusion, because the Black woman realizes that the Jew is just another crazy white-appearing guy who wants a relationship with Blacks that will benefit him. This is the reality that stands against the beautiful dream of *Watchmen*'s Black-Jewish relations. And it is the reality that contextualizes Spike Lee's depiction of those relations in *Blackkklansman* (2018).

In addition to dramatizing the amazing story of Colorado Springs policeman and real-life hero Ron Stallworth (played in the film by John David Washington), *Blackkklansman* sends a wake-up call to American Jews who imagine themselves to be perceived as white by the Americans who have indisputable white status. Unlike his predecessor in infiltrating the Ku Klux Klan, Walter Francis White, who was the son of freed slaves and a member of the NAACP but could pass for white, Stallworth is easily recognizable as Black. So he used an undercover police officer, Philip (Flip) Zimmerman (Adam Driver), as his surrogate within the KKK. The film's message to Jews comes through Flip's experience. With his long hooked nose, dark complexion, and black curly hair, he looks stereotypically Jewish, but it is credible that Flip could pass for Gentile because Driver is a Gentile.

Flip does fall under suspicion by the Klansmen of being Jewish, but thanks to help from a distraction created by Stallworth, he is accepted and even placed on protection duty for David Duke, then the Grand Wizard of the Ku Klux Klan. Inside the KKK, Flip quickly comes to understand that to American racists, Jews are not white, as he had always previously believed himself to be, and moreover "Jewish" is not a religious identity to white supremacists but a race. His lack of interest in Judaism is no protection from their hateful agenda to end the lives of as many people of color, very much including Jews, as they can. Suddenly, when he narrowly escapes being murdered, he sees his mission not as an amusing game in which he makes fools of racists on behalf of other people, such as Stallworth, who suffer persecution, but as vital solidarity with his fellow embattled racialized subjects.

Fig. C.1 *Blackkklansman*: The KKK is a big joke until it isn't.

Lee's treatment of Flip as needing to be awakened to his situation as a racialized subject stands in contrast to Charles Burnett's story of a Black and Jewish police pair in *The Glass Shield* (1994). This film, an exposé of racist corruption in the Los Angeles Sheriff's Department, is also based on a true story. It follows the awakening of a naive Black rookie, J. J. Johnson (Michael Boatman), to the reality that police routinely frame Black people for crimes and also murder Black people in custody. Initially his desire to be accepted and fulfill his lifetime dream of being a cop causes him to collude in the framing of a Black man for a murder committed by a prominent white man. But when his only real friend on the force, the other "token" hire, Deborah Fields (Lori Petty), is beaten almost to death for persisting in her claim that the framed man is not guilty, J. J. realizes that he must value his relations with racialized people, like the wrongly accused man and also Deborah, who has been subjected to hazing because she is a Jew, above being accepted by corrupt racists.

But whether their film depicts Jews or African Americans as the ones needing to wake up to reality, the message Burnett and Lee advance is the same: we need each other in the fight against racism. As the concluding footage of *Blackkklansman*, taken from the 2017 Unite the Right rally in Charlottesville; Trump's defense of the white supremacist marchers at the same rally; and David Duke's statement in support of the rally tell us, so should we all.

It is important for Jews to make common cause with all America's minoritized people for ethical reasons and because there is strength in numbers. This reason is lightly touched on in the BBC miniseries *The City and the City* (2018), adapted from China Miéville's 2009 novel. This complex speculative fiction concerns an imaginary Eastern European city divided into two parts, each of whose citizens are conditioned by their governments literally not to see each other. The situation brings up questions about what regional cultures allow us to perceive about othered people and what we are forced to "unsee," as the inhabitants of these cities term it. One of the cities, Ul Qoma, provides a vision of contemporary Eastern Europe as prosperous, highly dependent on technology, and ruled by oligarchs. The other city, Besźel, represents the old Eastern Europe of the impoverished 1990s, as the DVD "making of" documentary explains. Despite the hardships of life in Besźel, it at least has the virtue of strong resistance to the efforts of wealthy American technological firms, Ul Qoma's criminally exploitive government, and its own rising nativist faction, whose leader, Major Yorj Syedr (Danny Webb), tries to sell his city-state out to American exploiters. The resistance comes from a Muslim-Jewish alliance created by Islamic refugees settling in the old Jewish quarter, where they live in harmony with the Jews, even sharing the same café that offers kosher food on one side and halal on the other.

Both groups are subjected to hostile racialization from both Americans and the citizens of Ul Qoma. When the hero, Tyador Borlú (David Morrissey), confronts Mike Gorse (Robert Firth), the American technocrat villain, with having financed Syedr's campaign, Gorse dismisses him, saying, "Go back to your shtetl." But once his traitorous collaboration with a foreign power is exposed, Syedr resigns and suicides in disgrace. Among other ideas this very political miniseries promotes is that Jewish-Muslim alliances are crucial to democracy in our current political climate in which the whole world is endangered by the rise of power-hungry billionaires and the technocrats who aid them, some of whom just happen to hate progressive Jews and Muslims and all people of color.

However, the group that it is most crucially important that we Jews listen to are African Americans, since they are the group that has endured the brutality of American racialization the longest and the most horrifically. And as their voting records demonstrate, they are the group in America most resistant to politicians with racist agendas. As Ishmael Reed writes, African Americans have "developed a seventh sense to detect the hate barometer at any given time. For us, like the European Jews and the early Native Americans, extermination has always been on the table." For that reason I give Reed's comments in his essay in *Tablet Magazine* on Jewish racial identity close attention here.

Reed has published extensively on the need for a new Black-Jewish alliance to fight the resurgence of white supremacy in the United States. In this essay, "Do American Jews Still Believe They're White?", he calls for Jews to awaken from the dream that we became white folks in the United States post–World War II just because we were allowed into some spaces previously designated as being for whites only. This assimilationist story erases from the historical record Jews of color and Jews who are not now and have never been affluent as well as completely ignores not only the continued racialization of Jews in this country, so evident now that the neo-Nazis have come out into the open, but also the obvious facts that throughout the rest of the Western world and much of the East, Jews have remained racialized and that violence against people racialized as Jews has historically occurred throughout our history in this county and continues today.

Reed's essay is particularly meaningful to me because I am a professor at Washington State University, whose main campus is in Pullman, Washington, a locus of anti-Semitic hatred, as Reed has identified repeatedly. In this essay, he reminds us of his observation, recounted in *Another Day at the Front*, that Jews who think anti-Semitism among white people is a thing of the past and that the only American anti-Semites for many years have been Black followers of Louis Farrakhan "might be cured by a trip to Pullman, Wash., near the Idaho border, the scene of a 1984 shootout between the FBI and the American Nazi group called Order. Townsfolk were cheering for the Nazis." I can attest to this. In the early part of the twenty-first century, local white supremacists slid death threats under the doors of WSU professors of color and some of us received phone calls reiterating the threats. One professor remarked to the caller that he was not Jewish but Latino and was told, "I don't care what kind of nigger you are, we are going to kill you." If hearing that does not wake up the Jews who continue to claim whiteness, I do not know what can.

As many scholars of contemporary Jewish life and attitudes have noted, some Jews believe that we must embrace our supposed whiteness not in order to feel superior to people of color but, instead, as a way of acknowledging our white privilege. Since many of the Ashkenazi can pass for white, as I discuss in this book's introduction, this does have some logic. However, I think it is misguided. Rather than expressing guilt and shame that passing is possible for many of us, it would be better for us to cease trying to pass. As Barbara Smith does in the quote with which I began this conclusion, Reed persuasively explains that Black people, and presumably other people of color, do not generally resent or criticize Jews for acknowledging that they are not considered white by people to whom being white is seen as a virtue. One thing they do dislike is when we try to capitalize on our exclusion from pure whiteness by appropriating the cultural signifiers and practices of other racialized people, especially when those signifiers and practices are considered hip by political Progressives. The notorious black-face performances by Jewish entertainers like Al Jolson and Sophie Tucker exemplify appropriative identifications with a toxic effect on solidarity between Black and Jewish Americans. And while the passing for Black that the Jewish superhero achieves in *Watchmen* is less pernicious, it is still not only self-erasure through appropriation but an identification that falsifies the differences in Black and Jewish racializations, as I hope my comparison of the television series to *Joker* shows. Let us, instead, follow the lead of *Broad City* in heaping disapproval on Jews masquerading as other racialized subjects, such as what happens when the character Ilana wears outsized earrings that spell out "Latina." We should always also keep in mind that what other racialized people strongly dislike, and understandably so, is when Jews compete with them about which group has been the most persecuted and oppressed, not when Jews act in solidarity with them.

Reed emphasizes that Black people in America have good reason to criticize Jews in that many who are prominent in the entertainment industry, mentioning in particular that "David Simon, Steven Spielberg, and David Mamet offer products to the public that depict black men as sexual predators" in ways that closely parallel the way German Nazis depicted Jews. Instead of all the infighting and promulgation of hateful stereotypes that make alliances between people of color difficult, Reed demands that Jews face reality and act accordingly. "The United States has never been a white nation and it never will be," as he proclaims. If this seems at all exaggerated, one might consider the presence of Marjorie Taylor Greene as a Representative in the US Congress. Greene shared with her followers the conspiracy theory that "the record 2018 'Camp Fire' wildfire in California was orchestrated by California politicians and wealthy Jewish bankers via a space laser beam, in order to clear a path for a high-speed railway" (Azmi Haroun) and the Great Replacement theory that "Jews are orchestrating the mass migration of nonwhite immigrants into predominantly white countries in order to wipe out the populations there." And as Ben Sales reminds us, "The gunman who killed 11 people in the 2018 Pittsburgh synagogue shooting espoused the Great Replacement theory, as did marchers in the 2017 far-right rally in Charlottesville." Like the other anti-Semitic conspiracy theories, these also group the putatively genocidal Jews with other

POC, including African Americans and Muslims.¹ Consequently we who are designated people of color by racists must unite against the Right and stop vilifying each other.

However, we cannot begin to immediately effect these needed changes in the way entertainment media depicts us if we are not in the position to write screenplays, direct films, or run television series. Few of us can exert any direct influence over those who do. We Jews are such a small minority in America that even boycotting films and television series that include racist stereotypes would have no real effect. So what can we do? In addition to voicing our disapproval of hostile and undermining representations of other racialized subjects, we can stop praising every film and television series that gives us any representation at all, no matter how unpleasant. Yes, there are some very bad Jews and some very damaged Jews, but why must we be so quick to say that it is wonderful to see these realistic, fully developed characters, when their character development consists of a bunch of ugly stereotypical traits? And we can stop being good sports about anti-Semitic humor, whether it is generated by Gentiles or other Jews. We can learn from Black people who are seldom, if ever, heard praising the comedy of Stepin Fetchit or *Amos 'n' Andy*. Instead, we can say to our Gentile friends, when they enthuse about such comedy, that we find it offensively racist. And we can stop acting ashamed of mentioning the Holocaust, as if it happened thousands of years ago rather than in the lifetimes of many people who are still with us. Instead, we might consider mentioning that this event has an impact on how Jews think about law and morality, just as the existence of slavery as part of American history and the continuing police violence against Black people have an impact on how they think about these things. We can take issue with studies like Nancy Wang Yuen's *Reel Inequality: Hollywood Actors and Racism* that rely on the view that Jews in America are unmarked white subjects and have always been presented in US films as such.² And finally we can follow the example set by Spike Lee's film and acknowledge that we are racialized subjects who should accept that we are not white to racists and that, as a consequence, we should make common cause with other people of color.

I live in hopes that more films and television series will reflect this important truth. But until that glorious day, we can at least recognize that, like all racialized subjects, we must respond not only to the ways we are seen by our enemies but also to the ways they construct a system of racialization that impacts the lives of many people in addition to Jews. Think how much more compelling the anonymous commentator's argument about anti-Semitic racism in *Breaking Bad* would have been had they also addressed the series' other instances of racial stereotyping and if they had also talked about shows that are Islamophobic rather than ignoring that part of the question. They might have even pointed out that the term *Islamophobia* is part of the problem because, like the categorization of all crimes against Jews as deriving from religious prejudice, it obfuscates the racialization of the victims.[3] Hatred of Jews for following Judaism or Arabs for following Islam is not the real problem; racism is. And until we make that clear, solidarity will be sporadic or missing.

As I have attempted to show throughout this book, Jews have everything to gain by allying with other racialized Americans and refusing identification as white. And as chapter 6 demonstrates, if we cannot ourselves create minoritarian art, we can at the very least show appreciation of it. We need to extend the practice of reading as Jewish, discussed by Henry Bial, to an ability to interpret the visual entertainments that shape our worldviews from the position of nonwhite subjects within a society and culture where white supremacy is still in effect. As I have discussed throughout this book, we have a duty to be aware of the historical contexts that impact meaning-making and, within artworks, world-making, and that duty extends beyond exclusive focus on Jews. We might think about the members of the L'Simcha Congregation (Tree of Life Synagogue) who lost their lives because they were Jews who supported the human rights of Latinx asylum seekers. The survivors remain undaunted by those white supremacists who fear that we racialized people will replace them. Their motto proudly displayed on their website is "Stronger Together," and with people like this on our side, we will replace the racist murderers. I whole-heartedly agree with this call to action by Yvette Alt Miller: "It's crucial that we all stand up to hate, no matter where it occurs. . . . It's our urgent task to build bridges with our fellow citizens, to support them when they are in need, and call on allies to help us when our communities are targeted. Today, more than ever, we need to be vigilant in condemning attacks on our fellow citizens and to insist that others stand by us in our hour of need as well."

In addition we must maintain awareness that race is never articulated as independent of sexuality. The repression of sexual freedom, the demonization of nonheteronormative and nonpatriarchal gender identifications cannot be separated from racialization, as I have discussed in every chapter of this book. By both those who hate us and those who admire us, Jews have been identified as leaders in the transformation of concepts of gender and sexuality. We have a great responsibility to continue these efforts in ways that give full acknowledgment to the importance of intersectionality. We can see this exemplified in the works of many of the women in feminism's third wave, such as the writings of Rosario Morales in *This Bridge Called My Back*, who draws on her Puerto Rican and Jewish heritage to insist of the people minoritized by their sexuality, gender identity, and/or race "we are all in the same boat" (87). Fortunately, a new generation of Jews who contest the old fantasy of assimilation and so resist the pressure to pass as white carry on this important work.

The work of Marla Brettschneider on Jamaica Kincaid is one of many examples of this type of contestation within academic feminism. Brettschneider points out that "the internationally known diasporic writer and Afro-Caribbean writer Kincaid is also Jewish," and consequently analysis of the intersectionality in her writing can help "in imagining a renewed Jewish feminist social justice movement and new paths for antiracist Jewish feminism" (52, 59). We can see this in many areas of contemporary life, and one that was deeply moving to me and the audience I saw it with at Lincoln Center was Julia Wolfe's 2019 oratorio, "Fire in My Mouth," about the Triangle Shirtwaist Factory fire and its repercussions, very much including the labor organizing work of Jewish immigrants. However, what seemed to move the audience most was the way the performance was designed to address the anti-immigrant actions of Trump's government, to put revolutionary fire in all our mouths about the race-hatred manifested in the caging of asylum seekers' children, the abuse of undocumented workers, and the shocking rise in attacks on nonwhite people. We must show that to us, Black lives matter as do all the lives of people of color who are currently under assault. The solidarity that can set us free of complicity in these outrages and instead mark us as the enemies of racists begins with our refusing to think of Jews as white. And it continues through exploring all the many ways our identities are intersectional and that this intersectionality connects us to other people of color and others demonized for their sexual and gender identifications.

Notes

1. CNN reports that Democratic representative Cori Bush of Missouri, an African American, has repeatedly asked Congress to take action against Greene for her social media posts expressing hostility toward Black Lives Matter, and Bush personally, but despite the

obvious racism of these posts, some of which include calls for the "execution" of Democratic politicians, "GOP leadership has so far shown no steps toward reprimanding Greene for her comments or previous posts" (Grayer).

2. Although Yuen does a fine job of reporting and discussing the results of her interviews with many actors of color, her two references to the portrayal of Jews in film and on television draw on Brodkin's book to dismiss any claims we have to being minoritized. Instead, she argues that the depiction of Jews as white in visual entertainments was determined by "Jewish studio magnates in the 1920s and 1930s" and apparently has not wavered since (10). She attributes Lena Dunham's failure to depict the real, multiracialism of New York City to the "'write what you know rationale' that results in white writers leaving out the stories of people of color" (58). She dismisses Dunham's objection that she is not white but "half Jewish" as irrelevant, again repeating that Jews are white. Maybe if Yuen had interviewed some of the actors who play the grotesquely stereotyped Jews in the films and television shows I have discussed, she might have come to a different conclusion.

3. See Ivan Davison Kalmar, "Race by the Grace of God."

FILMOGRAPHY

American Beauty. Directed by Sam Mendes. Jinks/Cohen, 1999.

Annie Hall. Directed by Woody Allen. United Artists, 1977.

Antichrist. Directed by Lars von Trier. Zentropa, 2009.

At the Suicide of the Last Jew in the World in the Last Cinema in the World. Directed by David Cronenberg. In *To Each His Own Cinema.* Commissioned for the Cannes Film Festival, 2007.

Barton Fink. Directed by Joel Coen. Twentieth-Century Fox, 1991.

Basic Instinct. Directed by Paul Verhoeven. Carolco, 1992.

Better Call Saul. Created by Vince Gilligan and Peter Gould. AMC, 2015–.

The Big Lebowski. Directed by Joel Coen. Working Title Films, 1998.

Black Book (Zwartboek). Directed by Paul Verhoeven. AVRO Television, 2006.

Blessed Is the Match: The Life and Death of Hannah Senesh. Directed by Roberta Grossman. Katahdin Productions, 2008

Breaking Bad. Created by Vince Gilligan. High Bridge Entertainment, 2008–13.

Breaking the Waves. Directed by Lars von Trier. October Films, 1996.

Brokeback Mountain. Directed by Ang Lee. River Road Entertainment, 1997.

The Brood. Directed by David Cronenberg. New World Pictures, 1979.

Call Me by Your Name. Directed by Luca Guadagnino. Frenesy Film Company, 2017.

Capturing the Friedmans. Directed by Andrew Jarecki. Magnolia Pictures, 2003.

Casino. Directed by Martin Scorsese. Syalis D.A., 1995.

The City and the City. Directed by Tom Shankland. Mammoth Screen, 2018.

The Color Purple. Directed by Steven Spielberg. Warner Brothers, 1985.

Crazy Love. Directed by Dan Klores and Fisher Stevens. Dan Klores, 2007.

Dancer in the Dark. Directed by Lars von Trier. Zentropa, 2000.

A Dangerous Method. Directed by David Cronenberg. Recorded Picture Company, 2011.

Dead Ringers. Directed by David Cronenberg. Morgan Creek Productions, 1988.

Defiance. Directed by Edward Zwick. Bedford Flats Productions, 2008.

Denial. Directed by Mick Jackson. Bleecker Street, 2016.

Desperately Seeking Susan. Directed by Susan Seidelman. Orion, 1985.

The Dirty Dozen. Directed by Robert Aldrich. Metro-Goldwyn-Mayer, 1967.

Dogville. Directed by Lars von Trier. Filmek A.B., 2003.

Eastern Promises. Directed by David Cronenberg. BBC Films, 2007.

An Education. Directed by Lone Scherfig. BBC Films, 2009.

The Eternal Jew. Directed by Fritz Hippler. Terra Film, 1940.

Europa (released as *Zentropa* in North America). Directed by Lars von Trier. Det Danske Filminstitut, 1991.

Exodus. Directed by Otto Preminger. United Artists, 1960.

The Expanse. Created by Mark Fergus and Hawk Ostby. Syfy, 2015–18; Prime Video, 2019–.

Fiddler on the Roof. Directed by Norman Jewison. United Artists, 1971.

A Fist Full of Dollars. Directed by Sergio Leone. Jolly Film, 1964.

Friends. Created by David Crane and Marta Kauffman. Warner Brothers, 1994–2004.

Funny Girl. Directed by William Wyler. Rastar, 1968.

Get Out Your Handkerchiefs. Directed by Bertrand Blier. Compagnie Commerciale Française, 1978.

Girls. Created by Lena Dunham. HBO, 2012–17.

The Glass Shield. Directed by Charles Burnett. Miramax, 1994

Hannah's War. Directed by Menahem Golan. Golan-Globus Productions, 1988.

Hannibal. Created by Bryan Fuller. Dino De Laurentiis Company, 2013–15.

The Heartbreak Kid. Directed by Elaine May. Twentieth-Century Fox, 1972.

Hester Street. Directed by Joan Micklin Silver. Midwest Films, 1975.

A History of Violence. Directed by David Cronenberg. Benderspink, 2005.

Hostel. Directed by Eli Roth. Next Entertainment, 2005.

I Do Not Care If We Go Down in History as Barbarians. Directed by Radu Jude. Micro Film, 2018.

Ida. Directed by Pawel Pawlikowski. Canal + Polska, 2013.

The Idiots. Directed by Lars von Trier. Arte, 1998.

I'm Not There. Directed by Todd Haynes. Endgame Entertainment, 2007.

Inglourious Basterds. Directed by Quentin Tarantino. A Band Apart, 2009.

Inside Amy Schumer. Created by Amy Schumer and Daniel Powell. Comedy Central, 2013–16.

Inside Llewyn Davis. Directed by Joel Coen. StudioCanal, 2013.

The Jazz Singer. Directed by Alan Crosland. Warner Brothers Pictures, 1927.

Jew Süss. Directed by Lothar Mendes. Gaumont British, 1934.

Joker. Directed by Todd Philips. Warner Brothers, 2019.

Judgment at Nuremberg. Directed by Stanley Kramer. Roxlom Films, 1961.

Keetje Tipple. Directed by Paul Verhoeven. Rob Houwer Film, 1975.

Last Embrace. Directed by Jonathan Demme. United Artists, 1979.

Little Fockers. Directed by Paul Weitz. Dreamworks Pictures, 2010.

Lolita. Directed by Stanley Kubrick. Metro-Goldwin-Mayer, 1962.

The Man in the High Castle. Created by Frank Spotnitz. Amazon Studios, 2015–19.

The Marvelous Mrs. Maisel. Created by Amy Sherman-Palladino. Prime Video, 2017–.

The Mary Tyler Moore Show. Created by James L. Brooks and Allan Burns. CBS, 1970–77.

Mean Girls. Directed by Mark Waters. Paramount Pictures, 2004.

Meet the Fockers. Directed by Jay Roach. Tribeca Productions, 2004.

Melancholia. Directed by Lars von Trier. Zentropa, 2011.

Miller's Crossing. Directed by Joel Coen. Twentieth Century Fox, 1990.

Mr. Mercedes. Created by David E. Kelley. Audience, 2017–20.

The Nanny. Created by Fran Drescher. TriStar Television, 1993–99.

Night and Fog. Directed by Alain Resnais. Argos Films, 1956.

Nice Jewish Girls. Directed by Matthew Blade. Dollhouse Digital, 2009.

Nymphomaniac. Directed by Lars von Trier. Artificial Eye, 2013.

Once Upon a Time in America. Directed by Sergio Leone. The Ladd Company, 1984.

One Night in Miami. Directed by Regina King. Amazon Studios, 2020.

Orange Is the New Black. Created by Jenji Kohan. Netflix, 2013–19.

Orphan Black. Created by Graeme Manson and John Fawcett. Temple Street Productions, 2013–17.

The Owl and the Pussycat. Directed by Herbert Ross. Rastar, 1970.

Oz. Created by Tom Fontana. HBO, 1997–2003.

Paris Is Burning. Directed by Jennie Livingston. Academy Entertainment, 1990.

The Prince of Tides. Directed by Barbra Streisand. Columbia Pictures, 1991.

Princesses: Long Island. Created by True Entertainment. Bravo, 2013.

Private Benjamin. Directed by Howard Zieff. Warner Brothers, 1980.

Queer as Folk. Created by Russell T. Davis. Red Production Company, 1999–2000.

Rabid. Directed by David Cronenberg. Dunning/Link/Reitman, 1977.

Radio Days. Directed by Woody Allen. Orion Pictures, 1987.

Rear Window. Directed by Alfred Hitchcock. Paramount Pictures, 1954.

The Sarah Silverman Program. Created by Sarah Silverman, Dan Harmon, and Rob Schrab. Comedy Central, 2007–10.

Schindler's List. Directed by Steven Spielberg. Amblin Entertainment, 1993.

Secretary. Directed by Steven Shainberg. Secretary, Inc., 2002.

A Serious Man. Directed by Joel Coen and Ethan Coen. Working Title Films, 2009.

The Seven-Per-Cent Solution. Directed by Herbert Ross. Alex Winitsky/Arlene Sellers Productions, 1976.

Shalom Bollywood: The Untold Story of Indian Cinema. Directed by Danny Ben-Moshe. Menemsha Films, 2017.

Shame. Directed by Steve McQueen. See-Saw Films, 2011.

Shivers. Directed by David Cronenberg. Cinépix Films, 1975.

Shoah. Directed by Claude Lanzmann. New Yorker Films, 1985.

Showgirls. Directed by Paul Verhoeven. Carolco Pictures, 1995.

Soap. Created by Susan Harris. ABC, 1977–81.

Sons of Anarchy. Created by Kurt Sutter. 20th Television, 2008–14.

Spider. Directed by David Cronenberg, Sony Pictures Classics, 2002.

The Strain. Created by Guillermo del Toro and Chuck Hogan. FX, 2014–17.

Suddenly Susan. Created by Clyde Phillips. Warner Brothers Television, 1996–2000.

The Third Man. Directed by Carol Reed. London Films, 1949.

Uncut Gems. Directed by Josh Safdie and Bennie Safdie. A24, 2019.

UnREAL. Created by Marti Noxon and Sarah Gertrude Shapiro. A-E Studios, 2015–.

Vertigo. Directed by Alfred Hitchcock. Alfred J. Hitchcock Productions, 1958.

Videodrome. Directed by David Cronenberg. Canadian Film Development Company, 1983.

Villain. Directed by Michael Tuchner. Anglo-EMI, 1971.

Watchmen. Created by Damon Lidelof. HBO, 2019.

The Way We Were. Directed by Sydney Pollack. Rastar, 1973.

The Wire. Created by David Simon. HBO, 2002–8.

X-Men: First Class. Directed by Matthew Vaughn. Marvel Entertainment, 2011.

Yojimbo. Directed by Akira Kurosawa. Kurosawa Production, 1961.

BIBLIOGRAPHY

Abrams, Nathan. "Jews in Contemporary Cinema and Television." In *The New Jewish American Literary Studies*, edited by Victoria Aarons, 216–31. Cambridge: Cambridge University Press, 2019.

———. "Kubrick's Double: 'Lolita's' Hidden Heart of Jewishness." *Cinema Journal* 55.3 (Spring 2016): 17–39.

———. *The New Jew in Film*. New Brunswick, NJ: Rutgers University Press, 2012.

———. "Triple Exthnics." *Jewish Quarterly* 51.4 (Winter 2004): 27–31.

Ahmed, Sara. *Living a Feminist Life*. Durham, NC: Duke University Press, 2017.

Anderson, Benedict. *Imagined Communities: Reflections on the Origin and Spread of Nationalism*. Rev. ed. New York: Verso, 1991.

Anderson, John. "Job in Minnesota: The Coen Brothers Tackle Suffering in 'A Serious Man.'" *America Magazine*, November 2, 2009, 42–42.

Anti-Defamation League. "ADL Audit: Anti-Semitic Assaults Rise Dramatically across the Country in 2015." Press release, June 22, 2016. http://www.adl.org/press-center/press-releases/anti-semitism-usa/2015-audit-anti-semitic-incidents.html#.V2rOJOsrJaQ.

Antler, Joyce. "Hester Street." In *Past Imperfect: History According to the Movies*, edited by Mark C. Carnes, 178–81. New York: Henry Holt, 1996.

———. *The Journey Home: How Jewish Women Shaped Modern America*. New York: Schocken Books, 1997.

Appadurai, Arjun. *Modernity at Large: Cultural Dimensions of Globalization*. Minneapolis: University of Minnesota Press, 1996.

Bachman, Andy. "'Inside Llewyn Davis' and Judaism: What's the Connection?" *Reform Judaism*, January 7, 2014. https://reformjudaism.org/blog/inside-llewyn-davis-and-judaism-whats-connection.

Badley, Linda. *Contemporary Film Directors: Lars von Trier*. Champaign: University of Illinois Press, 2011.

Bahr, Robyn. "'UnREAL' Is Back and More Biting Than Ever in Season 2." *Forward*, June 6, 2016. https://forward.com/sisterhood/342018/unreal-is-back-and-more-biting-than-ever-in-season-2/.

Bainbridge, Caroline. *The Cinema of Lars von Trier: Authenticity and Artifice*. London: Wallflower, 2007.

Baron, Lawrence. "Holocaust and Genocide Cinema: Crossing Disciplinary, Genre, and Geographical Borders: Editor's Introduction." *Shofar: An Interdisciplinary Journal of Jewish Studies* 28.4 (2010): 1–9.

Barry, Robert. "Talking about the Talking Cure: *A Dangerous Method* Reviewed." *Quietus*, February 8, 2012. http://thequietus.com/articles/07934-dangerous-method-david-cronenberg-review.

Barthes, Roland. *The Pleasure of the Text*. Translated by Richard Miller. New York: Wang, 1975.

Bartov, Omer. *The "Jew" in Cinema: From "The Golem" to "Don't Touch My Holocaust."* Bloomington: Indiana University Press, 2005.

Bassani, Giorgio. *The Garden of the Finzi-Continis*. Reprint. Translated by William Weaver. New York: Harcourt Brace Jovanovich, 1977.

Beck, Evelyn Torton. *Nice Jewish Girls: A Lesbian Anthology*. Boston: Beacon Press, 1989.

Behan, Dani Ishai. "No Such Thing as a 'White European' Ashkenazi Jew." *Times of Israel*, February 21, 2019. https://blogs.timesofisrael.com/there-is-no-such-thing-as-a-white -jew/.

Beiser, Vince. "The Heretic." *Tablet Magazine*, April 22, 2011. https://www.tabletmag.com /jewish-arts-and-culture/65548/the-heretic.

Benson, Sheila. "'Miller's Crossing': Stylish but Remote." *L.A. Times*, October 5, 1990. https:// www.latimes.com/archives/la-xpm-1990-10-05-ca-1531-story.html.

Berlant, Lauren. *Cruel Optimism*. Durham, NC: Duke University Press, 2011.

Berman, Judy. "8 Ways of Looking at Lars von Trier's 'Nymphomaniac: Volume 1.'" *Flavorwire*, March 14, 2014. http://flavorwire.com/444644/8-ways-of-looking-at-lars -von-triers-nymphomaniac-volume-1.

Bernstein, Arielle. "The End of *UnREAL*: Why It's Time to Say Goodbye to TV's Darkest Comedy." *Guardian*, July 20, 2018. www.theguardian.com/tv-and-radio/2018/jul/20 /unreal-season-4-review-shiri-appleby-constance-zimmer.

Beyerstein, Lindsay. "Is *Breaking Bad* Racist?" *In These Times* 45.9 (September 13, 2012). https://inthesetimes.com/article/is-breaking-bad-racist.

Bial, Henry. *Acting Jewish: Negotiating Ethnicity on the American Stage and Screen*. Ann Arbor: University Michigan Press, 2005.

Bianco, Robert. "Ten Reasons We Still Love TV." *USA TODAY* 30, May 26, 2004. https:// usatoday30.usatoday.com/life/television/news/2004-05-26-tv-mvps_x.htm.

Bickart, Noah Benjamin. "'Overturning the "Table"': The Hidden Meaning of a Talmudic Metaphor for Coitus." *Journal of the History of Sexuality* 25.3 (September 2016): 489-507.

Billington, Michael. "The Talking Cure." *Guardian*, January 14, 2003. http://www.theguardian .com/stage/2003/jan/14/theatre.artsfeatures.

Bloom, Murray Teigh. *The 13th Man*. New York: Macmillan, 1977.

Bloomer, Naomi. "Surviving the Holocaust in 2015: Recent Cinematic Representations of the Jewish Holocaust Survivor." Paper, LCUL4001, University College London. Academia. edu, accessed October 25, 2019. https://www.academia.edu/16296408/Surviving_the _Holocaust_in_2015_Recent_cinematic_representations_of_the_Jewish_Holocaust _survivor.

Bogdanovich, Peter. "The Importance of Seeing Ernst." *Observer*, August 4, 2008. http:// observer.com/2008/04/the-importance-of-seeing-ernst/.

Boyarin, Daniel. "Goyim Naches, or Modernity and the Manliness of the Mentsh." In *Modernity, Culture and "The Jew,"* edited by Bryan Cheyette and Laura Marcus, 63–87. Stanford CA: University Press, 1998.

———. "Homophobia and the Postcoloniality of the 'Jewish Science.'" In Boyarin, Itzkovitz, and Pellegrini, *Queer Theory and the Jewish Question*, 166–98.

———. *Unheroic Conduct: The Rise of Heterosexuality and the Invention of the Jewish Man*. Berkeley: University of California Press, 1997.

Boyarin, Daniel, Daniel Itzkovitz, and Ann Pellegrini. *Queer Theory and the Jewish Question*. New York: Columbia University Press, 2003.

———. "Strange Bedfellows: An Introduction." In Boyarin, Itzkovitz, and Pellegrini, *Queer Theory and the Jewish Question*, 1–18.

Bragin, Irina. "British Film Gives 'An Education' in Anti-Semitism." *Jewish Journal*, December 2, 2009. https://jewishjournal.com/culture/arts/74638/.

Branfman, Jonathan. "'Plow Him Like a Queen!' Jewish Female Masculinity, Queer Glamor, and Racial Commentary in *Broad City*." *Jewish Television and New Media*, June 2019, 1–19.

Brener, Anne. "When the Truth Is Found to Be Lies: The Coen Brothers' Rorschach for Serious People." *Jewish Journal*, March 1, 2010. https://jewishjournal.com/culture/arts/77077/when-the-truth-is-found-to-be-lies-the-coen-brothers-rorschach-for-serious-people/.

Brettschneider, Marla. *Jewish Feminism and Intersectionality*. Albany: State University of New York Press, 2016.

Brodkin, Karen. *How Jews Became White Folks and What That Says about Race in America*. New Brunswick, NJ: Rutgers University Press, 1998.

Brody, Richard. "The Empty, Sanitized Intimacy of 'Call Me By Your Name.'" *New Yorker*, November 28, 2017. https://www.newyorker.com/culture/richard-brody/the-empty-sanitized-intimacy-of-call-me-by-your-name.

Brook, Vincent. "The Gospel According to Woody: From *Annie Hall* through *To Rome with Love*." In *Woody on Rye: Jewishness in the Films and Plays of Woody Allen*, edited by Vincent Brook and Marat Grinberg, 3–33. Waltham, MA: Brandies University Press, 2014.

Brostoff, Marissa. "Is 'The Marvelous Mrs. Maisel' in on the Joke?" *Jewish Currents*, December 7, 2018. https://jewishcurrents.org/marvelous-mrs-maisel-season-two/.

Brownfield, Paul. "Shtick, Stereotypes, and Self-Parody: How 'The Marvelous Mrs. Maisel' Gets Jewish Culture Wrong." *Los Angeles Times*, January 5, 2019. https://www.latimes.com/entertainment/tv/la-et-st-marvelous-maisel-and-judaism-20190105-story.html.

Bulkin, Elly, Minnie Bruce Pratt, and Barbara Smith. *Yours in Struggle: Three Feminist Perspectives on Anti-Semitism and Racism*. Ithaca, NY: Firebrand Books, 1984.

Burack, Emily. "The Best Jewish References in 'The Marvelous Mrs. Maisel' Season 2." *Kveller*, December 12, 2018. https://www.kveller.com/the-best-jewish-references-in-the-marvelous-mrs-maisel-season-2/.

Burnetts, Charles. "Of Basterds and the Greatest Generation: The Limits of Sentimentalism and the Post-Classical War Film." *Journal of Film and Video* 68.2 (Summer 2016): 1–13.

Butler, Judith, and Athena Athanasiou. *Dispossession: The Performative in the Political*. Polity: Cambridge: 2013.

Carby, Hazel V. "It Jus Be's Dat Way Sometime: The Sexual Politics of Women's Blues." In *The Jazz Cadence of American Culture*, edited by Robert O'Meally, 470–83. New York: Columbia University Press, 1998.

Carras, Christi. "'Transparent's' Trace Lysette on Accusing Jeffrey Tambor of Sexual Harassment: 'It Was Hell.'" *Variety*, August 7, 2018. https://variety.com/2018/tv/news/transparent-trace-lysette-jeffrey-tambor-sexual-harassment-1202898144/.

Clark, Travis. "HBO's 'Watchmen' Director Shares How Being from Charlottesville Made the Series Incredibly Personal, and Her Thoughts on a Season 2." *Business Insider*, October 21, 2019. https://www.businessinsider.com/hbos-watchmen-director-how-charlottesville-made-series-personal-2019-10.

Cohen, Debra Nussbaum. "How Jill Soloway Created 'Transparent'—The Jewiest Show Ever," *Forward*, October 21, 2014. http://forward.com/culture/207407/how-jill-soloway-created-transparent-the-jewiest/.

Cohen, Jeffrey Jerome. "Monster Culture (Seven Theses)." In *The Monster Theory Reader*, edited by Jeffrey Andrew Weinstock, 905–1396. Minneapolis: University of Minnesota Press, 2020. E-book.

Cohen, Steven M. "The Shrinking Jewish Middle—And What to Do about It." David W. Belin Lecture in American Jewish Affairs, 27. Jean & Samuel Frankel Center for Judaic Studies, University of Michigan, 2017. http://hdl.handle.net/2027/spo.13469761.0027.001.

Copeland, Libby. "DNA Test Results in Century-Old Mystery." *Oregonian*, August 4, 2017, C1, C6–C8.

Coughlin, Paul. *"Miller's Crossing, The Glass Key,* and *Dashiell Hammett."* Senses of Cinema 19, March 2002. http://sensesofcinema.com/2002/cteq/millers/.

Crews, Frederick. "The Unknown Freud." *New York Review of Books*, November 18, 1993, 55–67.

Dahl, Julia. *Run You Down*. London: Minotaur, 2015.

Danzig, Micha. "No, Ashkenazi Jews Are Not 'Functionally White.'" *Forward*, July 9, 2018. https://forward.com/scribe/405016/no-ashkenazi-jews-are-not-functionally-white/.

Davis, Angela Y. *Blues Legacies and Black Feminism*. New York: Vintage, 1999.

Davis, Nick. The Desiring-Image: Gilles Deleuze and Contemporary Queer Cinema. New York: Oxford University Press, 2013.

Decolo, Kendra. "Jew Kid on the Block: From Aspirational to Political—Becoming the Feminist Jewish Mother I Want to See in the World." *Bitch* 74 (Spring 2017): 25–28.

Deleuze, Gilles. *Cinema 2: The Time-Image*. Translated by Hugh Tomlinson and Robert Galeta. Minneapolis: University of Minnesota Press, 1989.

Deleuze, Gilles, and Félix Guattari. *Kafka: Toward a Minor Literature*. Translated by Dana Polan. Minneapolis: University of Minnesota Press, 1986.

Deloia, Shlomi, and Hannah Adelman Komy Ofir. "Jewish Characters in *Weeds*: Reinserting 'Race' into the Postmodern Discourse on American Jews." In Sicher, *Race, Color, Identity*, 129–43.

de Young, Mary. *The Day Care Ritual Abuse Moral Panic*. Jefferson, North Carolina: McFarland, 2004.

Doherty, Thomas. "Quentin Tarantino's *Inglourious Basterds*." *Cineaste* 35.1 (Winter 2009): 59–61.

Douglas, Susan J. "Single Bright Females." *In These Times* 40.5 (May 2016): 16.

Drake, Susanna. *Slandering the Jew: Sexuality and Difference in Early Christian Texts*. Philadelphia: University of Pennsylvania Press, 2013.

Eagleton, Terry. *Literary Theory: An Introduction*. Minneapolis: University of Minnesota Press, 1983.

Ebert, Roger. "To Hell with the History Books, This Is Tarantino's Own War." Review of *Inglourious Basterds*. RoberEbert.com, August 19, 2009. https://www.rogerebert.com/reviews/inglourious-basterds-2009.

Epstein, Helen. *Children of the Holocaust: Conversations with Sons and Daughters of Survivors*. Reprint. New York: Penguin, 1988.

Epstein, Jason. "A Dissent on 'Schindler's List.'" *New York Review of Books*, April 21, 1994. https://www.nybooks.com/articles/1994/04/21/a-dissent-on-schindlers-list/.

Erens, Patricia. *The Jew in American Cinema*. Bloomington: Indiana University Press, 1984.

Erickson, Sean. Review of *Nymphomaniac*. *Trash.Art.Movies*, March 21, 2014. http://trashartandmovies.com/film/2014/3/21/nymphomaniac-parts-1-2.

European Union Agency for Fundamental Rights. "Discrimination and Hate Crime against Jews In EU Member States: Experiences and Perceptions of Anti-Semitism." *FRA*, November 5, 2013. http://fra.europa.eu/en/press-release/2013/combating-antisemitism -more-targeted-measures-needed.

Fanon, Frantz. *Black Skin, White Masks*. Translated by Charles Lam Markmann. New York: Grove Press, 1968.

Ferrante, Elena. *My Brilliant Friend*. Translated by Ann Goldstein. New York: Europa Editions, 2012.

Fishman, Sylvia Barack. *The Way into Varieties of Jewish Experience*. Woodstock, VT: Jewish Lights, 2007.

Forster, E. M. *A Passage to India*. New York: Harcourt, Brace, and World, 1952.

Foucault, Michel. *Discipline and Punish: The Birth of the Prison*. Translated by Alan Sheridan. New York: Random House, 1979.

Foundas, Scott. "Kino Uber Alles: Is Quentin Tarantino's 'Inglourious Basterds' the War Movie to End All War Movies?" *Film Comment* 45.4 (July/August 2009): 28–33.

Freedman, Jonathan. "Graves and Images: *Once Upon a Time in America* and the Unmaking of Jewish Memory." *TDR: The Drama Review* 55.3 (Fall 2011): 124–33.

Friedman, Amy. "The Genius of *Broad City*: At Last a Comedy That Speaks to My World." *Guardian*, April 14, 2014. http://www.theguardian.com/tv-and-radio /tvandradioblog/2014/apr/14/broad-city-comedy-genius.

Funk, Steven, and Jaydi Funk. "An Analysis of *Transparent* through Dispossession." *International Journal of TV Serial Narratives* (Spring 2016): 69–80.

Gabler, Neal. *An Empire of Their Own: How the Jews Invented Hollywood*. New York: Random House, 2010.

Garber, Marjorie. *Vested Interests: Cross-Dressing and Cultural Anxiety*. New York: Routledge, 1992.

Gilbey, Ryan. "Days of Gloury." *Sight & Sound* 19.9 (2009): 16–21.

Gilman, Sander L. *Freud, Race, and Gender*. Princeton, NJ: Princeton University Press, 1993.

Gilroy, Paul. *The Black Atlantic: Modernity and Double Consciousness*. Cambridge, MA: Harvard University Press, 1992.

Glenn, Susan A. "The Jewish Cold War: Anxiety and Identity in the Aftermath of the Holocaust." David W. Berlin Lecture in American Jewish Affairs, vol. 24 (2014). Jean & Samuel Center for Judaic Studies, University of Michigan. https://quod.lib .umich.edu/b/belin/13469761.0024.001/--jewish-cold-war-anxiety-and-identity-in-the -aftermath?rgn=main;view=fulltext.

Goldberg, Jeffrey. "Hollywood's Jewish Avenger." *Atlantic*, September 2009. https://www .theatlantic.com/magazine/archive/2009/09/hollywoods-jewish-avenger/307619/.

Goldberg, Michelle. "Democrats Are Moving Left. Don't Panic." *New York Times*, July 23, 2018, A20.

Goldman, Eric A. *The American Jewish Story through Cinema*. Austin: University of Texas Press, 2013.

Goldstein, Eric L. *The Price of Whiteness: Jews, Race, and American Identity*. Princeton, NJ: Princeton University Press, 2006.

Goldstein, Richard. "The New Anti-Semitism: A Geshrei." *Village Voice*, October 1, 1991, 33–38.

Gordan, Rachel. "Alfred Kinsey and the Remaking of Jewish Sexuality in the Wake of the Holocaust." *Jewish Social Studies* 20.3 (Spring/Summer 2014): 72–99.

Grant, Michael. *The Modern Fantastic: The Films of David Cronenberg.* Trowbridge, UK: Flicks Books, 2000.

Grayer, Annie. "Cori Bush Says She Is Moving Offices to Get Away from Marjorie Taylor Greene after Mask Altercation." *CNN Politics,* January 29, 2021. https://www.cnn .com/2021/01/29/politics/cori-bush-marjorie-taylor-green-office-move/index.html.

Green, Emma. "Are Jews White?" *Atlantic,* December 5, 2015. https://www.theatlantic.com /politics/archive/2016/12/are-jews-white/509453/.

———. "Why the Charlottesville Marchers Were Obsessed with Jews." *Atlantic,* August 15, 2017. https://www.theatlantic.com/politics/archive/2017/08/nazis-racism -charlottesville/536928/.

Greenblatt, Stephen. "Shakespeare's Cure for Xenophobia." *New Yorker,* July 3, 2017. https:// www.newyorker.com/magazine/2017/07/10/shakespeares-cure-for-xenophobia.

Greenberg, Cheryl. "I'm Not White—I'm Jewish." In Sicher, *Race, Color, Identity,* 35–55.

Greenberg, Yudit Kornberg. "Breaking Taboos: Jewish Women Performing the Vamp on the Indian Screen." *AJS Perspectives* (Fall 2019): 29–31.

Haag, Matthew. "Robert Jeffress, Pastor Who Said Jews Are Going to Hell, Led Prayer at Jerusalem Embassy." *New York Times,* May 14, 2018. https://www.nytimes .com/2018/05/14/world/middleeast/robert-jeffress-embassy-jerusalem-us.html.

Halberstam, J. Jack. *Trans*: A Quick and Quirky Account of Gender Variability.* Berkeley: University of California Press, 2018.

———. "*Transparent*: The Highs, the Lows, the Inbetweens." *Bully Blog,* January 7, 2015. https://bullybloggers.wordpress.com/2015/01/07/transparent-2014-the-highs-the-lows -the-inbetweens/.

Hammerman, Shaina. *Silver Screen, Hasidic Jews: The Story of an Image.* Bloomington: Indiana University Press, 2018.

Hammett, Dashiell. *The Glass Key.* 1931. Reprint, New York: Vintage, 1989.

———. *Red Harvest.* 1929. Reprint, New York: Random House, 1992.

Hampton, Christopher. *The Talking Cure.* New York: Faber and Faber Plays, 2002.

Hancock, Laura. "Some Ohio Coronavirus Protestors Using Anti-Semitic Symbolism." Cleveland.Com. Updated April 21, 2020. https://www.cleveland.com/open/2020/04 /some-ohio-coronavirus-protesters-using-anti-semitism-symbolism.html.

Haroun, Azmi. "Marjorie Greene Pushed an Anti-Semitic Conspiracy Theory in 2018 That a Space Laser Ignited California's Worst Wildfire of All Time." *Business Insider,* January 25, 2021. https://www.msn.com/en-us/news/us/marjorie-greene-pushed-an -anti-semitic-conspiracy-theory-in-2018-that-a-space-laser-ignited-california-s-worst -wildfire-of-all-time/ar-BB1dc4Gi.

Harris, Malcolm. "Walter White Supremacy." *New Inquiry,* September 27, 2013. https:// thenewinquiry.com/walter-white-supremacy/.

———. "The White Market." *New Inquiry,* September 8, 2012. https://thenewinquiry.com /the-white-market/.

Heller, Nathan. "Mind and Body: The Director Luca Guadagnino." *New Yorker,* October 15, 2018, 60–69.

Heng, Geraldine. "Reinventing Race, Colonization, and Globalism across Deep Time: Lessons from the Longue Dureé." *PMLA* 130.2 (2015): 358–66.

Heritage, Stuart. "10 Reasons Why Today's TV Is Better Than Film." *Guardian,* October 23, 2013. https://www.theguardian.com/tv-and-radio/tvandradioblog/2013/oct/23/10 -reasons-tv-better-movies.

Hoberman, J. "Coen Bros. Torture Another Schlemiel While Imagining They Are Dylan's True Heirs." *Tablet Magazine*, November 20, 2013. http://www.tabletmag.com/jewish -arts-and-culture/153484/coen-brothers-inside-llewyn-davis.

———. "'Joker' Is the Movie of the Year." *Tablet Magazine*, February 5, 2020. https://www .tabletmag.com/jewish-arts-and-culture/297804/joker-is-the-movie-of-the-year?utm _source=tabletmagazinelist&utm_campaign=38699fc08b-.

hooks, bell. "The Oppositional Gaze: Black Female Spectators." In *The Film Theory Reader: Debates and Arguments*, edited by Mark Furstenau, 229–41. London: Routledge, 2010.

Huddleston, Tom. "Quentin Tarantino: Interview." *Time Out London*, August 18, 2009. https://www.timeoutbahrain.com/films/features/10372-quentin-tarantino-interview.

Husain, Atiya. "Are Jews White?" *Slate*, August 14, 2018. https://slate.com/news-and -politics/2018/08/are-jews-white-a-judge-tries-to-answer-the-question-in-a-messy -lawsuit.html.

Ilany, Ofri. "'Call Me by Your Name' Is the Straightest Gay Movie Ever." *Haaretz*, August 17, 2018. https://www.haaretz.com/life/film/call-me-by-your-name-is-the-straightest-gay -movie-ever-1.5792649.

Ingall, Marjorie. "Why *The Marvelous Mrs. Maisel* Is More Subversive Than You Think It Is." *Town and Country*, December 4, 2018. https://www.townandcountrymag.com/leisure /arts-and-culture/a25399462/marvelous-mrs-maisel-jewish-feminism/.

Jacobson, Harlan. Review of *A Serious Man*. *Film Comment* 46.7 (January/February 2010): 47.

James, Nick. "Analyse This." *Sight & Sound* 22.3 (2012): 22–26.

Jenkins, Philip. *Moral Panic: Changing Concepts of the Child Molester in Modern America*. New Haven, CT: Yale University Press, 2004.

Jerusalem Post staff. "Louis Farrakhan: Pedophilia, Homosexuality, Sex Trafficking is Talmudic." *Jerusalem Post*, July 26, 2019. https://www.jpost.com/Diaspora /Antisemitism/Louis-Farrakhan-pedophilia-homosexuality-sex-trafficking-is -Talmudic-596860.

JewOrNotJew.com. Accessed November 12, 2011. http://www.jewornotjew.com/profile .jsp?ID=625.

Johnson, Paul Elliott. "Walter White(ness) Lashes Out: Breaking Bad and Male Victimage." *Critical Studies in Media Communication* 34.1 (2017): 14–28.

Joselit, Jenna Weissman. *Our Gang: Jewish Crime and the New York Jewish Community, 1900–1940*. Bloomington: Indiana University Press, 1983.

JTA. "'UnREAL' Star Shiri Appleby: Jewish, Feminist Antihero." *New York Jewish Week*, July 19, 2016. https://jewishweek.timesofisrael.com/unreal-star-shiri-appleby-jewish -feminist-antihero/.

Kafrissen, Rohkl. "Sorry, but 'The Marvelous Mrs. Maisel' Has a History Problem." *Alma*, January 18, 2018. https://www.heyalma.com/sorry-but-the-marvelous-mrs-maisel-has -a-history-problem/.

Kahn-Harris, Keith. "The Politics of Brisket: Jews and 'The Wire.'" *Darkmatter* 4 (May 29, 2009). http://www.darkmatter101.org/site/2009/05/29/the-politics-of-brisket-jews-and -the-wire/#foot_src_2.

Kalmar, Ivan Davidson. "Race by the Grace of God: Race, Religion, and the Construction of the 'Jew' and the "Arab." In Sicher, *Race, Color, Identity*, 324–43.

Kang, Inkoo. "Transparent's Jill Soloway Continues TV's Sexual (R)evolution." *Village Voice*, September 30, 2014. http://www.villagevoice.com/film/transparents-jill-soloway -continues-tvs-sexual-r-evolution-6442732.

Kaplan, Arielle. "'Orange Is the New Black' Wraps Up with a Very Jewish Final Season." *Alma*, August 28, 2019. https://www.heyalma.com/orange-is-the-new-black-wraps-up -with-a-very-jewish-final-season/.

Kaufman, Debra Renee. "Embedded Categories: Identity among Jewish Young Adults in the U.S." *Race, Gender, and Class: American Jewish Perspectives* 6.4 (1999): 76–87.

Kellerman, Henry. *Greedy, Cowardly, and Weak: Hollywood's Jewish Stereotypes.* Fort Lee, NJ: Barricade Books, 2009.

Kerr, John. *A Most Dangerous Method: The Story of Jung, Freud, and Sabina Spielrein.* New York: Vintage, 1994.

Kestenbaum, Sam. "Anti-Semitic 'Alt-Right' Pounces On Harvey Weinstein Scandal to Bolster Conspiracy Theories." *Forward*, October 10, 2017. https://forward.com/news /384669/anti-semitic-alt-right-pounces-on-harvey-weinstein-scandal-to-bolster -consp/.

Kirkpatrick, Scott. "Should You Write a TV Series or Feature Film?" *Filmmaking Stuff*, February 7, 2020. https://www.filmmakingstuff.com/write-a-tv-series/.

Klawans, Stuart. "Undercover of the Night." *Nation*, April 23, 2007, 34–36.

Kornhaber, Spenser. "The Brilliant Challenge of *Transparent*." *Atlantic*, December 14, 2015. http://www.theatlantic.com/entertainment/archive/2015/12/transparent-season-two -review/419943/.

Kramer, Larry. *Faggots.* New York: Warner Books, 1978.

Kupfer, Ruta. "Breaking Bad, The Wire, Orange Is the New Black: Jewish Stereotypes, without the Guilt." *Haaretz*, July 11, 2019. https://www.haaretz.com/jewish/.premium -two-dimensional-jews-1.5280361.

Lacan, Jacques. "The Signification of the Phallus." Translated by Alan Sheridan. In *Écrits: A Selection*, 281–91. New York: W. W. Norton & Co, 1977.

Lambert, Josh. *Unclean Lips: Obscenity, Jews, and American Culture.* New York: New York University Press, 2014.

Launer, John. *Sex vs. Survival: The Life and Ideas of Sabina Spielrein.* New York: Overlook Duckworth, 2015.

Lee, Nathan. "The Agony and the Ecstasy: Paul Verhoeven's Carnal Knowledge." *Film Comment* 43.2 (March/April 2007): 26–30.

Leibovitz, Liel. "Lars von Trier's 'Nymphomaniac' Isn't Porn. It's a Defense of Jewish Theology." *Tablet Magazine*, March 27, 2014. http://www.tabletmag.com/jewish-arts -and-culture/167406/lars-von-trier-nymphomaniac.

Levi, Lawrence. "Best Nazi-Loving Role Model." *Tablet Magazine*, December 19, 2007. https://www.tabletmag.com/jewish-arts-and-culture/books/955/best -of-2007.

Levine, Elana. *Wallowing in Sex: The New Sexual Culture of 1970s Television.* Durham, NC: Duke University Press, 2007.

Levine, Elana, and Michael Z. Newman. "Jewish Media Power: Myth and Reality." *AJS Perspectives* (Spring 2018): 42–43.

Levine, Judith. *Harmful to Minors: The Perils of Protecting Children from Sex.* Minneapolis: University of Minnesota Press, 2002.

Levinson, Marcy J. "AJFF Review: Shalom to Jewish Stars of Bollywood." *Atlanta Jewish Times*, January 11, 2018. https://atlantajewishtimes.timesofisrael.com/ajff-review -shalom-to-jewish-stars-of-bollywood/.

Li, Shirley. "The Importance of *Watchmen*'s Latest Twist." *Atlantic*, December 9, 2019. https://www.theatlantic.com/entertainment/archive/2019/12/why-latest-watchmen-twist-so-important-doctor-manhattan/603301/.

Liphshiz, Cnaan. "15% of Italians Say Holocaust Never Happened—Poll." *Times of Israel*, February 1, 2020. https://www.timesofisrael.com/15-of-italians-say-holocaust-never-happened-poll-finds.

Lipstadt, Deborah E. *Antisemitism Here and Now.* New York: Schocken Books, 2019.

———. *Denying the Holocaust: The Growing Assault on Truth and Memory.* New York: Free Press, 1993.

Lipton, Sara. *Dark Mirror: The Medieval Origins of Anti-Jewish Iconography.* New York: Metropolitan Books, 2014.

Loeffler, James. *Rooted Cosmopolitans: Jews and Human Rights in the Twentieth Century.* New Haven, CT: Yale University Press, 2018.

Lopate, Phillip. "Berlin: Paramount." *New York Review of Books*, June 28, 2018, 52–54.

Lowenstein, Adam. "'A Dangerous Method': Sight Unseen." *Film Quarterly* 65.3 (2012): 25–29.

Madej, Seth. "Is 'The Wire' Anti-Semitic?" *Crasstalk*, July 19, 2011. https://crasstalk.com/2011/07/is-the-wire-anti-semitic/.

Markowitz, Fran. "Blood, Race, Soul, and Suffering: Full-Bodied Ethnography and Expressions of Jewish Belonging." In Sicher, *Race, Color, Identity*, 261–80.

Marmer, Jake. "An André Aciman Movie?" *Tablet Magazine*, November 28, 2017. https://www.tabletmag.com/sections/arts-letters/articles/an-andre-aciman-movie.

Mathijs, Ernest. *The Cinema of David Cronenberg: From "Baron of Blood" to "Cultural Hero."* London: Wallflower, 2008.

Mayer, Sophie. "Shine a Light: Jill Soloway's *Transparent*." *Sight & Sound*, February 2, 2015. http://www.bfi.org.uk/explore-film-tv/sight-sound-magazine/sight-sound-articles/reviews-recommendations/tv/shine-light-transparent.

McDonald, Jordan. "Racial Passing as Chosen Exile." *Bitch: A Feminist Response to Pop Culture* 79 (Summer 2018): 70–71.

Meis, Morgan and J. M. Tyree. "Is It Okay to Read the Coen Brothers as Literature?" *Gettysburg Review* 19.1 (2006): 61–73.

Merodeadora, Andrea. "The Problem with 'Call Me by Your Name.'" *Medium*, August 3, 2017. https://medium.com/@puentera/the-problem-with-call-me-by-your-name-a8369de0b489.

Michels, Tony. "Jews and American Freedom." *AJS Perspectives* (Fall 2016): 20–23.

Miller, Yvette Alt. "The United States of Hate." *Aish*, March 1, 2017. https://www.aish.com/jw/s/The-United-States-of-Hate.html?s=mm.

Mizejewski, Linda. "1990: Movies and the Off-White Gangster." In *American Cinema of the 1990s: Themes and Variations*, edited by Chris Holmlund, 24–44. New Brunswick, NJ: Rutgers University Press, 2008.

———. *Pretty/Funny: Women Comedians and Body Politics.* Austin: University of Texas Press, 2014.

Momigliano, Anna. "Angst or Reality: How Bad Is Anti-Semitism in Italy?" *Haaretz*, February 26, 2015. https://www.haaretz.com/whdcMobileSite/jewish/.premium-how-bad-is-anti-semitism-in-italy-1.5311214.

Morales, Rosario. "We Are All in the Same Boat." In *This Bridge Called My Back: Writings by Radical Women of Color*, 4th ed., edited by Cherríe Moraga and Gloria Anzaldúa, 87–89. Albany: State University of New York Press, 2015.

Mülhäuser, Regina. "Reframing Sexual Violence as a Weapon and Strategy of War: The Case of the German Wehrmacht during the War and Genocide in the Soviet Union, 1941–1944." *Journal of the History of Sexuality* 26.3 (2017): 366–401.

Nathan, Ian. *Masters of Cinema: Ethan and Joel Coen*. London: Phaidon, 2012.

Nayman, Adam. "Inside Llewyn Davis (Joel and Ethan Coen, US)." *Cinema Scope* 57. http://cinema-scope.com/currency/inside-llewyn-davis-joel-ethan-coen-us/.

Nolan, William. "*Miller's Crossing*'s Tom Reagan: 'Straight as a Corkscrew, Mr. Inside -Outsky.'" *Postscript* 27.2 (2008): 48–60.

Nussbaum, Emily. "The Cloying Fantasia of 'The Marvelous Mrs. Maisel.'" *New Yorker*, December 11, 2018, 88–89.

Oppenheimer, Mark. "An Apology." *Tablet Magazine*, October 10, 2017. https://www.tabletmag.com/scroll/246857/an-apology.

———. "The Death of Civility on the Digital Age." *New Republic*, March 6, 2018. https://newrepublic.com/article/147276/death-civility-digital-age.

———. "The Specifically Jewish Perviness of Harvey Weinstein." *Tablet Magazine*, October 9, 2017. https://www.tabletmag.com/scroll/246724/the-specifically-jewy-perviness-of -harvey-weinstein.

Orr, Christopher. "Thirty Years of Coens: *Miller's Crossing*: An Overdue Love Letter to the Extraordinary Meta Gangster Movie." *Atlantic*, September 10, 2014. https://www.theatlantic.com/entertainment/archive/2014/09/30-years-of-coens-millers -crossing/379895/.

Ostrer, Harry. *Legacy: A Genetic History of the Jewish People*. Oxford: Oxford University, Press, 2012.

Parr, Adrian, ed. *The Deleuze Dictionary*, s.v. "Minoritarian + Cinema." By Constantine Verevis, 165. New York: Columbia University Press, 2005.

Paulus, Tom. "A Critique of Judgment: Movies and Morality." *Photogenie*, February 26, 2014. https://cinea.be/a-critique-judgment-movies-and-morality.

Penley, Constance. "Brownian Motion: Women, Tactics, and Technology." In *Technoculture*, edited by Constance Penley and Andrew Ross, 135–62. Vol. 3 of *Cultural Politics*. Minneapolis: University of Minnesota Press, 1991.

Perry, David M. "The Wisdom of Science Fiction in the Age of Trump." *Pacific Standard*, February 8, 2017. https://psmag.com/news/the-wisdom-of-science-fiction-in-the-age -of-trump.

Peters, Florian. "Remaking Polish National History: Reenactment over Reflection." *Cultures of History Forum*, October 3, 2016. http://www.cultures-of-history.uni-jena.de/politics /poland/remaking-polish-national-history-reenactment-over-reflection/.

Pew Research Center. "A Portrait of Jewish Americans." October 1, 2013. http://www.pewforum.org/2013/10/01/jewish-american-beliefs-attitudes-culture-survey/.

Pildis, Carly. "In Light of Rising Anti-Semitism, Rethinking Black Jewish Relations." *Tablet Magazine*, January 28, 2020. https://www.tabletmag.com/sections/news/articles /rethinking-black-jewish-relations.

Plotz, David. "Week 10: Spoiler Alert! Maury Levy Is Jewish?" *Slate*, March 10, 2008. https://slate.com/culture/2008/03/week-10-spoiler-alert-maury-levy-is-jewish.html.

Polland, Matthew. "Broad City: Season Two." *Slant Magazine*, January 9, 2015. http://www.slantmagazine.com/tv/review/broad-city-season-two.

Prioleau, Chris. "Walter White and Bleeding Brown: On *Breaking Bad*'s Race Problem." *Apogee*, October 3, 2013. https://apogeejournal.org/2013/10/03/walter-white-bleeding -brown-on-breaking-bads-race-problem/.

Rabin, Nathan. "I'm Sorry for Coining the Term Manic Pixie Dream Girl." *Salon*, July 16, 2014. https://www.salon.com/2014/07/15/im_sorry_for_coining_the_phrase_manic _pixie_dream_girl/.

Ragussis, Michael. *Figures of Conversion and the "Jewish Question" and English National Identity*. Durham, NC: Duke University Press, 1995.

Reed, Ishmael. "Do American Jews Still Believe They're White?" *Tablet Magazine*, November 8, 2018. https://www.tabletmag.com/jewish-news-and-politics/274414/american-jews -white.

Reznik, David L. *New Jews: Race and American Jewish Identity in 21st-Century Film*. Boulder, CO: Paradigm Publishers, 2012.

Robinson, Ira. *A History of Antisemitism in Canada*. Waterloo, ON: Wilfred Laurier University Press, 2015.

Robinson, Tasha. "How SyFy's *The Expanse* Cast Its Multiracial Future." *Verge*, February 25, 2016. https://www.theverge.com/2016/2/25/11103434/syfy-the-expanse-series-diverse -cast.

Rogin, Michael. *Blackface, White Noise: Jewish Immigrants in the Hollywood Melting Pot*. Berkeley: University of California Press, 1996.

Romney, Jonathan. "Review: *Nymph()maniac*, Vol. 1." *Sight & Sound* 24.3 (2014): 86.

———. "Songs of Innocence and Experience." *Film Comment* 49.6 (2013): 18–22.

Rosenbaum, Judith. "American Jews, Race, Identity, and the Civil Rights Movement." Intoductory essay for Living the Legacy, unit 1, lessons 1–4. Jewish Women's Archive. Accessed March 25, 2020. https://jwa.org/teach/livingthelegacy/american-jews-race -identity-and-civil-rights-movement.

Rosenberg, Yair. "Jews Will Not Replace Us: Why White Supremacists Go After Jews." *Washington Post*, August 14, 2017. https://www.washingtonpost.com/news/acts-of -faith/wp/2017/08/14/jews-will-not-replace-us-why-white-supremacists-go-after -jews/?utm_term=.ab8faea27a22.

Rosenfeld, Alvin H. *The End of the Holocaust*. Bloomington: Indiana University Press, 2011.

Rowe, Kathleen. *The Unruly Woman: Gender and the Genres of Laughter*. Austin: University of Texas Press, 1995.

Ruggieri, Dominique G., and Elizabeth J. Leebron. "Situation Comedies Imitate Life: Jewish and Italian-American Women on Prime Time." *Journal of Popular Culture* 43.6: 1266–81.

Ryan, Maureen, "'Transparent' on Amazon Is Terrific and Belongs in TV's Top Tier." *Huffington Post*, September 25, 2014. http://www.huffingtonpost.com/2014/09/25 /transparent-amazon-review_n_5883154.html.

Ryan, Mike S. "TV Is Not the New Film." *Filmmaker*, July 23, 2015. https:// filmmakermagazine.com/95009-tv-is-not-the-new-film/#.Xq8TW817mUk.

Sales, Ben. "Marjorie Taylor Greene Shared Antisemitic and Islamophobic Video." *Jerusalem Post*, August 27, 2020. https://www.jpost.com/diaspora/antisemitism/marjorie-taylor -greene-shared-antisemitic-and-islamophobic-video-640093.

Samberg, Joel. *Reel Jewish*. Middle Village, NY: Jonathan David Publishers, 2000.

Samuel, Sigal. "Does 'Orange Is the New Black' Have a Jewish Problem?" *Daily Beast*, July 18, 2013. https://www.thedailybeast.com/does-orange-is-the-new-black-have-a-jewish-problem.

San Filippo, Maria. "'Art Porn Provocateurs': Queer Feminist Performances of Embodiment in the Work of Catherine Breillat and Lena Dunham." *Velvet Light Trap* 77 (Spring 2016): 28–49.

Schepelern, Peter. "Forget about Love: Sex and Detachment in Lars von Trier's *Nymphomaniac*." *Kosmorama* 259 (2015). https://www.kosmorama.org/en/kosmorama/artikler/forget-about-love-sex-and-detachment-lars-von-triers-nymphomaniac.

Schleier, Curt. "Wire Creator Finds a Muse on the Streets of Baltimore." *Jewish News of Northern California*, October 6, 2006. https://www.jweekly.com/2006/10/06/wire-creator-finds-a-muse-on-the-streets-of-baltimore/.

Schwadron, Hannah. *The Case of the Sexy Jewess: Dance, Gender, and Jewish Joke-Work in U.S. Pop Culture*. New York: Oxford University Press, 2018.

Sedgwick, Eve Kosofsky. *Between Men: English Literature and Male Homosocial Desire*. New York: Columbia University Press, 1985.

Sen, Sharmila. *Not Quite White: Losing and Finding Race in America*. New York: Penguin, 2018.

Setka, Stella. "Bastardized History: How *Inglourious Basterds* Breaks through American Screen Memory." *Jewish Film and New Media* 3.2 (2015): 141–69.

Sharrett, Christopher. Review: *Gilda*. *Cinéaste* 41.3 (Summer 2016): 67–68.

Shire, Emily. "'Girls,' Sex and the All New JAP." *Forward*, February 16, 2020. https://forward.com/culture/157915/girls-sex-and-the-all-new-jap/.

Sicher, Ephraim, ed. *Race, Color, Identity: Rethinking Discourses about "Jews" in the Twenty-First Century*. New York: Berghahn, 2013.

Silow-Carroll, Andrew. "Harvey Weinstein and Al Franken Are Jews, but Are They Jewish News?" *Jerusalem Post*, November 22, 2017. https://www.jpost.com/Diaspora/Harvey-Weinstein-and-Al-Franken-are-Jewish-but-are-they-Jewish-news-514926.

Simsolo, Noël. *Conversations avec Sergio Leone*. Paris: Stock, 1987.

Smyth, J. E. "Babylon Revisited." *Cineaste* 43.2 (Spring 2018): 4–9.

Snyder, Timothy. *Black Earth: The Holocaust as History and Warning*. New York: Tim Duggan Books, 2015.

Sobchack, Vivian. "Phenomenology and the Film Experience." In *Viewing Positions: Ways of Seeing Film*, edited by Linda Williams, 36–58. New Brunswick, NJ: Rutgers University Press, 1994.

Sochen, June. "Fanny Brice and Sophie Tucker: Blending the Particular with the Universal." In *From Hester Street to Hollywood: The Jewish-American Stage and Screen*, edited by Sarah Blacher Cohen. Bloomington: Indiana University Press, 1983.

———. "From Sophie Tucker to Barbra Streisand: Jewish Women Entertainers as Reformers." In *Talking Back: Images of Jewish Women in Popular American Culture*, 68–84. Hanover, NH: Brandeis University Press, 1998.

Spillers, Hortense. "Mama's Baby, Papa's Maybe: An American Grammar Book." *Diacritics* 17.2: 64–81.

Sticchi, Francesco. "Inside the 'Mind' of Llewyn Davis: Embodying a Melancholic Vision of the World." *Quarterly Review of Film and Video* 35.2 (October 24, 2017): 137–52.

Stone, Alan A. "The Jewish Question." *Boston Review* 35.1 (2010): 49–50.

Stratton, Jon. "Not Really White—Again: Performing Jewish Difference in Hollywood Films since the 1980s." *Screen* 42.2 (Summer 2001): 142–66.

Taubin, Amy. "Minds on Fire." *Film Comment*, September/October 2011. http://www .filmcomment.com/article/david-cronenbergs-a-dangerous-method.

Taylor, Charles. "Violence as the Best Revenge: Fantasies of Dead Nazis." *Dissent*, Winter 2010. https://www.dissentmagazine.org/article/violence-as-the-best-revenge-fantasies -of-dead-nazis.

Taylor, Ella. "Quentin Tarantino: The *Inglourious Basterds* Interview." *Village Voice*, August 18, 2009. https://www.villagevoice.com/2009/08/18/quentin-tarantino-the-inglourious -basterds-interview/.

Timm, Annette F. "Introduction: The Challenges of Including Sexual Violence and Transgressive Love in Historical Writing in World War II and the Holocaust." *Journal of the History of Sexuality* 26.3 (2017): 351–65.

Tuchman, Aryeh. "Generational Changes in the Holocaust Denial Movement in the United States." In *Deciphering the New Anti-Semitism*, edited by Akvin H. Rosenfeld, 350–72. Bloomington: Indiana University Press, 2015.

Vance, Carole S., ed. *Pleasure and Danger: Exploring Female Sexuality*. Boston: Routledge, 1984.

Wall, Harry D. "A New Museum Explores 2,000 Years of Jewish Life in Italy." *New York Times*, April 24, 2019. https://www.nytimes.com/2019/04/24/travel/jewish-history -museum-ferrara-italy.html.

Walters, Ben. "Debating Inglourious Basterds." *Film Quarterly* 63.7 (2009–10): 19–22.

Wang, Feifei. "The Marvelous Mrs. Maisel and the Celebration of White Feminism." *Colored Lenses*, February 10, 2018. https://medium.com/colored-lenses/the-marvelous-mrs -maisel-and-the-celebration-of-white-feminism-3396a66563c1.

Weisman, Jonathan. *((Semitism)): Being Jewish in America in the Age of Trump*. New York: St. Martin's Press, 2018.

Wenger, Beth S. "Memory as Identity: The Invention of the Lower East Side." *American Jewish History* 85.1 (March 1, 1997): 3–27.

White, Armond. "Review: Inside Llewyn Davis." *City Arts*, December 13, 2913. https://www .nyfcc.com/2013/12/inside-llewyn-davis-reviewed-by-armond-white-for-cityarts/.

Wilkerson, Isabel. *Caste: The Origins of Our Discontent*. New York: Random House, 2020.

Williams, Linda. "Film Bodies: Gender, Genre, and Excess." *Film Quarterly* 44.4 (1991): 2–5.

Williams, Linda Ruth. "Sleeping with the Enemy." *Sight & Sound* 17.2 (2007): 18–20.

Wilson, Scott. *The Politics of Insects: David Cronenberg's Cinema of Confrontation*. New York: Bloomsbury, 2013.

Winant, Howard, and Andreas Wimmer. "Race, Ethnicity and Social Science." *Ethnic and Racial Studies* 38.13 (2015): 2176–85. https://doi.org/10.1080/01419870.2015.1058514.

Wisse, Ruth R. "A Serious Film." *Commentary* (December 2009): 69–71.

Yelsey, Lisa. "Will *UnREAL* Be 'Four And Done' On Hulu?" *Forward*, May 22, 2018. https:// forward.com/schmooze/401659/will-unreal-be-four-and-done-on-hulu/.

Yuen, Nancy Wang. *Reel Inequality: Hollywood Actors and Racism*. New Brunswick, NJ: Rutgers University Press, 2016.

INDEX

CAROL SIEGEL is Distinguished Professor of English, Film, and Women's, Gender, and Sexuality Studies at Washington State University Vancouver. She is the author of *Sex Radical Cinema* (2015) and *New Millennial Sexstyles* (2000), among other monographs and collections.